Studies in Modern History

Cold War to *Détente*

## Studies in Modern History

# COLD WAR TO
# *DÉTENTE*
# 1945–85

### Second edition

*Colin Bown*
*Peter J. Mooney*

Heinemann Educational Publishers,
Halley Court, Jordan Hill, Oxford OX2 8EJ
a division of Reed Educational & Professional Publishing Ltd

OXFORD   MELBOURNE   AUCKLAND
JOHANNESBURG   BLANTYRE   GABORONE
IBADAN   PORTSMOUTH (NH) USA   CHICAGO

ISBN 0 435 32132 3
© Colin Brown and Peter J. Mooney 1976, 1981
First published 1976
98 99 00   18 17 16

Printed in Great Britain by
Athenæum Press Ltd, Gateshead, Tyne & Wear

For our sons:
Tamas, Christopher, James and Thomas

# CONTENTS

# ABBREVIATIONS

| | |
|---|---|
| A.B.M. | Anti Ballistic Missile |
| A.C.C. | Allied Control Council |
| A.L.B.M. | Aircraft Launched Ballistic Missile |
| A.R.V.N. | Army of the Republic of (South) Vietnam |
| A.S.E.A.N. | Association of South-East Asian Nations |
| C.E.W.C. | Council for Education in World Citizenship |
| Comecon | Council for Mutual Economic Co-operation |
| C.P. | Communist Party |
| C.S.C.E. | *Conférence de la Sécurité et de la Co-opération Européenne* (European Conference on Security and Co-operation) |
| D.D.R./G.D.R. | *Deutsche Demokratische Republik*/German Democratic Republic (East Germany) |
| E.D.C. | European Defence Community |
| E.E.C. | European Economic Community |
| E.R.W. | Enhanced Radiation Weapon |
| F.D.P. | Free Democratic Party (West German Liberal Party) |
| F.N.L.A. | National Front for the Liberation of Angola |
| G.N.P. | Gross National Product |
| I.C.B.M. | Intercontinental Ballistic Missile |
| I.I.S.S. | International Institute for Strategic Studies |
| I.M.F. | International Monetary Fund |
| I.N.F. | Intermediate Nuclear Force |
| I.R.B.M. | Intermediate Range Ballistic Missile |
| K.P.D. | *Kommunistische Partei Deutschlands* (German C.P.) |
| M.B.F.R. | Mutual and Balanced Force Reductions (now officially called Mutual Force Reductions and Associated Measures) |
| M.I.R.V. | Multiple Independently Targetable Re-entry Vehicle |
| M.P.L.A. | Popular Movement for the Liberation of Angola |
| M.R.B.M. | Medium Range Ballistic Missile |
| M.R.V. | Multiple Re-entry Vehicle |
| M.L.F. | Multilateral Nuclear Force |
| N.A.T.O. | North Atlantic Treaty Organization |
| N.L.F. | National Liberation Front |
| N.P.T. | Non-Proliferation Treaty |

| | |
|---|---|
| N.V.A. | North Vietnamese Army |
| O.P.E.C. | Organization of Petroleum Exporting Countries |
| P.L.A. | People's Liberation Army |
| P.L.O. | Palestine Liberation Organization |
| P.O.W.s | Prisoners of war |
| P.R.C. | People's Republic of China |
| P.U.W.P. | Polish United Workers Party |
| S.A.C. | Strategic Air Command |
| S.A.L.T. | Strategic Arms Limitation Treaty |
| S.A.M. | Surface to Air Missile |
| S.E.A.T.O. | South-East Asia Treaty Organization |
| S.E.D. | *Sozialistiche Einheitspartei Deutschlands* (East German Socialist Unity Party – Communist Party) |
| S.L.B.M. | Submarine Launched Ballistic Missile |
| S.P.D. | *Sozialdemokratische Partei Deutschlands* (West German Social Democratic Party) |
| S.T.A.R.T. | Strategic Arms Reduction Talks |
| S.W.A.P.O. | South-West African People's Organization |
| U.N.I.T.A. | National Union for the Total Independence of Angola |
| Vc | Vietcong |

# LIST OF MAPS

*Notes to map on facing page:*

## United States Alliances

| | |
|---|---|
| NATO 1949 | U.S., U.K., Canada, Norway, Iceland, Netherlands, Belgium, Denmark, Luxembourg, Portugal, France, Italy, Greece, Turkey, West Germany. (Joint resistance to external attack.) France opted out of the military aspects of NATO in 1966. |
| Baghdad Pact 1955 | Called CENTO in 1958 – including the U.K., Iraq, Turkey, Iran and Pakistan. (Joint resistance to external attack.) Iraq left in 1958. |
| SEATO 1954 –77 (Manila Pact) | U.S., U.K., France, Australia, New Zealand, Pakistan (left November 1972), Philippines, Thailand. (Joint consultation in the event of aggression against a member, or the countries of ex-Indo-China.) |
| ANZUS 1951 | U.S., Australia, New Zealand. (Joint resistance to aggression.) |
| OAS 1948 | U.S., Mexico, Haiti, Dominica, Honduras, Guatemala, Salvador, Nicaragua, Costa Rica, Panama, Colombia, Peru, Venezuela, Ecuador, Brazil, Bolivia, Paraguay, Uruguay, Chile, Argentina. (Joint resistance to external attack.) Cuba expelled in 1962. |
| Individual Treaties | Mutual defence treaties with Japan (1951), Philippines (1952), South Korea (1954), Taiwan (1955). U.S. bases established in Spain (1953) and Libya (ended by Colonel Gadaffi in early 1970). |

## Soviet Alliances

| | |
|---|---|
| Warsaw Pact 1955 | E. Germany, Poland, Czechoslovakia, Bulgaria, Rumania, Hungary. (Yugoslavia did not join this alliance, and Albania took the Chinese side in the post-1960 Sino-Soviet split.) |
| Individual Defence Treaties | With China 1950 (of doubtful use after 1960, if not before. See Chapter 14). North Korea, Cuba 1962, India 1971, and also with Mongolia, Bangladesh, Vietnam, Sri Lanka and Afghanistan. |

(European countries remaining neutral in the Cold War are Switzerland, Sweden, Austria – as a prerequisite of its de-occupation in 1955 – and Finland, obliged to by its proximity to the U.S.S.R.)

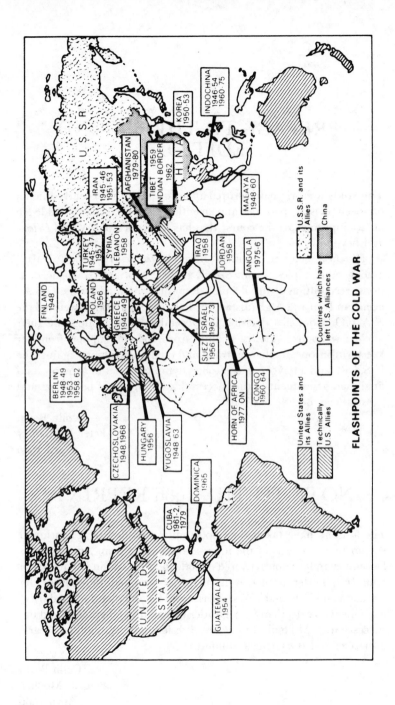

**FLASHPOINTS OF THE COLD WAR**

INDOCHINA
1946-54
1960-75

KOREA
1950-53

AFGHANISTAN
1979-80

TIBET 1959
INDIAN BORDER
1962

IRAN
1945-46
1951-53

MALAYA
1948-60

TURKEY
1945-47
1957

SYRIA
LEBANON
1958

IRAQ
1958

JORDAN
1958

ANGOLA
1975-6

FINLAND
1948

POLAND
1956

GREECE
1945-49

ISRAEL
1967-73

BERLIN
1948-49
1953
1958-62

SUEZ
1956

CONGO
1960-64

CZECHOSLOVAKIA
1948-1968

HUNGARY
1956

YUGOSLAVIA
1948-63

HORN OF AFRICA
1977 ON

DOMINICA
1965

CUBA
1961-2
1979

GUATEMALA
1954

U.S.S.R. and its
Allies

China

United States and
its Allies

Countries which have
left U.S. Alliances

Technically
U.S. Allies

# PREFACE TO THE SECOND EDITION

This study was originally written up to 1975. For this second edition it has been revised up to 1980 and an entirely new final chapter added in an attempt to chart the course that has led from Cold War to *Détente* and beyond ...

The new chapter, entitled 'Beyond *Détente*, 1975–80', deals – among other topics – with SALT 2; the Egyptian–Israeli negotiations; recognition of the People's Republic of China by the U.S.A.; events in Iran and Afghanistan; the balance of nuclear power and the N.A.T.O. Council's decision in December 1979 to upgrade their nuclear weapons; America's call in April 1980 for support from her Western European allies on trade and credit restrictions against the U.S.S.R., and a boycott of the 1980 Olympic Games in Moscow; and finally an assessment of the successes and failures of both East and West after a decade of *détente*.

Colin Bown
Peter J. Mooney
April 1980

# NOTE TO THE 1986 REPRINT

The authors have taken the opportunity provided by a reprint to extend their analysis of the international scene from April 1980 to December 1985. Topics covered include the 1982 war in Lebanon; the Iran–Iraq border conflict; events in Soviet-occupied Afghanistan; the Grenada and Falkland crises; the rise and fall of Poland's 'Solidarity' movement; the death of Soviet leader Konstantin Chernenko and the succession of Mikhail Gorbachev; President Reagan's 'Star Wars' initiative; and the Geneva Summit.

Colin Bown
Peter J. Mooney
April 1986

*One*

# INTRODUCTION

A century before the term 'Cold War' entered the vocabulary of international relations, Karl Marx and Friedrich Engels published *The Communist Manifesto* (1848). Their treatise ended with a clarion call: 'Communists . . . openly declare that their ends can be attained only by the forcible overthrow of all existing social conditions. Let the ruling classes tremble at a Communistic revolution. The proletarians have nothing to lose but their chains. They have a world to win.'[1] But in 1848 there was no state that could provide a home for the revolution or the arms to accompany the call to battle. In October 1917, as Leon Trotsky's Red Guards stormed the Winter Palace in Petrograd, that state came into being. In 1919, its leader Ilyich Ulanov Lenin prophesied: 'We are living not merely in a state, but in a system of states; and it is inconceivable that the Soviet Republic should continue to exist for a long period side by side with imperialist states. Ultimately one or the other must conquer. Until this end occurs, a number of terrible clashes between the Soviet Republic and bourgeois states is inevitable.'[2]

This was the language of international civil war – 'communist' against 'democrat' – to be fought the world over until one truth emerged victorious. But in 1919 the Western world intervened in the Russian Civil War, stung into action by the dictates of counter-revolution. It was a half-hearted intervention and, according to Churchill, a horrific defeat, since the West failed 'to strangle Bolshevism at birth'. Yet Lenin – and after 1924 his successor Joseph Stalin – had learnt the lesson and acted upon it. For until the Soviet Union was strong – until it had industry, munitions factories and millions of men under arms – provoking attack from the imperialists by pressing the Comintern to stir up world revolution would be the action of an 'infantile leftist'.

In 1945 the Union of Soviet Socialist Republics was strong, and the collapse of the '1000 Year' Reich left a power vacuum across central and eastern Europe. On 2 April 1945, the Fuehrer mused on the future of Europe and the world. He concluded that: 'With the defeat of the Reich and pending the emergence of the Asiatic, the African and perhaps the South American nationalisms, there will remain in the world only two Great Powers capable of confronting each other – the United States and Soviet Russia. The laws of both history and geography will compel these two powers to a trial of strength either militarily or in the fields of economics and ideology.'³ The motive power of ideological beliefs is admittedly very strong: but, of course, it would be foolish to ignore the dictates of great power rivalry as a basis for the birth and continuance of Cold War relationships between the super-powers of this century.

By 1947 the 'trial of strength' forecast by Hitler had begun – between the United States, her partners and allies and the Soviet Union and hers, apparently contending for a world ideological monopoly. Although each of the opposing blocs possessed their 'deviants', basically one side supported the advance of a totalitarian and egalitarian social and political structure, while the other championed the concept of individual liberty in a multi-party democracy. Of course, the United States has welcomed to her camp countries such as Spain, Greece, South Korea and South Vietnam, all of which have been less than democratic, but each of which possessed the virtue of being anti-communist. The Soviet Union, on the other hand, has fostered relations with countries not initially belonging to either Western or communist worlds – 'Third World' countries such as India, Indonesia and Egypt – on the basis that their anti-communism was offset by their anti-imperialism.

The Cold War, then, has been fought in the 'hearts and minds' of people on all the globe's continents, and occasionally that ideological sparring has involved military conflict. But the conflict has been fought – from Korea, to Malaya, to Vietnam, to the Middle East – by and with proxy states. The super-powers themselves have not engaged in 'hot war', for with the development and deployment of nuclear weapons, both the U.S.S.R. and the U.S. became increasingly aware of the 'unacceptable losses' to themselves and to mankind that a Third World War would entail. Yet both states have, since 1945, maintained an advanced state of readiness for war which gave confrontation situations a horrific aspect of Armageddon to many people throughout the world – situations like Berlin in 1948–9 and again from 1958 to 1962; like the Middle East in 1956–7 and again in 1973; like the Taiwan Straits in 1955 and 1958; like Cuba in 1962 (and the list is by no means complete). In his Inaugural Address of 1961, the American President, John F. Kennedy, declared: 'Let every nation know . . . that we shall pay any price, bear any burden, meet any hardship, support any friend, oppose any foe to assure the survival and success of liberty.'[4]

But the price could be enormous, and neither side wished – nor wishes – to pay with the lives of democrats or proletarians: the alternative is *détente*. Paradoxically, the immense nuclear arsenals and global interests of both super-powers has given them, to quote President Nixon, 'a certain common outlook, a kind of interdependence for survival. Although we competed, our conflict did not admit of resolution by victory . . . we seemed compelled to coexist.'[5] Nixon was hinting as the lowest common denominator of *détente* – the fact that it involved a 'relaxation of tension' and an increase in co-operation, sometimes, in some geographical areas, but not necessarily in all. Neither Kremlin nor White House compromised their ideologies or their national interests in promoting *détente* and yet, although the parameters of *détente* were fully grasped in the chancelleries of East and West, public opinion in general – especially in the West – had higher expectations of *détente* than reality warranted. The West may have attempted to pursue *détente* as a strategy, but the Soviets made no secret of the fact that for them it was only a tactic, and in 1979–80 when *détente* did not deliver, first the Soviets and then the Americans were quite prepared to reappraise *détente* and pull back, however temporarily, from many of the ties they had so recently cemented with each other.

# Two

# THE UNLIKELY PARTNERS

On 1 January 1942, in Washington D.C., the representatives of twenty-six countries, including the United Kingdom, the United States and the Soviet Union, signed the 'Declaration of the United Nations' in which they pledged – among other things – to destroy the Axis Powers of Germany, Italy and Japan. This apparent amity between the 'Big Three' was in striking contrast to the relations between them which had existed from 1917. Both Britain and the United States had intervened militarily in the Russian Civil War from 1918–20 in opposition to the Bolshevik revolutionaries.

Britain and France only extended diplomatic recognition to the U.S.S.R. in 1924, the U.S.A. waited until 1933. Public opinion in the West was outraged by the Russo–German treaty and partition of Poland in 1939. Furthermore, having failed to negotiate an anti-Hitler alliance with the Soviet Union in the summer of 1939, Britain and France seriously considered going to war with her early in 1940 to protect Finland. The element of distrust and of ideological hostility between the Soviet Union and the West must not be underestimated. Both sides expected the worst from each other, so co-operation between the wartime allies was always limited and cautious.

There was very little in the way of joint military planning between the U.S.S.R. and the West during the war and contact between ordinary Russians and their allied counterparts remained minimal. The Anglo–Americans sent massive amounts of war *matériel* to Russia but the Soviet attitude to this aid was always ambiguous. For example, the Russians received thousands of trucks which, as they were better than Russian models, were militarily valuable but politically dangerous because they might be seen by the ordinary Russian to be products of superior societies. The Soviet Union, reeling under the hammer-blows of the German army from 1941–3, was desperate for the Western Allies to open a second front against the Germans in France, and Stalin – who embodied supreme authority in the U.S.S.R. – remained deeply suspicious of Western motives for not doing so until 1944, fearing that his two Western allies, their military power largely intact, might seek to profit from a war in which both the U.S.S.R. and Germany were being very seriously weakened. When, on 5 June 1944, Stalin was informed that the Anglo–Americans were to invade France the next day, his scepticism remained: 'Yes, there'll be a landing, if there is no fog. Until now there has always been something that put it off. I suspect tomorrow it will be something else. Maybe they'll meet with some Germans! What if they meet with some Germans? Maybe there won't be a landing then, but just promises as usual.'[1]

Once the Second World War had come to an end the differences between the Big Three, which had been largely submerged during the war, began to come to the surface and between 1945–8 it became increasingly obvious that the policies and priorities of the Soviet Union had little in common with those of her allies.

In the spring of 1939, Britain and France guaranteed the frontiers of Poland. They declared war on Germany in September 1939 after the German invasion of Poland. Having gone to war over Poland, it was only to be expected that Britain would attach great importance to the future of that country, but so too did the U.S.S.R. Poland was the traditional invasion route to Russia from the West and as far as the Soviet leadership was concerned, Poland, in successfully obstructing Russian offers of help to Czechoslovakia in 1938, by denying transit rights – Russian troops could only reach Czechoslovakia through Poland – had to share some of the responsibility for the Second World War. During the war, Stalin repeatedly made clear that whatever else happened to Poland after the war, the Soviet Union would not accept the existence on her frontiers of a Poland which was unfriendly to Russia. To some extent the Western Allies sympathized with this Soviet preoccupation and at the Big Three Conference at Teheran in November 1943, Churchill was prepared to accept a westward shift in Poland's frontiers;

however, the Polish Government (the London Poles) in exile in London was not.

Relations between the London Poles and Stalin – always poor in the light of the Soviet invasion of Poland in 1939 – worsened when news broke of the Katyn Woods massacre. Since 1939, the London Poles had been unsuccessfully trying to find out what had happened to large numbers of Polish officers, who, it was believed, had been captured by the Russians. In April 1943 the German army revealed that it had discovered a mass grave in the Katyn Forest of some 10,000 Polish officers and N.C.O.s. The matter has not been finally proven but it appears likely that it was the Russians rather than the Germans who were responsible; certainly this is the interpretation that the London Poles accepted. The London Poles demanded a Red Cross inquiry into the incident and on 25 April 1943 the Kremlin broke off diplomatic relations with the London Poles, and in July 1944 set up a rival Polish Government the 'Polish Committee of National Liberation' – or 'Lublin Committee' – which was dominated by communists and could be relied upon to implement Soviet policy. Matters were further complicated in August 1944 when, with the Red Army just six miles from Warsaw, the Polish underground Home Army rose against the Germans. The Russians made no move to help and refused permission for Anglo–American aircraft to drop supplies to the Home Army and then land in Soviet-occupied territory to refuel. The Warsaw rising lasted over two months, cost the lives of 300,000 Poles and devastated Warsaw, and for the duration the Red Army made no move to cross the river obstacle that lay between them and Warsaw. If the rising had succeeded, Stalin would have been faced with an armed, well-organized group of non-communist Poles who had liberated the Polish capital in the name of the London Poles. The Lublin Committee would have been shown to be the unrepresentative creature of the Kremlin that it was and Stalin's policy in Eastern Europe would have received a major setback. As it was, a major row broke out between the Western Allies and the Soviet Union when on 5 January 1945, the Kremlin recognized the Lublin Committee as the legal government of Poland thus ignoring the claims of the London Poles.

If Stalin's policy at Katyn and during the Warsaw uprising was to remove the intellegentsia and potential non-communist Polish leadership, then a further example occurred soon after the death of the American President, Roosevelt, in April 1945. Key figures of the Polish Home Army and leaders of Polish non-communist parties were arrested by the Russians and on 2 June 1945 thirteen of them were given prison sentences for 'anti-Soviet' activities. On his way to the United Nations Conference in San Francisco in April 1945, the Soviet Foreign Minister, Molotov, had two meetings with Truman at which he was to discover that the new President was not prepared to be as conciliatory towards Stalin as the old. Truman left Molotov in no doubt that the United States regarded the Polish question as 'the symbol of the future development of our international relations'. In his second meeting with Molotov, Truman was even more direct. He told Molotov: 'the failure to go forward at this time with the implementations of the Crimean decision* on Poland would seriously shake confidence in the unity of the three governments.'[2]

By the time of the Potsdam Conference in July 1945, the Soviets had accepted Mikolajczyk, the leader of the London Poles, as Vice-President of the Polish Government. The Potsdam Agreement also promised that free elections would be held in Poland but the Western Allies could win no more concessions. Within eighteen months Mikolajczyk had to flee for his life from Poland, his Peasant Party was banned and Poland was firmly in the hands of a communist government depending for its support not upon the Polish electorate, but upon the presence in strength of the Red Army and the Soviet Secret Police.

Although the Western Allies had agreed to Poland's eastern frontiers before Potsdam they were not prepared for the fact that on 2 April 1945 the U.S.S.R. had unilaterally signed an agreement with the Warsaw Government handing over to them the former German territory east of the Oder and Western Neisse rivers. However, the U.K. and the U.S.A. were able to obtain agreements at Potsdam that the western frontier of Poland had not been finally settled and must await a peace settlement. To some extent Western arguments on this issue lacked force as Churchill – who was replaced as Prime Minister by Attlee during the Potsdam Conference – was known to be in favour of Poland acquiring lands at Germany's

* At the Yalta Conference in February 1945 the Allies had disagreed over the Western frontier of Poland but had reached an agreement in principle by which some of the London Poles would join the Lublin Committee and this would then receive diplomatic recognition from the Governments of the Big Three.

expense and de Gaulle's Provisional French Government – which
was not represented at Potsdam – had already accepted the Oder–
Neisse frontier. It was not Poland's acquisition of these German
lands as such that the U.K. and U.S.A. objected to, but the way
in which the question had been decided.

The Yalta and Potsdam conferences were high points of co-
operation between the Big Three, but already at Potsdam attitudes
were changing, and with them personalities. Truman had succeeded
Roosevelt and Churchill had lost a General Election to Attlee. Both
were men whom Stalin did not know. They were heads of peacetime
governments and therefore did not have the wide powers of decision-
making and discretion which their predecessors enjoyed. No longer
could difficult questions be settled between three old statesmen;
matters now had to be referred back to Washington and London –
a process which the dictator Stalin cannot have fully appreciated.
Roosevelt had pinned great hopes upon a post-war world in which
the peace would be kept by the Big Three acting in concert through
the United Nations Organization and had been prepared to go a
long way to obtain this. He reluctantly accepted Soviet demands
that the Big Four – including China – could have a veto in the
U.N. Security Council, which meant that any one Great Power
could block any U.N. action. Also, the Americans had to accept at
Yalta that the U.S.S.R. would have three votes in the U.N. General
Assembly – the Soviet Union, Ukraine and Byelorussia – although
Roosevelt did reject Soviet demands that all fifteen of the constituent republics of the U.S.S.R. could have votes. Soviet tactics
over the U.N. appeared to be merely obstructionist, but they were
more than that. When the U.N. Charter came into force in October
1945, of the Organization's fifty member states, the U.S.S.R. could
depend only upon the votes of her Mongolian and East European
satellites: she could be out-voted on any issue. In fact, by the end
of 1949, the U.S.S.R. had used the veto in the Security Council
forty times and Roosevelt's high hopes of co-operation between the
wartime allies had come to nothing.

Truman however, had few illusions about U.N.O. and his
patience with the Russians quickly ran out, until in January 1946
he could write: 'I'm tired babying the Soviets.'[3]

# Three

# THE COLD WAR BEGINS

During the war, the Soviet Union had been bound to the Western Allies, and especially to Britain, by the common threat to their political systems and to their national existence. When survival was assured by the beginning of 1943, their link had become the drive for victory. Their very serious ideological differences remained, as did the inherent distrust with which two opposing political systems regarded each other. At the wartime conferences of the Big Three a number of agreements were made on the conduct of the peace after fighting had ceased, but they were largely agreements on vague matters of principle.

The delegations of the Big Three gathered at Potsdam, bringing with them their suspicions and their very different conceptions of what victory over Germany meant.

The wartime experience of the United States, coupled with her recent history of isolation, her democratic traditions, her continental size and her relative self-sufficiency, meant that her territorial security was not threatened by anyone. The United States had not been occupied or bombed during the war. Battles had not been fought on her soil and, protected by the oceans, no one in the immediate post-war world had the military capacity to inflict damage on the American homeland. The Americans did not share the fears of the Europeans of a resurgent revanchist Germany. For the Americans, the multi-party democracy built upon a republican constitution like theirs and upon American concepts of freedom and private enterprise was almost enough in itself to stand as a bulwark against dictatorship, fascist or communist. They opposed colonialism in all its forms – despite the presence in the American cupboard of the skeletons of the Philippines and Puerto Rico – and were unhappy about the imperial status of some of their allies in Europe.

The British too believed that the erection of democratic systems, not necessarily republican, in the countries of east and central Europe would do much to ensure their own security, because those states might then become natural allies of Britain against any European great power seeking once again to establish a continental hegemony. The British still tended to look at European affairs in terms of 'balance of power' politics, a concept that the Americans, especially President Roosevelt, found abhorrent. They wanted a revitalized France to take her place in Europe once more so that Britain would have an ally against a Germany whose recovery was possible, and a Soviet Union whose hostility was expected. The British Government did not share Roosevelt's trust in the future peaceful and co-operative intentions of Stalin, nor did they view decolonization in the same light as the Americans. Britain was already preparing to give independence to the Indian subcontinent but was reluctant to do the same for her other imperial possessions. The Empire had contributed men, money and bases in the war and there was a widespread fear in Britain that if the Empire were to go, then Britain's 'great power' status might go with it. At Yalta when Churchill pressed his partners to accept France back into the 'great power club', Stalin responded that the entrance fee was 5 million soldiers. Churchill corrected this to 3 million, but nevertheless, if 'great power' status depended upon the number of divisions that a state could put into the field, then Britain would have been hard pressed without her Empire.

The Soviet Union had defeated Nazi Germany and in so doing had demonstrated to itself the truth of the Marxist–Leninist idea that communism was inherently stronger than its opponents. The soldiers of the Soviet Union had fought whether they realized it or not not only for Mother Russia but also to preserve the Stalinist system and all it represented. Stalin looked with contempt upon the democratic systems so beloved by his Western allies. These same systems had in the past proved too weak to prevent the rise of Hitler and Mussolini, the 'betrayal' of Czechoslovakia in 1938 and, most important of all, the attack upon the Soviet Union in 1941. Russia did not possess any natural barriers along her western borders. She had no English Channel, Atlantic Ocean or mountain range to deter or hinder an invader. All she had was space and the more space she had, the more her security was assured. In annexing the Baltic States and part of Rumania, and in pushing the U.S.S.R.'s

**Legend:**
- ——— The 'Iron Curtain' from 1948
- —·—·— Germany since 1945
- ———— 1937 frontiers
- Allied control zones of Germany and Austria
- Ceded to Russian zone by Britain & America
- Annexed by Russia in 1945
- States which became Communist between 1945 & 1948
- Yugoslav gains from Italy 1945

FINLAND

Porkkala · Viborg · Leningrad

ESTONIA

Pskov

SWEDEN

LATVIA · Riga

LITHUANIA

DENMARK · BALTIC SEA · Memel · Konigsberg · Vilna · Minsk

Danzig

American · Bremen · Szczecin (Stettin) · Berlin · Poznan · Warsaw · RUSSIA

HOLLAND

BRITISH

Annexed by Poland

FRENCH · Erfurt · Prague · Wroclaw (Breslau) · Cracow · Lvov

Nuremberg (Trials 1945-46) · CZECHOSLOVAKIA · Czernowitz

FRANCE

SWITZERLAND · AMERICAN · Vienna · Uzhgorod · Kishinev

USA · AUSTRIA · BRITISH · FRENCH

Budapest · HUNGARY · RUMANIA (Monarchy abolished 1947)

Trieste (British & US occupation 1945-1955)

ITALY · ADRIATIC SEA · Bucharest

(Monarchy abolished June 1946) · Belgrade

YUGOSLAVIA (Monarchy abolished 1945) · BULGARIA (Monarchy abolished 1946)

Sofia

ALBANIA (Monarchy abolished 1946) · Communist activity 1946-49

GREECE (Monarchy restored after plebiscite September 1946)

TURKEY

AEGEAN SEA

0 — 100
miles

## SOVIET EXPANSION IN EUROPE, 1945-48

**Annexed or under Soviet administration**

| YEAR | COUNTRIES | POPULATION millions | AREA sq. mls |
|---|---|---|---|
| 1940 | Part of Finland | 0.5 | 17,600 |
| 1940 | Estonia | 1.1 | 18,300 |
| 1940 | Latvia | 2.0 | 25,400 |
| 1940 | Lithuania | 3.0 | 21,500 |
| 1945 | Part of German East Prussia | 1.2 | 5,400 |
| 1945 | Part of Poland | 11.8 | 69,900 |
| 1945 | Part of Czechoslovakia | 0.7 | 4,900 |
| 1945 | Part of Rumania | 3.7 | 19,400 |
| | TOTAL: | 24.0 | 182,400 |

**Controlled by U.S.S.R.**

| | | | |
|---|---|---|---|
| 1945 | Soviet Zone of Germany | 18.8 | 42,900 |
| 1945 | Poland | 26.5 | 120,355 |
| 1948 | Czechoslovakia | 12.3 | 49,381 |
| 1947 | Hungary | 9.8 | 35,902 |
| 1948 | Rumania | 16.1 | 91,584 |
| 1946 | Bulgaria | 7.2 | 42,796 |
| 1946 | Albania | 1.2 | 10,629 |
| | TOTAL: | 91.9 | 393,547 |

frontiers westwards at the expense of Poland, Germany and Czechoslovakia, Stalin – however immoral or illegal these actions may have
been – was merely bowing to the necessities of the Soviet Union's
geography. Stalin agreed at Yalta that the countries of Eastern
Europe would be allowed free elections to decide their own futures,
and the Western Allies sympathized with Stalin's desire to have
only 'friendly' governments on his western frontier. But what was a
'friendly' government? As the U.S. believed that the peace she
wanted could only be guaranteed by democracies in Eastern Europe,
so Stalin too it seems came to accept that the peace he wanted
could only be guaranteed if the East European governments were
communist. The Yugoslav Communist, Milovan Djilas, wrote of
him: 'As a result of his ideology and methods, his personal experience
and historical heritage, he trusted nothing but what he held in his
fist, and everyone beyond the control of his police was a potential
enemy.'[1] Also, it must be said that if Stalin did believe fully in
Marxism, and this point has been widely debated, then it was his
duty to carry the gospel of communism to those countries which,
owing to the presence in strength of the Red Army, would provide
receptive audiences.

Given these preoccupations of the Big Three, dispute in the post-
war world was inevitable. Relations between the Big Three had
begun to deteriorate even before Potsdam. During the war, the U.S.
gave more than $46,000 million of military aid under the Lend–
Lease programme to her allies. Most of this went to Britain and the
Soviet Union and to their consternation, on 8 May 1945, President
Truman effectively stopped Lend–Lease. There had been a mis-
understanding and deliveries to these two countries were resumed
until 19 August 1945. Truman was new to the office of the Presidency and his decision to stop Lend–Lease was due to his inexperience; but in an interview with Truman's emissary, Harry Hopkins,
at the end of May 1945, Stalin specifically mentioned the Lend–
Lease decision as one of those events which had led him to believe
that 'the American attitude towards the Soviet Union had per-
ceptibly cooled once it became obvious that Germany was defeated,
and that it was as though the Americans were saying that the
Russians were no longer needed'.[2]

In the remaining unresolved conflict of the Second World War,
the Russians were no longer needed. At Yalta, the Americans had
been anxious to secure Soviet help in the war against Japan, fearing

that the invasion of Japan could cost up to 1 million American casualties. By the summer of 1945, the U.S. had developed the atom bomb which gave her a way of avoiding those casualties and bombing Japan into surrender. On 8 August Soviet forces began the attack on Japanese positions in Manchuria, Korea, South Sakhalin and the Kuriles, but Stalin received little thanks or credit in the West and no share in the occupation regime in Japan.

Against Japan, Stalin did what the Yalta agreement required of him, but viewed alongside Soviet actions in Germany, Eastern Europe and the Middle East, Soviet policy indicated to many in the West a desire for expansion which was alarming. The possession of the atomb bomb altered Anglo–American attitudes towards the Soviet Union. Ian Gray made the interesting point that 'This change in the attitude of the Americans and British at Potsdam gave dramatic confirmation of Stalin's worst fears and suspicions. Moreover, it offended him deeply as an act of ingratitude and rejection.'[3]

The Soviet Union's first move outside Europe after the war was seen by her allies as overtly hostile. It came in Iran. For a century, although nominally independent, northern Persia had been accepted as lying within Russia's sphere of influence and the southern part in Britain's. In September 1941, Britain and the U.S.S.R. occupied their erstwhile spheres of influence, thus securing their valuable pipeline for Lend–Lease supplies to the Soviet Union. In January 1942, Iran, Britain and the U.S.S.R. signed a treaty, reaffirmed at the Teheran Conference of 1943, according to which the occupying powers would withdraw their troops within six months of the end of the war. In September 1944, Britain and Iran agreed to set up the joint Anglo–Iranian Oil Company – the American Standard Oil Company was also included – to exploit an oil exploration concession in the old British sphere of influence. Stalin tried to extract a similar concession, but the Iranian Government under Western pressure, refused. The U.S.S.R. tried another tactic. Russian support was given to the Teudeh party which opposed the Iranian monarchy, and to the Kurdish and Azarbaijani separatists of Northern Iran.

After the war, the British withdrew from Iran but the Soviets did not. In the autumn of 1945, an 'independent' republic of Azarbaijan was set up with Red Army backing and the important posts in the new government went to communists. The Iranian

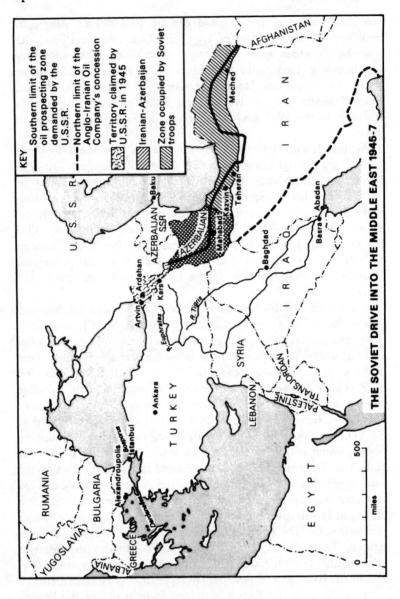

KEY

Southern limit of the oil prospecting zone demanded by the U.S.S.R.

Northern limit of the Anglo-Iranian Oil Company's concession

Territory claimed by U.S.S.R. in 1945

Iranian-Azerbaijan

Zone occupied by Soviet troops

THE SOVIET DRIVE INTO THE MIDDLE EAST 1945-7

Government and the Western Allies were furious. In a letter to Secretary of State Byrnes, President Truman wrote:

> Iran was our ally in the war. Iran was Russia's ally in the war. Iran agreed to the free passage of arms, ammunition and other supplies running into millions of tons across her territory from the Persian Gulf to the Caspian Sea. Without these supplies furnished by the United States, Russia would have been ignominiously defeated.* Yet now Russia stirs up rebellion and keeps troops on the soil of her friend and ally – Iran. There isn't a doubt in my mind that Russia intends an invasion of Turkey and the Black Sea Straits to the Mediterranean. Unless Russia is faced with an iron fist and strong language war is in the making. Only one language do they understand – 'How many divisions have you?'[4]

On 19 January 1946, the Iranian Government complained to the U.N. Security Council about Soviet actions and in March the U.S.S.R. began the six-week process of withdrawing from Iran. However, the Azarbaijani republic remained and continued to receive Soviet help. When the Iranian authorities moved to crush the separatists, Soviet forces massed on the border. Britain and the U.S. threatened to intervene and Britain moved a brigade to Basra in support of the Iranians. The Russians stood down and Teheran restored its control over Azarbaijan. But almost immediately a new crisis emerged.

At Teheran, Churchill had said that Russia was entitled to better access to the world's main sea routes. Stalin appears to have taken this as a hint that Britain would be prepared to acquiesce in the establishment of a Soviet base in the Turkish Dardanelles Straits. In March 1945, the U.S.S.R. demanded a revision of the treaty governing the use of the Straits. Three months later, Soviet demands became more insistent: a permanent base in the Dardanelles and the return of the old Tsarist provinces of Kars, Ardahan and Artvin from Turkey. Stalin broached this subject at Potsdam and also demanded a base on the Aegean at Alexandroupolis in Greece. Soviet pressure on Turkey was maintained throughout 1945–6, but Turkey received British support and declared that she was ready to defend herself. Stalin obviously believed that he had a reasonable case in this issue. In April 1946, Stalin told the American Ambassador: 'Turkey is weak and the Soviet Union is very conscious of the danger of foreign control of the Straits,† which Turkey is not

---

* The U.S.S.R. received Lend–Lease aid worth $10,982 million.

† Possibly Stalin was concerned that Britain – whose interests in the eastern Mediterranean had often clashed with Tsarist Russia's – was going to extend her influence over the Straits. The British did have a considerable military presence nearby at the time, in Palestine, Greece, Cyprus and Egypt.

strong enough to protect. The Turkish Government is unfriendly to us ... It is a matter of our own security.'[5] In August 1946, the U.S. parried the Soviet threat to Turkey with a counter threat. She stated that an attack on Turkey would justify action by the U.N. Security Council. As U.N. action could be blocked by a Soviet veto, Truman made his message plain by sending an aircraft carrier task force to join the battleship *Missouri*, which was already in Istanbul. Soviet pressure on Turkey eased, but only for a matter of weeks.

Meanwhile, in Greece the British had been engaged since December 1944 in attempting to prop up an unpopular monarchy widely associated with harsh, dictatorial methods. The most forceful opponents of the Greek regime were communist partisans who found ready sanctuaries and sources of supply in the communist states to the north. It seems that Yugoslavia and her puppet, Albania, were the chief supporters of the Greek insurgents, although this was not understood in the West at the time. Any communist activity anywhere was assumed to be in the interests of, if not dictated by, the Kremlin.

By early 1947, the United Kingdom was on her knees; drastic economies had to be made if she was to avoid collapse, and so on 21 February 1947 the British Government informed the U.S. that she had no choice but to end her assistance and support for Greece and Turkey. This marked a turning point in recent history for it resulted in the U.S. entering into military obligations to foreign countries in peacetime. On 12 March President Truman announced the Truman Doctrine in which he dedicated American support to the 'Free World' and summed up the issues in the 'Cold War' as they appeared to him:

> At the present moment in world history, nearly every nation must choose alternative ways of life. The choice is too often not a free one. One way of life is based upon the will of the majority, and is distinguished by free institutions, representative government, free elections, guarantees of individual liberty, freedom of speech and religion, and freedom from political oppression. The second way of life is based upon the will of a minority forcibly imposed upon the majority. It relies upon terror and oppression, a controlled press and radio, fixed elections, and the suppression of personal freedoms. I believe that it must be the policy of the United States to support free peoples who are resisting attempted subjugation by armed minorities or by outside pressures. I believe that we must assist free peoples to work out their own destinies in their own way.[6]

Truman then asked Congress to grant to Greece and Turkey aid totalling $250,000,000 and $150,000,000 respectively and Congress did so. The American action probably saved Greece and Turkey although the communist insurgency in Greece did not formally end until the summer of 1949. The Truman Doctrine was a response not just to communist activity in the eastern Mediterranean, but a reaction to Soviet activities across the board, not least in Central and Eastern Europe.

Towards the end of the war, Churchill had been worried about the future of Eastern Europe as it became increasingly likely that this area would be liberated by the Red Army. On a visit to Moscow in October 1944, the British Prime Minister made a deal with Stalin in which the two statesmen divided the Balkans into their respective spheres of influence. The U.S.S.R. was to have a 90 per cent interest in Rumania and 75 per cent in Bulgaria, Britain would have a 90 per cent interest in Greece. They would each have 50 per cent in Hungary and Yugoslavia. In making the agreement, Churchill was trying to do the best he could for Eastern Europe. He knew that the West would be powerless to prevent Stalin doing what he wished in the Balkans but hoped that a paper agreement would limit Stalin's actions.

The Second World War left the Red Army astride Eastern Europe and in complete control of the region, apart from Greece, Yugoslavia and Albania, but the two latter were in the hands of communist partisans. The Soviet Union annexed the Baltic States, parts of Finland, Poland, Germany, Czechoslovakia and Rumania, thus gaining an area of some 180,000 square miles with a population of 24 million. The presence of the Red Army and local communist parties supported by Moscow was to extend Soviet influence into Poland, Czechoslovakia, Rumania, Hungary, Albania, Bulgaria, Yugoslavia and the Soviet zone of Germany, an area of 393,500 square miles with a population of nearly 92 million. The prospect facing the West in 1945 was daunting, for if the U.S.S.R. ignored her promises to hold free elections in these countries and they were to go communist they would represent an immense accretion of power to the Soviet Union. What Britain fought the war to prevent – the domination of Central Europe by one country – had come about, but the dominant power was the Soviet Union not Germany.

As soon as the war ended, American forces began to pull out of Europe and Churchill, alarmed at the prospect of being left to face massive Russian forces, sent a telegram to Truman expressing his fears: 'I am profoundly concerned about the European situation . . .

What will be the position in a year when the British and American
armies have melted . . . when we may have a handful of divisions,
mostly French, and when Russia may choose to keep two or three
hundred on active service? An iron curtain is drawn down upon
their front. We do not know what is going on behind.'[7] Many
Americans regarded Churchill's views as exaggerations but he
returned to them the following year in a speech in Fulton, Missouri,
when he again spoke of an 'iron curtain' and said that the capitals
of Eastern Europe 'and the populations around them, lie in the
Soviet sphere, and all are subject in one form or another, not only
to Soviet influence, but to very high and increasing measures of
control from Moscow'.[8] Churchill was out of office at this time but
his statements were listened to in Moscow although they did not
produce the effect he desired in the United States where many were
still predisposed to co-operation with 'Uncle Joe' Stalin. Yet
Churchill's words were amply justified as events in Eastern Europe
were to show during 1947.

The Soviet Union appeared to be in no hurry to hold 'free
elections' in Eastern Europe, but in 1947 events began to move
quickly. On 10 February Russia signed peace treaties with Italy,
Finland, Bulgaria, Hungary and Rumania and this effectively
ended any Western ability materially to affect the fortunes of the
latter three countries. In the spring, the Truman Doctrine was
announced, the Foreign Ministers Conference in Moscow failed
(see Chapter 4), and on 5 June the U.S. Secretary of State, General
Marshall, published his Marshall Plan of massive financial aid to the
war-damaged countries of Europe. The American idea was to
restore the economies of Europe and so destroy the conditions of
deprivation and hopelessness which could stimulate the growth of
communism. Under the Marshall Aid Programme, the U.S. gave
$13,150,000,000 to sixteen European states,* but the U.S.S.R.
refused to join in the scheme. The Soviets did consider the Marshall
Plan carefully; Foreign Minister Molotov and a large team of
experts went to Paris at the end of June 1947 to confer with their
British and French opposite numbers. Meanwhile, to retain the
option of rejecting the plan, the Soviet press kept up a constant

---

* Recipients of Marshall Aid included: Austria, Belgium, Denmark, Norway,
Sweden, Iceland, Holland, Luxemburg, Britain, Portugal, Switzerland, Italy,
Greece, Turkey, France and Eire. The three Western zones of Germany also
received aid.

barrage of hostile criticism, denouncing it as 'foreign interference' and preparing Soviet and world opinion for Moscow's rejection of Marshall Aid. On 2 July, Molotov withdrew from the Paris conference, and any prospect of large-scale East–West economic cooperation was at an end. One by-product of the Soviet decision was that Hungary, Poland and Czechoslovakia who had shown interest in the Marshall Plan also had to withdraw. Many in the American Government were probably relieved that the Soviet Union did not participate, as the Aid Bill had a rough passage through the U.S. Congress and it might not have been passed at all if Congress had had to debate the giving of huge sums of aid to a country with which agreement in other spheres had become almost impossible.

In mid-July, in what appeared to be a reply to Marshall Aid, the Soviet Union began to draw the East Europeans closer to the Kremlin. By the end of August 1947, bilateral trade agreements had been signed between the U.S.S.R. on the one hand, and Bulgaria, Czechoslovakia, Hungary, Yugoslavia, Poland and Rumania on the other.

The West was offered a further example of Soviet attempts to extend her influence when the Cominform (Communist Information Bureau) was formally established on 5 October. Its membership consisted of the leaders of the Communist Parties of the U.S.S.R., Poland, Bulgaria, Czechoslovakia, Rumania, Hungary, Yugoslavia, France, Italy and (later) the Netherlands, and it provided a channel of communication and direction from the Kremlin to the other Communist Parties. The Cominform manifesto declared that the U.S. and U.K. had fought the war solely to rid themselves of German and Japanese competition. It also said 'that the world was divided into two fronts, one imperialist, the other socialist and democratic, and that there must be no Munich with the imperialists'.[9] This was seen in the West as a declaration of Cold War, and was doubly alarming because 20–30 per cent of those who voted in France and Italy voted communist. There were some fears – especially in the U.S. – of the possibility of attempted communist takeovers in these two countries.

A few weeks before this, the Soviet Communist Party theoretician Andrei Zhdanov made a speech in which he said: 'the time had come for the colonial people to "expel their aggressors".'[10] Largely as a result of this, the Western world accused the Soviet Union of

responsibility for communist-led unrest, strikes and insurgency
that sprang up in South and South-East Asia.

Nearer home, the Soviet Union consolidated its hold upon
Eastern Europe. Throughout this area, political parties of different
complexions had been set up but the process by which the communists came to power was inexorable. In Hungary early in 1947,
the Communist Party (C.P.) attacked the Smallholders' Party
and numbers of 'Smallholders' were arrested. Elections were held in
the summer in which the C.P. emerged as the largest party, although
it did not have a majority in Parliament. Nevertheless, the Hungarian C.P. formed a government and on 1 November all other political
parties were dissolved. The same pattern was followed in Bulgaria.
On 16 August 1947, the Bulgarian C.P. accused Petkov, the leader
of the Peasant Party of plotting a *coup*. He was arrested and his
party was dissolved on the grounds that it was 'fascist'. Petkov was
hanged in December 1947 and Georgi Dimitrov formed a government which was predominantly communist. In Rumania matters
were a little different as the country was a monarchy. Elections
were held but were denounced by the West as invalid. In October
1947 the opposition Peasant Party was dissolved and its leader
Maniu was sentenced to life imprisonment. Great pressure was
exerted against King Michael until on 1 January 1948 he abdicated
and fled the country. In Poland the leader of the London Poles,
Mikolajczyk, had to flee the country for his life and his opposition
party was dissolved in November 1947. By the end of 1947, the
Soviet Union and her client communist parties were in firm control
of all Eastern Europe except Czechoslovakia. The Western world
had a strong emotional interest in Czechoslovakia – a product of
guilt over the Munich Agreement – so when President Benes was
forced to resign and a Communist government took over in Prague,
and the last non-communist member of the Czech Government,
Jan Masaryk, died in mysterious circumstances in March 1948,
these events produced a shock wave in the West that others elsewhere
in Eastern Europe had failed to do. If there had been any doubt
about Soviet policy over the last year, Czechoslovakia removed it.

The events in Czechoslovakia combined with the Berlin Blockade
helped bring about what Western European Governments had been
hoping for – a firm American military commitment to the defence
of Western Europe. In June 1948, the U.S. Senate passed a resolution in which it declared America's intention to enter into a formal

military alliance with other countries. Twelve* nations signed the North Atlantic Treaty on 4 April 1949 and declared their commitment to common defence. For the first time in her history the U.S.A. had entered into a peacetime alliance and had finally and formally accepted the leadership of the Free World in the face of the commonly perceived menace. Initially the Americans hoped that their contribution would be limited to a 'nuclear umbrella' protecting Western Europe, but within a short time American troops returned in strength to Western Europe and old Second World War airbases were opened again for American forces. President Roosevelt had always declared his intention of withdrawing U.S. forces from Europe once the war was over. That intention was now reversed. In announcing the signing of the North Atlantic Treaty to the French National Assembly, the French Government representative spoke for the rest of Western Europe when he said: 'We have today obtained what we hoped for in vain between the two wars: the United States recognizes that there is neither peace nor security for America if Europe is in danger.'[11]

---

* The twelve were: the U.S.A., Canada, Britain, France, Belgium, Holland, Luxembourg, Italy, Denmark, Norway, Iceland and Portugal. Greece and Turkey joined in 1952 and West Germany in 1955.

# Four

# THE PARTITION OF GERMANY AND THE BERLIN BLOCKADE

All the Allies were determined that never again should Germany become a threat to them, but beyond this there was little substantial agreement either on the future of Germany or on a European peace settlement. It was agreed that Germany and Austria should be split into zones of occupation between Britain, the United States, the Soviet Union and France, and that Berlin and Vienna should be similarly divided. It was decided that supreme authority in Germany should be vested in the hands of the Allied Control Council (A.C.C.), consisting of the military governors of the four occupation zones and that subordinate to the A.C.C., but responsible for Berlin, would be the Allied *Kommandatura* which would consist of the four military Governors of Berlin. Further, Germany would be treated as one economic unit and would become once again one political unit. The desperate economic situation of Central Europe between 1945–8 coupled with the different occupation policies of the Four Powers meant that the Eastern and Western zones of Germany began to emerge as separate economic and political entities.

In the A.C.C. of 1945, the first difficulties did not come from the Russians but from the French. General de Gaulle's Provisional French Government had not been a party to the Teheran, Yalta and Potsdam Agreements and did not consider itself bound by any of them. Thus, although it was official allied policy that Germany should remain united, the French were adamant in their opposition to the recreation of a centralized Germany which they saw as a potential threat – France had been invaded by Germany three times in seventy years. In the latter part of 1945, the French in the

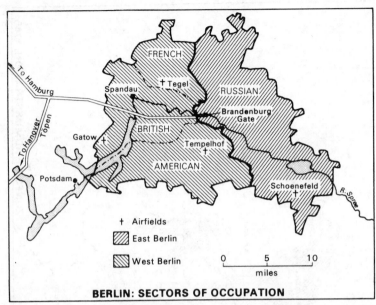

**BERLIN: SECTORS OF OCCUPATION**

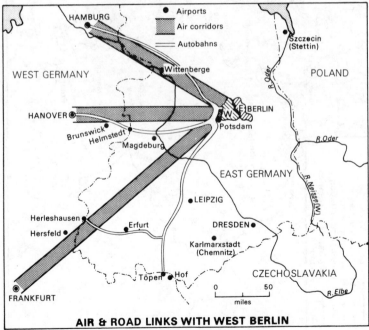

**AIR & ROAD LINKS WITH WEST BERLIN**

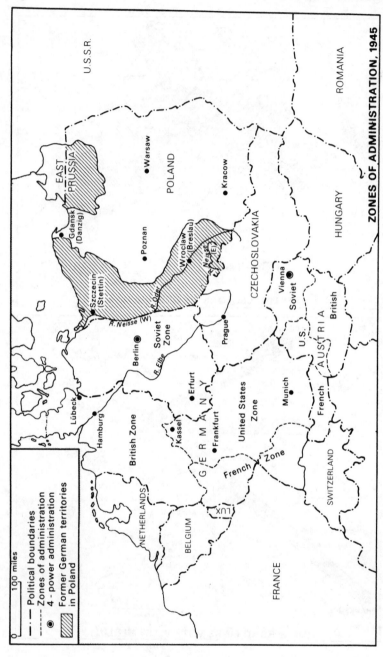

ZONES OF ADMINISTRATION, 1945

100 miles

- · — · Political boundaries
- - - - Zones of administration
- ⊙ · · 4 - power administration
- Former German territories
  in Poland

A.C.C. refused to allow the creation of a centralized administration of Germany, free passage of individuals between different zones, nationwide political parties, trades union, or a national railways directorate. If it was Soviet policy to prevent the rebuilding of a unified, centralized Germany – as many Western observers felt – then they did not need to implement this policy in the A.C.C. in 1945; the French were doing it for them. In the first few months of 1946, the A.C.C. had to deal with the difficult question of reparations and it was over this issue that the first big breach between the Anglo–Americans and the Russians came.

At Yalta, the Big Three had accepted that Germany should pay for the damage that she had done and that the bulk of the reparations should go to the U.S.S.R. The Soviets claimed a sum of $10,000,000,000 and the Western Allies accepted the principle but not the amount. It was agreed at Potsdam, that the U.S.S.R. could take reparations from its own zone of occupation. Also she should receive from the Western zones 25 per cent of all machinery and industrial plant that was unnecessary for Germany's peacetime economy. In return for this, the U.S.S.R. would send from her zone to the Western zones food, coal and raw materials to the value of 60 per cent of what she received from the West. Final details of just what was necessary to the German peacetime economy were left eventually to the A.C.C.

Article 13 of the Potsdam Agreement stated: 'In organising the German economy, primary emphasis shall be given to the development of agriculture and peaceful domestic industries.' Article 3 (ii) said that one of the purposes of the occupation was: 'To convince the German people that they have suffered total military defeat and that they cannot escape responsibility for what they have brought upon themselves, since their own ruthless warfare and the fanatical Nazi resistance have destroyed the German economy and made chaos and suffering inevitable.'[1] It was also agreed that the German standard of living should be reduced to a level not exceeding the average for other European countries. This level was estimated to be 74 per cent of Germany's figure for 1936.[2]

The Western Allies, then, were prepared to be punitive in their economic treatment of Germany, but Potsdam had ignored the prevailing realities of the German situation. When the Nazi Reich surrendered on 8 May 1945, the German state ceased to exist, so the Allies had to assume responsibility for administering the country.

The economy was shattered. In the British zone, which was the industrial heartland of Germany, coal production in June 1945 was running at a rate of 1 million tons per annum, whereas in 1943 production had been 38 million tons. The Western zones of occupation were not capable of producing sufficient food to feed themselves and if the Allies continued to insist upon the dismantling of German industry at the rate agreed at Potsdam, then industry in the Western zones would not be able to produce the exports needed to earn the money to pay for desperately needed food imports. Between 1945–7 the British and Americans had to import foodstuffs to the value of $700 million per annum into their zones just to prevent mass starvation. The problem was exacerbated for the West by the influx into their zones of millions of destitute refugees from Eastern Germany and people expelled from Poland and Czechoslovakia.

Meanwhile, the Russians were still exacting reparations from Germany and were making their zone live off its own resources. Moreover, the Russians refused to account for much of what they took from their own zone. This situation increasingly angered the British and American military authorities because they were having to import food into their own zones at their own cost, and they still had to send reparations to the Russians. By 1946 the Russians were holding up counter deliveries of food and raw materials because of the 'poor' economic state of Eastern Europe. This situation represented indirect payments for deliveries to the Russians by the British and Americans. 'Our first break with Soviet policy in Germany came over reparations,' wrote the American General Clay; '. . . in the spring of 1946, after repeated warnings had failed, I stopped delivery from our zone. I had no choice.'[3] The British followed suit. Stopping deliveries 'led to bitter altercations in the Control Council and in the meetings of the Foreign Ministers, and was a major contributing factor in the break-up of quadripartite government'.[4] In a speech in Stuttgart on 6 September 1946, the American Secretary of State, James Byrnes, formally acknowledged that the Potsdam economic agreements were not working. He proposed unifying the economy of the American zone with any or all of the other zones. Only Britain accepted and the two zones were formally merged into Bizonia on 1 January 1947. (The French zone joined in 1949.) So in 1946, the economic division of Germany between East and West was becoming a fact. The political division of Germany had begun even earlier.

The Potsdam Agreement had allowed for the setting-up in Germany of free democratic and anti-fascist political parties, but even before Potsdam, the Soviet Union had begun the process by which it tried to win communist and Russian control over any new German political parties. On 10 June 1945 the Military Governor of the Soviet zone, Marshal Zhukov, authorized the setting-up of democratic political parties, and so there quickly appeared a Communist Party (K.P.D.), a Social Democratic Party (S.P.D.) a Liberal Party (F.D.P.) and a Christian Democratic or Conservative Party. This represented an appeal by the Soviet Union to the German people to accept that the Russians were working in their interests. Soviet propaganda in the eighteen months after the war constantly offered a united Germany whose frontiers would be guaranteed by the Red Army. This offer was quite persuasive because it contrasted with the French who still wanted to annex the Saarland and separate the Ruhr from Germany, and the Anglo–Americans who still refused to boost the German economy as Russia claimed she wanted to do. Aware that the bulk of the German people associated communism with the Kremlin and were therefore frightened of both, the new K.P.D. issued a manifesto in Berlin on 25 June 1945, designed to set their fears at rest. The manifesto claimed:

> We consider it incorrect for Germany to open the path for implanting the Soviet system because such a path does not correspond with the conditions of the development of Germany at this moment. We consider that the real interests of the German people, under present conditions, dictate another path, that of establishing an anti-fascist democratic regime and a democratic parliamentary Republic with all democratic liberties.[5]

The pronouncement sought to convince those Germans who had never associated Russian communism with democracy, that the K.P.D. was an independent left-wing party which would be responsive to German rather than to Russian interests. Very many German socialists were not convinced.

In December 1945 representatives from the Soviet zone of the K.P.D. and the S.P.D. met in Berlin to discuss the merging together of the two parties. This alarmed S.P.D. members in the Western zones who met in Hanover the following January and overwhelmingly rejected the idea. The parties in the Eastern zone went ahead and held a referendum on the issue in Berlin on 31 March 1946. The Soviet commander in Berlin, General Kotikov, had agreed to the referendum but within an hour of the polls opening in the Soviet zone, it became clear that there was massive support for the S.P.D. faction which opposed the merger and so the polls in the Russian sector were closed because of 'irregularities'. Otto Grotewohl, the S.P.D. leader in the Soviet zone, told his followers in the other zones not to vote, but the result was a rejection of the merger and the communist control that went with it; 82 per cent of S.P.D. members voted against the fusion. Nevertheless on 22 April 1946, the new merged party, the Socialist Unity Party (S.E.D.), was established with Wilhelm Pieck of the K.P.D. and Otto Grotewohl of the S.P.D. as joint chairmen. The Russians had attempted to gain control over the new political parties and they had failed. But in making the attempt they had frightened off German political leaders in the Western zones who now went on to set up political parties only in the West.

By 1947 the wartime allies were at deadlock in Germany. The work of the A.C.C. was at a standstill and co-operation in the Berlin *Kommandatura* became more and more difficult as the Russians gradually showed their hand. In June 1947 the Berlin Parliament elected, by a majority of 89 votes to 17, the S.P.D. candidate, Ernst Reuter, as Mayor of the city but General Kotikov refused to accept the result because Reuter, an ex-communist, had reputedly called the Soviet Union a 'nation of slaves' and an 'ant-heap of a state'.[6]

Even before this, the Russians and Russian-controlled East German press had been attacking the West with increasing savagery until in the autumn of 1947 the American Governor, Clay, authorized the American press to 'attack Communism in every form wherever it existed and to cite each exposed example of its day-to-day work. We still would not attack governments or individuals; we would not sling mud but we would no longer refrain from exposing Communist tactics and purposes.'[7] The language of the Cold War had now appeared.

The Council of Foreign Ministers had been able to finalize peace treaties with Italy, Finland, Bulgaria, Hungary and Rumania and these were signed on 10 February 1947, but once these less important matters were out of the way the Foreign Ministers could no longer avoid confrontation on the major issue before them: peace treaties with Germany and Austria. The fourth session of the Council of Foreign Ministers opened in a tense atmosphere in Moscow on

10 March 1947, and two days later President Truman announced the Truman Doctrine which indicated an American determination to resist Soviet ambitions, especially in the eastern Mediterranean (see Chapter 3). As such, it could only worsen the atmosphere of the Moscow Conference. The Conference achieved nothing on the outstanding peace treaties and has been described as a 'fiasco' of 'accusations and counter-accusations'.[8] The American delegation had gone to Moscow 'prepared to stretch to the limit to meet legitimate Russian security interests in the structure of Germany and Europe', prepared to compromise and conscious of 'the consequences of failure in Moscow; a split Germany and Europe'.[9] The Moscow conference taught the Americans that they could only hope to negotiate successfully with the Russians from a position of strength. From this time on neither side was much interested in compromise; thus the Moscow Conference was central to the development of the Cold War.

As the Soviet Union could not get what she wanted in Germany by negotiation, she tried in 1948 to get it by other means: by trying to force the Western Allies out of their enclave in Berlin. 'The Berlin Blockade was in Russian eyes a substitute for war. It was a deliberate attack on the whole Western position in Germany and on the American commitment to Europe, which the Soviet policy of the preceding three years had brought about.'[10] Ostensibly the blockade was mounted as a protest against Western plans to introduce a currency reform into the Western zones. The Western Allies had decided to replace the old, worthless *Reichmark* with the new *Deutschmark* in the hope that this would spur the economic recovery of their zones. The new currency was introduced into the Western zones on 18 June 1948, but tension had been growing even before then. On 20 March 1948, the Soviet Military Governor, Marshal Sokolovsky, walked out of the Allied Control Council and declared that it had ceased to function. On 1 April, the Soviet Union began to impose restrictions on the road and rail links that Western allied traffic had to use between Berlin and their own zones.

On 16 June, the Russians left the Allied *Kommandatura* in Berlin and two days later the currency reform was introduced into the Western zones. All pretence at quadripartite government of Germany and Berlin had now ceased to exist and the Russians hurried to introduce their own currency reform into their zone of Germany

and sector of Berlin. On 23 June, East and West introduced their
new currencies into Berlin and the following day the Soviet Union
severed all rail, road and canal links to West Berlin. The blockade
was complete. West Berlin, stranded 100 miles deep in Soviet-
occupied territory, was dependent upon the Western zones for food,
clothing, coal and indeed for the necessities of life. The Western
Allies were faced with three options: they could send military con-
voys down the autobahns to West Berlin and attempt to run the
blockade; they could surrender, bring their forces out of the city
and hand over the whole of Berlin to Soviet administration; or
they could try to surmount the blockade, literally. The first option
was seriously considered by the Americans but was discarded
because it would have entailed too high a risk of war; also there
were only 6,000 Western troops in Berlin, but there were 18,000
Russian troops in the city and many divisions near by. Although
the United States enjoyed a monopoly of nuclear power at this
time her conventional forces were weak, as were those of her allies
in Europe, so the West could not risk provoking a conventional
conflict which they would certainly lose, initially at least. The
second option was never seriously considered. If the West had pulled
out of Berlin, then her credit in the world would have sunk dis-
astrously and anti-communist regimes throughout the world could
hardly have been expected to believe American assurances of help
against communist aggression. The third option was therefore
adopted. It was decided by the Western Allies to attempt to supply
West Berlin by air.

The civilian population of West Berlin at the end of 1948 was
2,108,000 and the Western authorities estimated that daily minimum imported tonnage of supplies would have to be 4,000 tons.
Also, 500 tons per day would be needed for the Western garrison.
This figure only represented the amount needed to keep the population alive, it took no account of the extra fuel that would be needed
for the winter or of tonnage needed to keep industry ticking over
and a subsistence economy going. The Western Allies mounted a
massive effort, the results of which surprised even themselves. The
Americans and British stripped their air forces in other parts of the
world of transport aircraft and sent them to Berlin. By the end of
winter, the West was flying in an average of 6,000 tons of supplies
each day. When the blockade was finally called off in May 1949,
2,300,000 tons of supplies had been flown into Berlin. The blockade

cost the lives of thirty-one American, thirty-nine British and nine German pilots and groundsmen.*

During the blockade, Stalin took pains to deny that there was a crisis. In early August 1948, he declared to the American Ambassador, Smith: 'After all we are still allies'[11] and the Russian military authorities described the blockade as 'only technical difficulties' of a 'temporary nature'. However, when he met the three Western Military Governors at Potsdam on 3 July 1948, Marshal Sokolovsky said that the 'technical difficulties' would continue until the West had abandoned their plans for a West German government.[12] Obviously Stalin wanted to achieve his objectives without incurring war. The Russians took pains to avoid violence between Western and Soviet troops and also were careful to ensure that none of the airlift planes was brought down as a result of Soviet interference. Indeed the Soviets kept an unusually 'low profile' throughout the crisis.

In the summer of 1948, the Americans and British imposed a 'counter-blockade' on goods going from the Western zones to the Eastern zone. This blockade was much more harmful to the East than to the West as the Soviet zone needed coking coal and steel from the only ready source of supply – in the West. Western Germany had access to the expanding economies of Western Europe and was being helped by the Marshall Plan, but Eastern Germany had no such advantages. It seems that Eastern Germany's economy was virtually at a standstill by early 1949, whereas Western Germany's 'economic miracle' had begun. When the blockade was lifted it was apparent that the West could have maintained the airlift indefinitely and that the continuation of the blockade was increasing the solidarity of the West Berliners and West Germans with the Western Allies.

The Berlin Blockade destroyed any illusions in the Western governments about agreement with the Russians in Germany, but it was significant in other ways too. 'The Berlin crisis marked the first time that nuclear weapons were seriously considered as a measure of last resort to check Soviet advances. It triggered the reversal of the post-war declining trend in United States defence budgets.'[13] On the other hand it also hastened the process by which two separate German states appeared.

* The Americans contributed about two-thirds of the aircraft and the British the rest. France had no large transport aircraft but fully supported her two allies.

On 12 May 1949 the A.C.C. (during Marshal Sokolovsky's absence) approved the Basic Law* of the new Federal Republic of Germany and on 23 May the Federal Republic came into existence. The West had seriously considered the establishment of an independent West Germany the previous year, and had come to the conclusion that Soviet action made a West German state and a partitioned Germany inevitable. Just a week after the full blockade of Berlin had started on 1 July 1948 the three Western Military Governors authorized the convening of a constituent assembly to draft a democratic constitution and set up a West German state. Once the Federal Republic was established, the constituent assembly dissolved itself and a general election was held. On 17 September 1949 the first freely elected members of Parliament in Germany since 1933 were sworn into the Federal Republic's Parliament and Konrad Adenauer became Chancellor. The final legal break in the German situation and the destruction of the last remnants of quadripartite control over the whole of Germany had been taken by the West.

At the Four Power Conference in Paris which took place after the end of the blockade, the Soviets demanded 'a return to Potsdam' and a halt in Western efforts to set up a West German state. But the concessions the Soviet Deputy Foreign Minister Vishinsky demanded were all one-sided. He refused to make any moves to dismantle the East German state that the Soviet Union was creating in her zone. The Paris Conference failed and the question of Germany was left on the table, unsolved and potentially dangerous for the world. No peace treaty with Germany had been signed. Both sides, however, appeared to have reached an unspoken understanding that they would accept the *status quo* in Central Europe.

Shortly after the first session of the West German Parliament opened, the German Democratic Republic (*Deutsche Demokratische Republik*) came into existence on 7 October 1949 in the Soviet zone. The D.D.R. was dominated by the S.E.D. which was in turn controlled by the communists. The Soviet Union refused to recognize the existence of the Federal Republic and the West refused to recognize East Germany. On 12 October 1949, the United States Secretary of State, Dean Acheson, declared: 'This new [D.D.R.]

---

* The Basic Law governs the functioning of the West German state and is designed to remain in force until Germany becomes reunited and is replaced by a constitution. To all intents and purposes the Basic Law is a constitution.

government was created by Soviet and Communist *fiat*. It was created by a self-styled People's Council which itself had no basis in free popular elections. This long expected Soviet creation thus stands in sharp contrast to the German Federal Republic at Bonn which has a thoroughly constitutional and popular basis.'[14]

With the appearance of the two German states in 1949 the partition of Germany was complete. Not only did the legal form of two German states separate people of the same nationality, but defended frontiers and the severing of most communications were soon to do so too. Along the 850 miles of the frontier between the two Germanies the East Germans began to guard their unpopular state with wire fences, watchtowers, mine fields, and armed patrols.

The Soviet Union and the Western Allies blamed each other for the creation of two German states and the breaking of the Potsdam Agreement, and each side was able to present a reasonably good case. But the fact was that both sides would have had great cause for concern about the future policies of a united, independent Germany – even a 'neutral' Germany – because this would have come to dominate Central Europe again simply by virtue of her size and industrial potential.

# Five

# THE COLD WAR TURNS EAST: THE 'LOSS' OF CHINA

To America, China was a special country. She had a great culture, great food, great charm and, according to an American novel of the 1930s, *The Good Earth* by Pearl Buck, her people were clean, hard-working, reverent, puritanical and cheerful – all those virtues which Americans admired. America had, admittedly out of economic self-interest, worked to prevent the fragmentation of China into European spheres of influence at the turn of the century. The U.S. had also sent missionaries to China (the Chinese leader Chiang Kai-shek became a Methodist during the 1930s) and set up schools there. A myth – not necessarily supported by facts – grew up about a very special relationship between the U.S. and China: America helped the Chinese, in return Chinese loved Americans. After a war of intensive propaganda films which showed, for example, the Japanese rape of China, American marines defending the Chinese, Chinese nurses saving American pilots and, of course, falling in love with them, the loss of China to the communist cause was a great shock.

As the previous chapters relate, U.S. attention was at that time focused on Europe. The possibility of a Soviet attack on Western Europe or at least of continued testing of the fringes of Europe in Greece, Turkey, Iran and elsewhere, reduced appreciation of the speed of events in China among U.S. government circles. As late as March 1947, when asked why China was not receiving massive U.S. aid, Dean Acheson replied: 'The Chinese Government is not at the present time in the position the Greek Government is in. It is not approaching collapse.'[1]

China had entered the twentieth century in a state of advanced decay – she was humiliated by foreign powers, she had failed to expand arable land sufficient to support her booming population, and she had failed to launch her economy into a commercial and industrial revolution. The Manchu Empire collapsed in a revolution inspired by the nationalist, republican, socialist Dr. Sun Yat Sen in 1911. The revolution was, however, perverted by 'warlords' and from 1912 to 1927 Sun and (after 1925) his heir, General Chiang Kai-shek, tried to regain control and reunify a divided China. In 1921, inspired by Russian success as much as by Russian ideology, a group of Chinese (including Mao Tse-tung) searching for a new truth, founded the Chinese Communist Party. Acting on the advice of Stalin, the C.C.P. co-operated with Chiang's Kuomintang Party, until Chiang attacked the Communists in 1927. The ensuing Chinese Civil War, lasted from 1927 to 1949 and was interrupted only by a temporary and unstable unity during the Japanese onslaught on China from 1937 to 1945.

By 1939, Mao controlled 30,000 square miles in north and central China and ruled 2 million people; by 1945 he controlled 400,000 square miles, ruled 100 million people, had a regular army of 470,000 and a force of 2 million guerrillas.[2] Chiang had American support. The Kuomintang was even recognized as the Chinese Government by the U.S.S.R. Chiang had control of industrial China and an army of $2\frac{1}{2}$ million regulars and $1\frac{1}{2}$ million militia. In December 1945, General Marshall arrived from America to try to prevent a rebirth of the civil war, but Chiang was determined to occupy Manchuria after the Soviets left in 1946. As early as 1944, American diplomatic personnel in China were recommending that the U.S. should help to produce a coalition government in China and foster reasonable relations with the Chinese Communists. The alternative appeared to be a Soviet-backed all-communist China. Few of these able Americans saw any chance for the shambling, corrupt, unpopular, feudal regime of Chiang.

America and Britain, attempting some degree of 'neutrality' – which must later have been sorely regretted – even banned military aid to Chiang between July 1946 and May 1947, in an attempt to force him to a political compromise. Congressman J. F. Kennedy commented on this in January 1949 at a political meeting in Massachusetts: 'Our policy in China has reaped the whirlwind. The continued insistence that aid would not be forthcoming unless a coalition government was formed was a crippling blow to the National Government. So concerned were our diplomats and their advisers . . . with the imperfections of the political system in China after twenty years of war, and the tales of corruption in higher places, that they lost sight of our tremendous stake in non-communist China.'[3] Yet during 1946, the U.S. did transport half a million of Chiang's troops around China, did arrange aerial reconnaissance for him, and between VJ Day and March 1949 did provide him with both military and economic aid amounting to $3,087 million. Thus, in Mao's eyes, America had intervened and was intervening in the Chinese Civil War just as thirty years previously she had intervened in the Russian Civil War. American concern for Soviet involvement in China was certainly unjustified, for in 1945 Stalin thought Chiang would win, and indeed recommended that Mao should seek a *modus vivendi* with Chiang. During a conversation in July 1947 Stalin stated: 'Now in the case of China, we admit we were wrong.'[4] (See Chapter 14.)

The vacated communist capital of Yenan fell by March 1947, but it was an empty victory: during 1946 inflation had run at 700 per cent, landlords in Chiang's government blocked land redistribution although 80 per cent of China's population was peasant and of those only 20 per cent owned any land, and during 1947, 400,000 of Chiang's army were either killed or deserted. In July 1948 Chiang's army possessed only a 2:1 superiority over the Communists. That military supremacy was nowhere near sufficient when one takes into consideration the greater morale of the Communists, their better tactics, and the massive support given them by the peasantry of northern China. In addition, by June 1948 the cost of living index was thousands of times what it had been in June 1946.[5]

In December 1948 America cancelled her aid to China. In October Marshall, then Secretary of State, had summarized the American analysis of the situation in China:

> To achieve the objective of reducing the Chinese Communists to a completely negligible factor in China in the immediate future, it would be necessary for the United States virtually to take over the Chinese government and administer its economic, military and governmental affairs. It would involve the United States Government in a continuing commitment from which it would practically be impossible to withdraw, and it would very probably involve grave consequences to this nation by making of China an arena of international conflict.[6]

By November 1948 Mukden, the capital of Manchuria, fell and the communist General Chu Teh headed for Soochow on the

Yangtse River, the symbolic division between North and South China. A sixty-five day battle commenced on 5 November between 600,000 troops on each side. By January 1949 the entire 'white' army had either been killed or were among the 327,000 prisoners or had deserted. Peking was also 'liberated' in January; in April, a million communist troops crossed the Yangtse on a 400-mile front; by October, Chiang's troops were fleeing towards Burma or across the 140-mile Formosan Straits to Taiwan and on 1 October Mao Tse-tung announced the foundation of the People's Republic of China. Within two years the P.R.C. had been recognized by the socialist world, Burma and Britain; she had signed a thirty-year treaty with the Soviet Union; she had occupied the 'roof of the world' in Tibet; and was fighting the U.N. forces in Korea.

The arrival of a 'Red' China of 500 million people completed the American sense of continuing failure that had begun with the 'loss' of Poland. The West (and Soviet Russia!) were faced with a new Asiatic form of communism – a rural, peasant, guerrilla communism which was the product of the non-industrial, coloured Han people – a different threat from that of the urban proletariat risings in the industrial cities of the rich, white world that Marx and Stalin had foreseen. America now had to watch for signs of revolution amongst the poor, coloured, colonial and ex-colonial worlds of South-East Asia, the Middle East, Africa, Central and South America. At the United Nations in 1948, Dr. T. F. Tsiang, Nationalist China's representative, made a prophesy: 'The fate of the entire Far East is linked to that of China, because the Chinese Communists will help the Communists in Indo-China, in Malaya, in Burma, in India, in all the Far East. Against this tide, you have built up in the West a solid dyke, in the form of material aid, from Scandinavia to the Persian Gulf. But now this tide will overflow in another direction.'[7]

# Six

# KOREA – THE LIMITED WAR

Although the Truman Doctrine had not been applicable to China and a 'bamboo curtain' had been added to the 'iron curtain' of Europe, President Truman reacted with speed and determination when a new threat was posed to the West in the Asia of June 1950.

During the Sino–Japanese War of 1895, Korea was wrested from the control of Manchu China by Japan. At the Cairo Conference of 1943 the Allies agreed that Korea, once liberated, would be granted total independence. On 12 August 1945 Soviet troops entered North Korea and reached the 38th Parallel before Japan surrendered: after 8 September the South was occupied by the Americans. The Soviets refused to allow democratic elections in their zone and gradually passed power to the communist Kim Il Sung. In the South, National Assembly elections were held under U.N. supervision in May 1948, and the anti-communist Dr. Syngman Rhee emerged as the President. By 1948 therefore two rival regimes, each claiming sovereignty over the entire country, had been formed – the Democratic People's Republic of Korea in the North and the Republic of Korea in the South. Russian forces withdrew from Korea in December 1948 and American forces withdrew in June 1949. Both sides had aided their 'client' states: the U.S. providing $466 million in civil and military aid, but no tanks, heavy artillery or planes to the 21 million people of South Korea; while the Soviets built up a 90,000 strong North Korean People's Liberation Army and equipped it with tanks and a supporting air force. Thus, although the North Korean population of 9 million was far smaller than that of the South, their armed forces were undoubtedly superior to the 65,000 troops of South Korea.

In January 1950 the U.S. Secretary of State, Dean Acheson, outlined the 'defence perimeter' of the United States in the Pacific and failed to include South Korea. U.S. budgetary economies partly account for the American evacuation of Korea, and some U.S. government officials either considered that Europe would provide the most probable future 'flashpoint', or presumed that the next Soviet–American clash would be global. In neither case did Korea at the time seem significant. However, this apparent ambiguity on America's part may have resulted in Moscow calculating that America might tolerate a forced unification of Korea – by the North Koreans. The Soviets had armed the North for an offensive war, and when seven North Korean Infantry and one Armoured Division attacked the South on 25 June 1950, they used Soviet T34 tanks, Soviet Yak fighters and had Soviet advisers. It seems inconceivable that North Korea would have attacked on its own initiative; that the newly proclaimed People's Republic of China knew of the impending attack is equally obvious, particularly since increased Soviet supplies built up from Vladivostok prior to the invasion. The Americans certainly presumed that Peking was in connivance with Moscow over the attack. Moreover South Korea was only 100 miles from Japan, and Soviet influence in that quarter would hearten Japanese communists as well as worry the Japanese authorities, who were at that time negotiating a defence treaty with the U.S.

Truman saw Korea as part of a new threat: 'The attack upon Korea makes it plain beyond all doubt that communism has passed beyond the use of subversion to conquer independent nations and will now use armed invasion and war.'[1] As he later reflected: 'I recalled some earlier instances: Manchuria, Ethiopia, Austria. I remembered how each time that the democracies failed to act it had encouraged the aggressors to go ahead . . . If this was allowed to go unchallenged, it would mean a third world war.'[2] Air and naval assistance were sent to the South, and within a week of the invasion General MacArthur sent ground troops from Japan. The U.N. Security Council also acted, and eventually seventeen nations sent forces to Korea, although the U.S. bore the brunt of the fighting. (The Soviet Union had absented herself from the Security Council since January 1950, apparently because communist China had not yet been invited to take its U.N. seat, but she may also have hoped to paralyse the Council. Her absence proved to be a major error, since with no Russian veto to impede it the U.N. intervened in Korea.)

Seoul fell on 28 June 1950. The American troops attempted to
hold the position, but tanks did not arrive until 7 July, the date on
which MacArthur was appointed U.N. Commander, as well as
U.S. Commander-in-Chief in the Far East. Meanwhile, on 3 July
the U.S. Seventh Fleet took up station in the Taiwan Straits since
'In these [new] circumstances the occupation of Formosa by Communist forces would be a direct threat to the security of the Pacific
area and to U.S. forces performing their lawful and necessary
functions in that area'.[3]

On 10 July Acheson stated that U.S. forces were in Korea 'solely
for the purpose of restoring the Republic of Korea to its status prior
to the invasion from the North'.[4] During the summer, American
and South Korean forces were pushed back towards Pusan. By early
September, the U.S. had suffered 8,000 casualties and although fifty
nations had pledged support, only a British force from Hong Kong
had actually arrived. On 1 September Truman broadcast to the
world: 'We do not want the fighting in Korea to expand into a
general war. It will not spread unless Communist imperialism draws
other armies and governments into the fight of the aggressors against
the United Nations.'[5] On 15 September, when the evacuation of
Korea seemed a possibility, MacArthur organized a brilliant
amphibious assault by one marine division on Inchon, 200 miles
behind enemy lines and only 20 miles from Seoul. Together with a
South Korean landing at Yongdok on the east coast, allied forces
severed the North–South supply system of the North Korean forces
and the enemy organization collapsed. By 21 September, Seoul was
reached, and by the end of the month, with the North Korean army
losses totalling 335,000, it was clear that U.S. firepower had won.

Rhee and MacArthur now wished to unify Korea and on 7
October 1950 the U.S. and U.N. changed their aim in Korea and
decided on 'the establishment of a unified, independent and
democratic government in the sovereign state of Korea'.[6] This was
no longer a war of 'containment' but an attempt to 'roll back'
communism. On 3 October, the U.S. received an ultimatum from
Chou En-lai, the Chinese Premier, through the Indian Ambassador:
'If the Americans cross the 38th Parallel China would be forced to
intervene in Korea – he was emphatic: the South Koreans did not
matter but American intrusion into North Korea would encounter
Chinese resistance.'[7] Pyongyang was taken on 19 October, but
350,000 men of the Chinese People's Liberation Army had entered

Korea by 16 October, and a major clash with the U.S. forces in North Korea took place on 25 November at Tokchon.

In 1960 the U.S. Air Force commissioned the 'think-tank' RAND Corporation to study China's entry into the war. It concluded that China had not intervened under Russian pressure 'but was "rationally motivated" to enter, assuming from statements issued by Mac-Arthur's headquarters that he intended to invade China. When the Report was released, General MacArthur confirmed that this had been his intention and that it remained an "unfulfilled ambition".'[8] But at the time the U.S. argued that, in the words of Dean Rusk, an Assistant Secretary of State, on 18 May 1951, China was 'a colonial government – a slavonik Manchukuo on a large scale'.[9]

By the end of November 1950, MacArthur's 'home for Christmas' drive on the Yalu had been smashed and by 5 December, the U.N. forces were back below the 38th Parallel. Truman and Attlee decided in Washington in December to abandon their aim of uniting Korea. Yet MacArthur believed that the war should be expanded to the 'privileged sanctuary' of Manchuria by bombing that region, that the Chinese coast should be blockaded and bombed, and that the U.S. should aid diversionary 'invasions' by Taiwanese troops against the mainland.[10] Truman, however, disagreed. In January 1951, new waves of Chinese volunteers crossed the Imjin River and headed for Seoul. The Chinese soldiers, each carrying only six days' rations, fought through the snow and relied on weight of numbers. They were met with the 'meatgrinder' tactics which, utilizing artillery, air bombardment and napalm, aimed at inflicting intolerable losses on the Chinese forces. In February 1951 the U.N. denounced 'Red' China as an aggressor, while China demanded U.S. evacuation of Korea, the removal of the Seventh Fleet from the Taiwan Straits and a U.N. seat. By April, U.N. forces were back over the 38th Parallel into the North, and the MacArthur incident erupted.

MacArthur, criticizing Truman's 'limited war', had publicly called for military operations against the interior and coast of China, aiming thereby to 'doom Red China to the risk of imminent military collapse',[11] and to remove China as a risk to peace in the Far East 'for generations to come'. MacArthur was dismissed on 11 April 1951 just as a new Chinese spring offensive began. Twelve thousand P.L.A. troops died on the first day and the success of firepower against fanatical courage became increasingly evident,

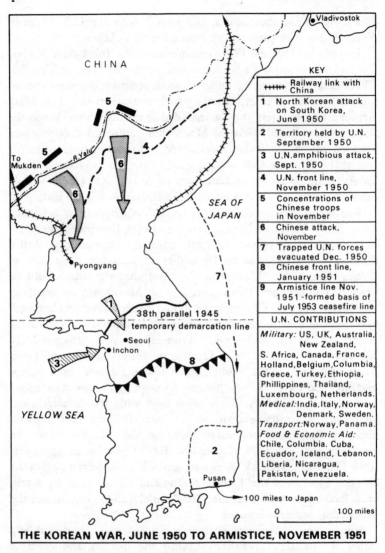

**KEY**

| ┿┿┿┿ | Railway link with China |
|---|---|
| **1** | North Korean attack on South Korea, June 1950 |
| **2** | Territory held by U.N. September 1950 |
| **3** | U.N.amphibious attack, Sept. 1950 |
| **4** | U.N. front line, November 1950 |
| **5** | Concentrations of Chinese troops in November |
| **6** | Chinese attack, November |
| **7** | Trapped U.N. forces evacuated Dec. 1950 |
| **8** | Chinese front line, January 1951 |
| **9** | Armistice line Nov. 1951 -formed basis of July 1953 ceasefire line |

**U.N. CONTRIBUTIONS**

*Military:* US, UK, Australia, New Zealand, S. Africa, Canada, France, Holland, Belgium, Columbia, Greece, Turkey, Ethiopia, Phillipines, Thailand, Luxembourg, Netherlands.
*Medical:* India, Italy, Norway, Denmark, Sweden.
*Transport:* Norway, Panama.
*Food & Economic Aid:* Chile, Columbia. Cuba, Ecuador, Iceland, Lebanon, Liberia, Nicaragua, Pakistan, Venezuela.

**THE KOREAN WAR, JUNE 1950 TO ARMISTICE, NOVEMBER 1951**

with the estimate that the Communist allies had suffered over 1 million casualties in the first year of war. In June 1951 the Chinese proposed an armistice, through the Soviets, but it was not signed until two years later. During this time the U.N. lost a further 60,000 troops. Any extension of the war against China herself would have lost the U.S. some of her allies, risked global war or alternatively 'delighted the Kremlin' by pinning down even more U.S. ground, air and naval forces in the Far East while the Soviets looked on. Omar Bradley, as chairman of the Joint Chiefs of Staff, testified to Congress in May 1951 that: 'Red China is not the most powerful nation seeking to dominate the world. Frankly, in the opinion of the Joint Chiefs of Staff, this strategy would involve us in the wrong war, at the wrong place, at the wrong time, and with the wrong enemy.'[12] In that same Congressional investigation of Korea and MacArthur's dismissal, George Marshall, the Defence Secretary, outlined 'containment' and the concept of the 'limited war' in answer to MacArthur's accusation that the Truman administration had 'no policy': 'There can be, I think, no quick and decisive solution to the global struggle short of resorting to another world war. The cost of such a conflict is beyond calculation. It is therefore our policy to contain communist aggression in different fashions in different areas without resorting to total war.'[14] The war continued throughout 1952, while Rhee declared martial law in May, arrested National Assembly representatives, and moved towards dictatorship.

In January 1953 the new President of the U.S., Eisenhower, hinted that Chiang Kai-shek might be unleashed against mainland China: this, coupled with the cost of maintaining a million Chinese troops in Korea against the U.N. force of 768,000, persuaded China to consider peace more seriously. Stalin died on 5 March 1953 and Russian thoughts turned towards a 'disputed succession'; this was not the time to confront the U.S. In May 1953, nuclear weapons were openly sent to the U.S.-garrisoned Japanese island of Okinawa. In July 1953, according to Eisenhower, the U.S. 'let the Communist authorities understand that in the absence of satisfactory progress at the truce talks, we intended to move decisively without inhibition in our use of weapons and would no longer be responsible for confining activities to the Korean Peninsula'.[15] An armistice was finally signed on 27 July 1953. It remained to count the casualties: South Korea suffered 1·3 million military and 1 million civilian deaths; the U.S. 142,000 and U.N. 17,000 (including 7,000

Commonwealth); the People's Republic of China 900,000 and North Korea 520,000 (for Korea at least it was not a 'limited war').

The outcome of the Korean War represented a clear-cut victory for neither side. From the U.S. point of view, South Korea and perhaps therefore Japan had been saved; the Communist momentum in Asia received a set-back; the U.S. military budget rose from $12 billion to $60 billion, thereby forcing the Soviet Union into an arms race that she could ill afford; the Chinese, after their heavy losses, were inclined to exercise greater caution regarding military confrontation with the U.S.; and the United Nations (or collective security as a general theory) was saved from the blow that had hit the League of Nations in Manchuria in 1931. On the other hand, with her nuclear superiority, perhaps the U.S. over-exaggerated the Soviet threat and could have used at least the full total of her conventional military hardware and gone nearer to the brink of world war than she did. North Korea, of course, had not been 'liberated'.

As for the Soviets, a chance had been taken, and little had been lost by its failure. The war had greatly exacerbated Sino–American hostility, which Stalin may have seen as advantageous. Yet the Chinese certainly gained in prestige; they had 'saved' North Korea from MacArthur, had inflicted major losses on U.N. forces by 'human wave' attacks, and had gone some way towards persuading the Pentagon that 'never again' must American forces be committed to the mainland of Asia. China had unified against the foreign threat, the P.L.A. had expanded, and China had earned the respect of foreign communist parties and sympathetic Asian governments. However, South Korea remained non-communist; Mao lost a son in the war; money needed for reconstruction in China had been diverted to the war effort and to repaying the Soviets for military supplies; the P.R.C. had been denounced as an 'aggressor' by the U.N.; the presence of the Seventh Fleet in the Taiwan Straits rendered impossible what might otherwise have been a relatively easy conquest of Taiwan in the early 1950s; and American hostility to China kept her commercially isolated from the West and its dependencies, and out of the U.N. for twenty-two years. Moreover, it was not to be the last time that China would be faced with an implicit nuclear war threat from America.

The armistice talks at Panmunjom continued into the 1980s, still with no peace treaty signed. Rhee resigned in April 1960 after massive demonstrations against his regime in which 127 people died: new elections brought in John Chang's Democratic Party which however was overthrown in a military coup in May 1961. But with U.S. aid the G.N.P. of South Korea was three times greater than that of the North in 1971 and her *per capita* income doubled between 1962 and 1971. Unification negotiations began and then collapsed in 1972-3, the South preferring to put trust in her own rising prosperity and the U.S. troops that still remained as her defence against communist aggression.

For three years during the early 1950s, Korea had been the 'storm centre' of world politics while the U.S. and Europe rearmed and contemplated whether the Soviets would risk invasion of West Germany to reunify that country as well. Just as the Berlin Blockade had drawn the line in Europe, so the Korean War had begun to draw a new line of the Cold War in Asia and in the early 1950s the storm continued in the Far East with Britain 'holding the line' in Malaya, and America, determined to 'contain' China, beginning its intervention in South-East Asia.

*Seven*

# INSURGENCY IN THE FAR EAST: MALAYA, THE PHILIPPINES AND FRENCH INDO-CHINA

Until December 1941, all of South and South-East Asia excluding Thailand – nearly 25 per cent of the world population – was controlled by Western colonial powers. In 1947/48 a nearly bankrupt Britain granted independence to India, Pakistan, Burma and Ceylon; in 1950 the Dutch, under pressure from the nationalist leader Sukarno (whose forces routed the Indonesian Communist Party during the anti-Dutch drive) supported by the U.S. and U.N. Security Council, gave Indonesia independence. But in British Malaya it was communism, as opposed to nationalistic anti-colonialism, which was far more significant.

Malaya was a polyglot society – large numbers of Chinese had been brought to Malaya in the 1920s to work on the rich rubber plantations and in the tin mines; there was also a sizeable Indian community. However, under British control, it was the Malays (numbering just under 50 per cent of the total population) who were officially regarded as the 'people of the country', and they alone were given special rights to land, and preferment in government employment. The Malayan Communist Party grew up based on the antagonism of the Chinese community to its lack of civic and political rights; communism found few adherents among the Malays and Indians. During the war, the Malayan Communist Party was accepted by Britain as part of the anti-Japanese resistance and given arms. In 1945 the M.C.P. held back from revolution, partly because at that time the reasonably successful Chiang Kai-shek might have offered troops to aid Britain against any rebellion by the Chinese Malayan community; more than 10,000 guerrillas

disbanded, handed in their arms and joined the trade union movement. Between 1945 and 1948, trade union strikes and occasional
violent demonstrations were organized by the Communists, but in
1948, perhaps emboldened by Communist successes in China and
Vietnam, the M.C.P. went into open rebellion against Britain.

The M.C.P. leader Chin Peng – who had visited Yenan, 'the
home of the revolution', in 1945 and 1946 – intended to follow the
Maoist doctrine of a three-stage war: guerrilla insurgency against
scattered plantations, tin mines and government outposts designed
to produce economic decline and political tension; land redistribution and political indoctrination in the liberated zones; and
conventional war leading to the takeover of government. The revolution, almost totally a Chinese affair, depended on willing or coerced
support from the 500,000 strong Chinese squatter community. The
Emergency was declared by Britain in June 1948 and officially
closed by Malaya in July 1960, though it effectively ended in 1954.
Great Britain promised to deal with the Communists and then to
grant independence to the Malayan Federation (which it did in
1957). The British reacted swiftly to the Emergency: it was essential
that planters should not be forced off outlying farms. Sten guns were
issued to estate workers, as were radio sets; the R.A.F. bombed
supposed communist hideouts in the jungle; and what the Americans
were later in Vietnam to call 'search and destroy' groups of British,
Malays and Gurkhas, with Dyak 'headhunter' trackers, went off
into the jungle to turn guerrillas into fugitives.

In April 1950 Lt.-General Sir Harold Briggs was put in charge
of counter-insurgency. Briggs' main initiative was the decision to
transplant squatter Chinese into 'new villages' or 'settlement areas';
break communist cells within those villages; set up an identity card
system within them; record the sale of all food within them; and
establish militia to police and defend them. The aim was to isolate,
starve and then seek out the guerrilla in the jungle – in Maoist
terms to prevent 'the fish' from 'swimming in the sea of the people'.
By spring 1952, 400,000 squatters had been moved to 400 new
barbed-wire surrounded villages. Every effort was then made to
provide schools, medical clinics and other services in the villages,
and to tie the squatters to the entangling webs of close government
control, government social services, government agricultural
advisers, etc.; 200,000 'home guards', primarily Malays with British
officers, were given the job of defending the communities.

A setback to Britain occurred when a new High Commissioner, Sir Henry Gurney, was assassinated by terrorists north of Kuala Lumpur, and Briggs was forced to retire due to ill health. However, the replacement High Commissioner, who also held the post of Director of Military Operations, was the very able General Sir Gerald Templar and the integration of responsibility under him was an important factor in British success against the Communists. Templar took from Britain in 1952 a detailed plan for the transference of power to Malaya, thus reinforcing the anti-communism of the Malays. He also instigated the distribution of secret questionnaires in the new villages and the jungle, offering rewards for information leading to the capture or death of terrorists. Villagers who aided terrorists were subject to collective reprisals against their crops and homes, and punitive curfews. Planes dropped leaflets urging guerrillas to surrender, offering 'safe conduct' passes. Detailed files on guerrillas made it possible for planes, as they cruised over the jungle, to broadcast offers to named individuals. Meanwhile, herbicides were dropped on communist food crops and trackways, while 'hunter-killer' patrols continued to search the jungle. By the time Templar left in 1954, some areas had been declared 'white' (free of guerrillas): by Merdeka (Independence) in August 1957, which removed most of the propaganda appeal of the M.C.P., there were only about 1,500 guerrillas left. In 1960, Chin Peng and his remaining five hundred or so followers had been pushed back to the Malayan border with Thailand, where they still were in 1980. Civilian casualties totalled 4,668; 2,702 communists had surrendered, 1,287 were captured and 9,520 killed during the twelve years of 'emergency'.

A number of lessons and comparisons can be drawn from the British success against a communist insurgency. By making an obviously sincere offer of independence (in contrast to the French in Vietnam in 1946), through the drive to win the 'hearts and minds of the people', and by expert application of jungle warfare counter-insurgency techniques, Britain enhanced her chances of victory. Nevertheless, one must remember that (apart from the 200,000 home guards) 40,000 British and Commonwealth troops and about 70,000 mainly Malayan police were used against what was at any one time a maximum of 8,000 insurgents. Thus Britain maintained a ratio of between 10 and 12 to 1 in her favour. Perhaps an even more important factor in British success was that the Chinese insurgents were ethnically distinguishable from the majority of the population. Even the transfer of the squatters was aided by their lack of attachment to the land on which they squatted – a far cry from America's removal of Vietnamese peasants to 'pacified hamlets' in the 1960s, for they had painstakingly nurtured the soil and prayed to their ancestors on land settled by their families for generations. Moreover, there was a Chinese alternative to Chin Peng – the Malayan Chinese Association. The Government gave every assistance to this body, which advocated co-operation with Malaya in the formation of a new, multi-racial state. Finally, one must acknowledge the relative isolation of the Malayan Communists from outside aid – unlike the Vietminh in Vietnam, who received aid from Communist China through its southern border. From 1949 onwards, the Malayan Communists received negligible outside aid and their only semi-secure 'sanctuary' – across the Thai border – was so far from the heavily populated areas of Malaya that resort to it virtually signified retreat and failure.

In 1946 the United States granted independence to the Philippines, but some military advisers like General Lansdale (who was later to advise the U.S. Ambassador in Vietnam) remained to give advice on the overthrow of an indigenous communist rising.

Unlike the Chinese insurgents in Malaya, the Hukbalahaps (or Huks) were members of the same ethnic group as the Government which they attacked; again in contrast to the Malayan episode, the Huks rose against an already independent government and were put down by the Filipino army, not the troops of an alien power. The Huks, led by Louis Taruc, and tempered in the guerrilla war against the Japanese invaders, took up arms after the Filipino Government refused to allow seven Huk candidates who had won seats in the 1946 Congressional elections to take their places. The Huks gained initial successes, owing primarily to the corruption and inefficiency within the post-war Filipino Government and army, but were effectively crushed by 1954. Taruc saw the movement as part of the world-wide communist revolution and obviously gained verbal support from the Soviet and Chinese Governments: but the Huk rising was neither directed nor materially aided by outside powers.

The rising failed for a number of reasons, but primarily because it was confined to central Luzon Island, north of Manila, which

was the only region in the Philippines where outright class antagonism existed. Furthermore, in October 1950 the Huks suffered a
crushing reversal when their entire political leadership was captured
in a raid on a communist headquarters in Manila. Equally
important to the eventual failure were the achievements of Ramon
Magsaysay, who became Minister of Defence in 1950 and President
in 1953. His integrity, his rise to power from social and economic
obscurity, his belief in democratic reform, the actions of the Economic Development Corps he founded in relieving a whole range
of rural inequities, and his promises of land reform, combined with
the military initiatives gained from, and possible after, the capture
of the Huk leadership, had all combined to doom the Huk movement
by 1953-4.

Neither the Huks nor the Malayan Communist Party were
completely eliminated, but both movements had faded into un-
threatening obscurity by the mid-1950s. Perhaps the dominant
common feature of both revolts was their failure to capture nationalist feeling and national identification: in Malaya isolated by their
race, in the Philippines isolated by peculiarly ripe conditions for
revolution in central Luzon only, both groups of insurgents stand
in stark contrast to Ho Chi Minh's Vietminh guerrillas in French
Indo-China.

The French occupied Indo-China (Vietnam, Laos and Cambodia) between 1862 and 1897 and, according to President Roosevelt in 1944, 'France has milked it for 100 years. The people of
Indochina are entitled to something better than that.' In 1930
Ho Chi Minh founded the Indo-Chinese Communist Party, but
France easily maintained her 'white' rule until the 'yellow' Japanese
shattered the apparent invincibility of the French by occupying
the country after France fell in Europe in 1940. In 1941, Ho founded
the Vietminh guerrillas with allied backing, to fight the Japanese
control. He presumably thought that after victory, France would
accept Indo-Chinese independence within some kind of French
'Commonwealth'. However, in the Brazzaville Declaration of 1944
De Gaulle stated that 'The attainment of self-government in the
colonies – even in the most distant future – must be excluded'.

In 1945, France was determined to resurrect the prestige of her
armed forces. It had been decided at Potsdam (with no French
representative present) that when Japan surrendered, Nationalist

Chinese forces should temporarily occupy northern Indo-China and British forces the southern part. In September 1945, Ho declared the independence of the Democratic Republic of Vietnam but Britain, possibly concerned for the status of her 'sister' Empire, allowed French troops to re-enter South Vietnam. With so many foreign troops on his soil. Ho was prepared to negotiate some kind of independence, as opposed to fighting for it. In 1946 it seemed possible that North Vietnam would become independent immediately (with French troops placed in strategic points for five years), and that plebiscites would occur in the South to determine the opinions of the people. But the referenda did not emerge and France ordered the Vietminh out of Hanoi and Haïphong in November 1946. The order was refused and the French bombed the two cities, causing 6,000 casualties. The first Indo-Chinese War had begun.

In 1946, 40,000 partially trained and poorly equipped Vietminh began their campaign against 63,000 'Free French' veteran troops.[1] The French idea of possible negotiation in 1947 envisaged the concept of five semi-independent states (Laos, Cambodia and three parts of Vietnam) entering the French 'Commonwealth' or Union. The French businessmen and colonial administrators were determined to hold on to the rice and rubber riches of southern Vietnam by arranging for 'puppet' states to be established. Ho refused, and in the North he began a full communist programme consisting of guerrilla attempts to control the countryside and strangle the cities by destroying inter-city communications; agitation-propaganda ('agitprop') teams of guerrillas roaming the villages; and peasant education and land redistribution. His was virtually a carbon-copy of Mao's strategy in northern China.

In 1949 the foundation of Communist China and the knowledge that the Vietminh would be given by the Chinese training facilities, rest areas, supplies and captured American arms and ammunition, prompted the French to grant independence within the French Union to Laos, Cambodia and to a Vietnamese Empire ruled by the last Vietnamese monarch – Emperor Bao Dai. The French then argued to the Americans that their colonial war must now be seen as part of the world-wide communist conspiracy against free, independent states and their Western allies. Truman accepted this, especially after the outbreak of the Korean War in June 1950. An American advisory military team was sent to Vietnam and the U.S., as well

as the U.K., recognized independent Vietnam. Inevitably, Ho's
Vietnam was recognized by China, the Soviet Union, North Korea
and a number of East European states during 1950. By 1954 the
U.S. was paying 78 per cent of French costs in fighting the Vietnam
war.

By March 1954, the French had lost control of the bulk of the
Vietnamese countryside, although the South, in which Frenchmen
had settled and spread Catholicism, was safer than the North where
the French had merely been represented through garrison forces in
the towns. General Navarre, last of the French military commanders,
hoped that he could tempt the Vietminh General Vo Nguyen Giap
into a pitched conventional battle, where the French presumed that
their more sophisticated army and its artillery and air support
could win a resounding victory. The confrontation finally came
from March to May 1954 at Dien Bien Phu, a French base set up to
prevent the Vietminh from crossing in and out of Laos. In the fifty-
five day siege of that base, Giap, bringing in men and supplies on
bicycles through the jungle trails, and using Chinese artillery and
anti-aircraft guns, killed 7,200 French and captured the remaining
11,000. The U.S. Secretary of State, Dulles, and Admiral Radford,
Chairman of the Joint Chiefs of Staff, advocated to President
Eisenhower the use of B-29 atomic bombers from the Philippine
bases against the encircling guerrillas at Dien Bien Phu. Eisenhower
rejected the advice, the French Parliament voted for French
evacuation from Vietnam, and the Geneva Conference, sitting to
deal with the German question, was given the task of settling a
cease-fire in Vietnam.

The war ended in July 1954. It had cost France approximately
$10 billion and the U.S. $1·1 billion. The French had lost 92,000
troops during the war, including 19,000 Frenchmen, and had been
defeated for a host of reasons. It is important to remember the scale
of their war in comparison with Malaya and the Philippines. The
French forces in Indo-China included, by 1954, a 'loyal' Vietnamese army of 200,000 regulars and 50,000 militia, and a Laotian–
Cambodian force of 50,000, as well as the 178,000-strong French
Expeditionary Force. The French faced, by 1954, 100,000 regular
Vietminh troops, 50,000 semi-regular regional troops and 225,000
guerrillas. The 8,000 Malayan and 15,000 Filippino insurgents
posed far more tractable problems, and very much smaller forces
over which it was conceivable to achieve a 10:1 superiority.[2]

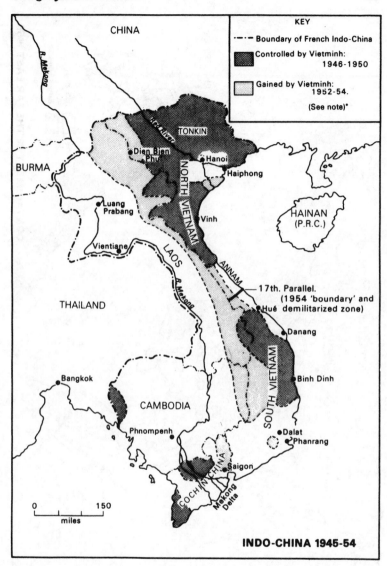

**KEY**
- – · – Boundary of French Indo-China
- Controlled by Vietminh: 1946-1950
- Gained by Vietminh: 1952-54. (See note)*

**INDO-CHINA 1945-54**

Areas of control varied from complete 'liberated zones' to countryside in Vietminh control by night and militarily contested during daylight hours.

It must also be noted that Vietminh 'control' of territory could be misleading – the majority of the Vietnamese population who lived in the Red River valley, Kekong Delta, and city areas were in government areas.

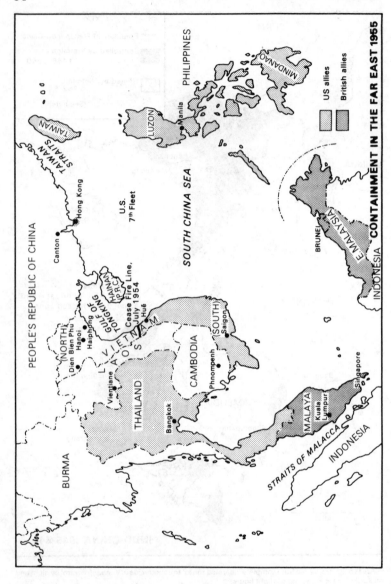

CONTAINMENT IN THE FAR EAST 1955

US allies

British allies

Moreover, it is indisputable that the communist Ho Chi Minh, the most active fighter against both Japanese invader and French colonialist, did capture the nationalist feeling of the majority of the Vietnamese people. In his memoirs, Eisenhower admitted that, 'I have never talked or corresponded with a person knowledgeable in Indochinese affairs who did not agree that, had elections been held [in 1956] . . . possibly 80 per cent of the population would have voted for the Communist Ho Chi Minh.'[3] The Vietnamese Communists were never isolated into limited areas – their guerrillas posed a threat to the French even in the Mekong Delta in the southern tip of Vietnam. They had an excellent leadership in Ho and Giap; they were singleminded in their purpose; they had the support of Soviet money and Chinese arms. Their enemies, the French, underestimated their power and determination; they lacked sufficient anti-guerrilla training; they were unsure of the political solution in Indo-China; and there were eight or more French generals in charge of operations during the war years. France herself required economic reconstruction after the Second World War and was forced to devalue the *piastre* in Vietnam; her people were disunited over the war effort – the left wing wanted France out, the politicians wavered and the French soldier wondered exactly what he was fighting for. Nevertheless, the French did not lose the Indo-China War in Paris, they lost it in 'the hearts and minds' of 80 per cent of the Vietnamese population.

Nevertheless, Ho was not entirely victorious – he commented in 1954 on those Vietminh who wished to continue the fighting that 'they see the French yet do not see the Americans'.[4] Neither the Soviets nor the Chinese represented at Geneva wished to press too far Americans like the violently anti-communist Dulles. Dulles had given his 'massive retaliation' speech (see Chapters 8 and 11) in January 1954, so Malenkov was nervous and preferred Soviet weaponry to be available in Europe, rather than given to Ho in Asia. Malenkov and Mao persuaded Ho to give up approximately 20 per cent of Vietnam that he controlled and to accept a temporary partition at the 17th Parallel prior to nation-wide elections to be held in 1956. France had already granted independence to South Vietnam and thus had a dubious right to sign this clause in the settlement on her behalf but nevertheless did so. South Vietnam itself refused to sign, as did the U.S. In fact, the U.S. had pressured the French to force Emperor Bao Dai to accept the Catholic artistocrat Ngo Dinh Diem as Prime Minister and America began to advise and arm what was by 1955 the new Republic of Vietnam, led by Diem. (It is important to note that, prior to 1954, the non-communist nationalists in Vietnam – the Catholics, Buddhists and democrats – had never united to form a viable alternative to Ho's nationalist communism, while the French had never given Bao Dai's regime sufficient semblance of power to make it appear 'respectable' to nationalists.) During 1956 the French, who had promised to help supervise the Vietnamese elections, decided to accept Diem's request to pull all troops out of Vietnam. They preferred to rid themselves of Vietnam – especially since troubles had begun in French North Africa – and thus they left the country, three months before the proposed elections. Eisenhower sent a letter to Diem 'committing' America to support South Vietnam and in September 1954 Dulles organized the South-East Asian Treaty Organization (S.E.A.T.O.) to 'stabilize' the entire Far-Eastern area of the Cold War. Eisenhower was determined to 'hold the line' in the East:

> The loss of Vietnam with Laos on the west and Cambodia in the southwest would have meant the surrender to Communist enslavement of millions. On the material side, it would have spelled the loss of valuable deposits of tin and prodigious supplies of rubber and rice. It would have meant that Thailand, enjoying buffer territory between itself and Red China, would be exposed on its entire eastern border to infiltration and attack. And if Indochina fell not only Thai but Burma and Malaya would be threatened with added risks to East Pakistan and South Asia as well as to all Indonesia.[5]

Within four short years, the Americans were obliged to act upon this 'domino' thesis as the situation in Vietnam again deteriorated – the Geneva Conference had no more 'settled' South-East Asia than it had solved the question of German elections or produced a satisfactory *rapprochement* with post-Stalinist Russia.

# Eight

# THE COLD WAR IN THE MID-1950s

The year 1953 opened with a paradox. On the one hand, Stalin – the man who must bear much of the responsibility for the Cold War – died on 5 March, leaving behind him a collective leadership in the U.S.S.R. which appeared to be committed to a measure of liberalization of policy both at home and abroad. On the other hand a new President and Secretary of State took office in the U.S.A. following an election campaign during which the previous administration had been accused of being 'soft on communism'.

Stalin had been feared in the West but had also been feared in the Soviet Union. From the end of the war, he had used the mechanism of the 'purge' to rid the Soviet Union of Western influence and potential or supposed opponents of the regime. A few months before Stalin died another purge was getting under way, but this was stopped after his death when the secret police chief, Beria, announced early in April that the reason for the purge, the 'Doctor's Plot', had been a fabrication. The collective leadership in the Soviet Union, fearing that one Stalin might be replaced by another from whom none of them might be safe, began a gradual and limited dismantling of the Soviet terror system. On 28 March, an amnesty was announced for some categories of prisoners in the vast Soviet prison network. In July, after the removal from power and subsequent 'execution' of Beria, measures were taken to reduce the status and power of the secret police.

The death of Stalin had a considerable impact outside the Soviet Union too. At the end of May, the U.S.S.R. wound up the Control Commission for Germany and continued to exercise authority in East Germany through a High Commissioner. This replacement of a military control with a political control marked a change in style in Soviet policy towards Eastern Europe but not necessarily a change in substance. The East German uprising in June (protesting against Soviet domination and wage cuts,) was quickly and ruthlessly put down by Soviet forces, but Soviet treatment of her satellite states did soften after this. The U.S.S.R. stopped exacting reparations from East Germany after 1953. The other satellites were given greater freedom to decide their own economic priorities, and numbers of East European communists who had opposed Soviet domination, like Gomulka in Poland and Gerö in Hungary, were released from prison.

To the West, it appeared to be no coincidence that Stalin's death was followed by the resumption of armistice negotiations in Korea, leading to an armistice coming into effect on 27 July. The reduction of tension went further. The U.S.S.R. re-established diplomatic relations with Israel, Yugoslavia and Greece. She withdrew her claims to the provinces of Kars, Ardahan and Artvin in Turkey and offered to normalize relations with Turkey and Iran. There was a change in Soviet propaganda which began to lose some of its stridency – especially towards Britain although the U.S.A. and West Germany were still the objects of repeated denunciation.

To many in the West the signs appeared optimistic. Even the power struggle in the Soviet leadership appeared hopeful, for the new Soviet Prime Minister Malenkov, favoured increased government spending on light industry, which produces consumer goods, at the expense of heavy industry, which produces armaments. To some extent the shift in emphasis in Soviet policy was a product of a position of strength. The Red Army was in complete command of the East European satellites, the Korean armistice removed a situation which was potentially highly dangerous to the Soviet Union and on 8 August 1953, Malenkov was able to announce that the U.S.S.R. possessed the H-bomb. No longer was the U.S.S.R. so militarily inferior to the U.S.A. and therefore she no longer needed to feel so vulnerable in the face of American nuclear superiority.

Meanwhile in the United States, Senator McCarthy made an unsubstantiated accusation of rampant communism in the State Department and so helped to produce a 'Reds under the bed' scare. The Korean War and the early Soviet development of nuclear weapons contributed to a public opinion and a government which had no wish to be seen as conciliatory. The Eisenhower administration inherited from its predecessor a cut in military spending which initially it could do nothing to alter, but this did not lead to a lessening of the Cold War military confrontation; quite the contrary. On 30 October 1953, President Eisenhower accepted the strategy suggestions of Admiral Radford, the Chairman of the U.S. Joint Chiefs of Staff. The Radford Plan suggested that the U.S.A. should base its defence – and the defence of its allies – upon the commitment to use nuclear weapons. Economic factors forced the U.S. to accept defence cuts but these were to be in conventional forces. This new American defence policy meant that the U.S.A. would no longer be able to maintain an effective nuclear strike force *and* the capability to fight major conventional wars as she had done in Korea. More 'Koreas' would be deterred in future by treating all wars except small local engagements – brushfire wars – as nuclear wars. This was the doctrine of 'massive retaliation' whereby any communist, i.e. supposed Soviet, aggression anywhere in the world could meet with instant U.S. massive nuclear retaliation against a target of its own choice. This strategy depended upon continued American nuclear superiority over the U.S.S.R. and so was obsolete almost as soon as it was announced. It also depended upon America's European allies raising enough conventional forces to be able to withstand a Soviet attack, but the death of Stalin and the end of the Korean War meant that the Europeans no longer saw the need to raise and equip the fifty divisions that the U.S.A. required of them. The new U.S. partnership of Eisenhower and his Secretary of State, John Foster Dulles, recognized the limitations of the 'massive retaliation' strategy and in April 1954 Dulles modified the policy when he said that the United States 'must not put itself in the position where the only response open to it is general war'.[1]

To the Soviet Union, the declarations of the U.S. Government on its new defence policy must have appeared contradictory. On 7 April 1954, Eisenhower explained the 'Domino Theory' to show how the U.S. could be drawn into the war in Indo-China and to show why the first 'domino' must not be allowed to fall. But within months France suffered a major military defeat in Vietnam, and by the terms of the Geneva Conference had to withdraw from Indo-China, and the U.S.A. reluctantly acquiesced in this. Although the U.S. considered the use of nuclear weapons in this instance she did not use them, and yet 'massive retaliation' gave the impression that she would.

But the United States was determined to prevent a similar occurrence by organizing a more effective defence around the communist bloc. N.A.T.O. was already in existence and on 8 September 1954, the Manila Pact was signed to unite those states which would be susceptible to 'falling dominoes', and those who had interests in the area. On 2 December 1954, the U.S. signed a treaty with Nationalist China and extended a nuclear guarantee to Chiang Kai-shek. The U.S.A. also effectively promoted the creation of a military alliance in the Middle East as a result of which the Baghdad Pact was formally established on 24 February 1955. In May 1955, West Germany became a fully sovereign state and a member of N.A.T.O. Dulles' diplomacy had resulted in the communist bloc on the Eurasian landmass being ringed by a system of interlocking alliances and defence agreements (see map page ix).

The alliances created around the Soviet Union's borders were designed to 'contain' Soviet expansionism. To the West they were symbols of a defensive attitude, but to the Soviets they must have appeared ominous. The Soviet Union attempted to break out of its encirclement by unsuccessfully pressuring France and other Western countries into opposing the rearmament of West Germany, and by trying to exploit the creaky foundations upon which the Baghdad Pact had been built. But parallel to this policy, the Soviet Union bound her satellites closer to her. Before becoming Secretary of State, Dulles had stressed the tenuousness of the U.S.S.R.'s hold over the hearts and minds of the populations of Eastern Europe and had said that a determined West could 'roll-back' Soviet influence in Eastern Europe. The events of 1955 and 1956 were to prove that the Russians had no intention of letting this happen.

Soviet activity in Eastern Europe in 1955–6 was largely the responsibility of the new First Secretary of the Soviet Communist Party, Nikita Khrushchev, the man who, in 1955, had replaced Malenkov as the front-runner in the continuing Kremlin power struggle. Together with Nicolai Bulganin, who replaced Malenkov as Prime Minister in February 1955, Khrushchev made trips to Peking, Delhi, Belgrade and London attempting to break out of the Soviet Union's political isolation. The Soviet Union initiated the negotiations with Austria that led on 15 May 1955, to the signing of the Austrian State Treaty by which the four occupying powers withdrew their forces and Austria became independent and neutral. At first sight, the Austrian treaty is difficult to explain from the Soviet point of view. It was a surrender of territory but it brought concrete advantages to the Kremlin. It could be used to indicate that the U.S.S.R. could be flexible and reasonable. It removed British occupation forces from the southern zone of Austria where they

used to border on Yugoslavia and Hungary. It also pushed back
N.A.T.O.'s front line and meant that there were no longer con-
tinuous lines of communication between the two N.A.T.O. allies,
Italy and West Germany (see map page 24).

Having limited Western territorial contact with Yugoslavia,
Khrushchev tried to remove the hostility that had existed between
Moscow and Belgrade since 1948. Alone among the occupied
countries of the Second World War, Yugoslavia liberated herself
from Nazi rule. The Yugoslav Communist leader, Marshal Tito,
owed little to Stalin and was not prepared to allow his country to
become a mere appendage of the Soviet Union. After being expelled
from the Cominform in June 1948, Tito declared Yugoslavia neutral
in the 'Cold War' and it was in the interest of the West that she
remained so. Yugoslavia was cut off from the economic bloc of
Eastern Europe and so she had to turn to the West for trade and aid.
To do this the Yugoslavs had to modify their earlier hostile attitudes
to the Western capitalists and had to compromise with Marxist
orthodoxy. While Stalin was alive, the Yugoslav Communist Party
was subjected to a propaganda campaign that rivalled in intensity
and hostility the similar campaign being waged against the West.
Belgrade was condemned by the Sino–Soviet bloc for 'Revisionism',
the sin of heresy against Marxist–Leninism, and attempts were made
to subvert Tito's regime. No Soviet military action had been taken
against Yugoslavia in the late 1940s because it seemed that Stalin
expected his adherents in the Yugoslav Communist Party to overthrow Tito. After 1950, military action was too dangerous. Tito
rebuilt his bridges with the West and in June 1951 the three major
Western Allies extended a £50 million loan to Yugoslavia for the
purchase of arms. The Western powers indicated that they would not
allow Yugoslavia to be forced back into the Soviet system.

Yugoslavia was an embarrassment to the Soviet Union. Belgrade
set an example to the East European satellites of a state that was
communist, nationalist and independent of Moscow. Yugoslavia
also gave the lie to Soviet claims that the East European states needed
protection from the West, because the West showed no interest in
attacking Yugoslavia and even helped her. The only country from
whom the Yugoslavs feared attack was the U.S.S.R. Possibly most
embarrassing of all, Yugoslavia showed that there was another way
to communism. If Yugoslavia could not be conquered and Tito
could not be overthrown, then at least the unfortunate example of

Yugoslavian independence from Moscow could be removed. In May 1955, Khrushchev and Bulganin went to Belgrade to make their peace with Tito, but Tito refused to come back into the Soviet bloc. Relations between the two states were normalized but Khrushchev had to pay the price of admitting that the Soviet Union had been at fault for the original dispute. Khrushchev could claim a measure of unity in the socialist world after his trip to Belgrade but some East Europeans still looked to the Yugoslav example, and more importantly Khrushchev had admitted that the Soviet Union had been wrong. The lesson of this was not lost upon other communist countries, especially China, but nor was it lost upon the U.S.S.R. Before the Belgrade trip, the Soviet leadership had created the Warsaw Pact on 14 May, thus establishing an even stronger control over their East European satellites.

In 1955, the Soviet Union mounted a 'peace offensive', the showpiece of which was the Geneva Summit conference in July. The Austrian treaty and the *rapprochement* with Belgrade had created a favourable impression in the West but the Americans wanted to test the seriousness of this new-found Soviet friendliness at Geneva. A measure of agreement appeared to have been reached on Germany – the final communiqué stated:

> The Heads of government, conscious of their joint responsibility concerning the settlement of the German question and the reunification of Germany, are agreed that the settlement of the German question and the reunification of Germany by means of free elections will be carried out in conformity with the national interests of the German people and in the interests of European security.[2]

The Western Allies regarded the agreement as a commitment to German unification at an unspecified date in the future. The Soviet Union however, interpreted 'national interests of the German people' and 'interests of European security' differently. The Soviet leaders began to talk about Geneva having proved that the Big Four accepted the *status quo* on Europe. They also began to talk about the existence of two Germanies.

Some relaxation of tension did follow Geneva. The U.S.S.R. returned the naval base of Porkkala to Finland, announced a reduction of 600,000 in the size of the Red Army, began an exchange with the U.S. of agricultural experts and sent a delegation to the U.S.-inspired international conference on the peaceful use of atomic energy. Diplomatic relations were established between West Germany and the U.S.S.R. But the 'spirit' of Geneva did not last long.

In the U.N. the U.S.S.R. voted for Algerian independence from France, and revitalized the dispute with the West over the question of the admission of the People's Republic of China. At the Foreign Ministers' Conference in October and November 1955, called to discuss further a European settlement, the Soviet Foreign Minister, Molotov, rejected Western proposals for increased East–West contacts, and no progress was made on Germany. President Eisenhower had had a heart attack and so was unable to exercise a moderating influence over his Secretary of State, Dulles, who clashed with Molotov at the conference. One factor which affected the failure of the Foreign Ministers' Conference was the announcement on 27 September, that Czechoslovakia had agreed to supply arms to Egypt. This evidence that the Soviet bloc was taking advantage of Western difficulties in the Middle East to extend its influence there and disrupt the Baghdad Pact disturbed Western statesmen. It indicated what was already widely believed in the West, that the outstretched hand of the Soviet Union in one area was matched by the clenched fist in another.

Whatever the seriousness of the U.S.S.R.'s 'peace offensive', there was no going back to Stalinism for the Soviet Union. The Soviet leadership was prepared to introduce some liberalization at home and abroad. In February 1956, at the Twentieth Congress of the Communist Party of the Soviet Union, Khrushchev in his 'secret speech' denounced Stalin's 'cult of personality', his departure from Marxist–Leninism and his use of terror to ensure obedience in the communist world. The speech sent a shock wave through the communist world. Soviet communism suffered a loss of prestige as a result of this speech and some of the Stalinist regimes in Eastern Europe began to totter as public opinion in Poland and Hungary demanded better living and working conditions.

In July 1956, unrest broke out in the Polish city of Poznan. The situation was potentially dangerous as Poland was still largely Catholic and Polish nationalism and opposition to Russian dominance were strong. To calm the situation, Moscow allowed some changes in the Polish Government to be made, accepting the dismissal from office of some Polish leaders who were too closely associated with Russian control. In mid-October the Polish C.P. decided to elect Wladislaw Gomulka to the post of First Secretary and to sack the Soviet Marshal Rokossovsky from the Ministry of Defence, a post he had held since 1949. Gomulka had been imprisoned in Stalin's time and his appointment alarmed the Soviet leadership. Khrushchev and three of his Politburo colleagues flew to Warsaw where they confronted the Poles. The talks were extremely tense. The Russians threatened to invade if they could not have their choice of personnel in the Polish Government, and the Poles said they would fight if they had to. The Poles had no intention of taking their country out of the Soviet bloc and eventually the Russians had to accept a form of national communism in Poland and much less Soviet control. The Polish crisis was resolved relatively happily for the Soviet Union. The Soviet bloc remained intact, as did the territorial balance between East and West, but Moscow faced a greater threat to her security in Hungary.

In the autumn of 1956, Hungary was shaken by some of the emotions that had affected Poland. In the face of mounting Hungarian unrest, the Soviet Union accepted the replacement of the Stalinist First Secretary of the Hungarian C.P. Rákosi by his deputy Ernö Gerö. In mid-October spontaneous demonstrations broke out in Hungary against 'hard-line' communist rule and Soviet influence. There were widespread strikes and fighting between Soviet troops and Hungarian civilians between 24–28 October. A new Hungarian Government was formed on 27 October, with Russian consent. The new government was headed by Imre Nagy and included two non-communists. It seemed that Moscow was prepared to accept a considerable diminution of influence in Hungary but events moved fast. On 25 October, Eisenhower declared: 'I feel with the Hungarian people.' Two days later, Dulles made a speech in which he congratulated the Hungarians on the way in which they were prepared to challenge the Red Army.[3] On 28 October, the West tried to discuss Hungary in the U.N. Security Council but the U.S.S.R. vetoed this as a provocative interference in the affairs of the communist bloc. Public opinion in Hungary demanded widespread reforms and rapidly outstripped the ability of the Government to introduce reforms and still stay in the Soviet bloc. On 1 November, the Nagy Government acceded to popular demand and prepared to declare the neutrality of Hungary, to set up a multi-party democracy and to bring Hungary out of the Warsaw Pact. Later Khrushchev said: 'We would have accepted another Finland but the Hungarians were in the process of bringing back fascism.'[4] But in fact the Soviet Union was not prepared to tolerate the neutrality of Hungary. On 4 November, Soviet troops moved into Budapest in strength, the uprising was crushed and a new Soviet-backed government under Janos Kadar was installed. (The uprising cost the lives of 7,000 Russian troops and 30,000 Hungarians and left a legacy of bitterness against the Soviet Union in Hungary.) The Hungarian tragedy was compounded by the fact that it appears many Hungarians had accepted at face value the American 'roll-back' argument and believed they would receive help from the West. The broadcasts of Radio Free Europe – an American financed radio station in Munich which beamed Western 'Cold War' propaganda at the Soviet bloc – had incited the Hungarians to overthrow the Government, but all the help the Hungarians got from the West was sympathy and an abortive debate in the U.N. on an American resolution that Soviet troops be withdrawn.

By the end of 1956, the U.S.S.R. held her satellites in a firm grip. Hungary was an example to any other state which might consider leaving the Soviet bloc. The U.S.S.R. had indicated a preparedness to accept some ideological differences in Eastern Europe as long as these were limited to purely domestic affairs, but she was not prepared to accept the disintegration of her satellite system and the *status quo* in Europe. Moreover, the moral outrage felt in the West at Soviet actions was soon transformed into acute embarrassment when what the Soviet Union had been condemned for doing in Hungary, the British and French were to try to do in Egypt. The difference between the Hungary and Suez incidents is that Hungary confirmed what the West suspected, that the U.S.S.R. would accept no compromise in Europe, but Suez appeared to threaten war between East and West.

The Suez incident (see Chapter 17) was a bonus for the Soviet Union and little short of a disaster for the West. It distracted world attention from Hungary for a while; it showed up the very different interests of the major Western Allies and the fact that the U.S.A. could not be counted on to defend the purely national interests of her allies; it seriously damaged Anglo–French and Western prestige in the Middle East; the leading Arab opponents of continued Western dominance in the area, Egypt and Syria, turned increasingly to the Soviet Union for the arms and aid that they needed, which the West was reluctant to supply. Suez gave the U.S.S.R. a foothold in the Middle East, and in effect demonstrated what had been suspected since the founding of the Baghdad Pact: the Cold War had arrived in the Middle East.

# Nine

# THE GERMAN PROBLEM
# AND THE BERLIN ANOMALY

East–West relations eased somewhat after the death of Stalin, but underlying all the questions that separated the Great Powers in the first sixteen years after the war was Germany. In 1947, while acting as adviser to the U.S. Secretary of State, Marshall, John Foster Dulles wrote: 'The Germans concededly are the heart of the problem of Europe. Never before has a people so numerous and so potentially powerful had so unique an opportunity to bargain between two opposing groups. If the Germans would combine again with Soviet Communism as they did in the fall of 1939, that combination could sweep Europe.'[1] Nevertheless, the Western Powers continued to stress their commitment to the ideal of a Germany which would become united after free elections had been held in each of the four occupation zones. They argued that such a German state would cherish the benefits of democracy and would automatically seek closer relations with the other democratic states – themselves.

The Soviet Union constantly opposed any idea of unification taking place after free elections, and in so doing indicated that the Kremlin also accepted the logic of the West's argument. But there were other factors at play in this Soviet policy. At the Berlin Foreign Ministers' Conference early in 1954, Molotov rejected free elections, arguing that when a united Germany had last held free elections, it had resulted in Hitler becoming Chancellor.

The formation of N.A.T.O. had indicated Western resolve to defend Germany, and Comecon, by integrating the East German economy into the Soviet system, indicated that Moscow intended to hang on to East Germany. Also in 1949, the West approved the establishment of the West German state and the U.S.S.R. approved the establishment of the East German state. Both Germanies were less than independent but their very creation limited the ability of their sponsors to accept their disappearance. Between

1949 and 1952 the Soviet Union put forward the idea of a disarmed, neutralized and united Germany. Just how serious these Soviet proposals were it is impossible to say but it is possible to identify the benefits the U.S.S.R. was hoping to accrue from her diplomacy. The Soviet Union and some of her satellites had good historical reason to fear a reunited and revivified Germany but they also had cause to worry about the potentialities of West Germany. West Germany, truncated as she was, was still the largest state in Western and Central Europe in terms of population and industrial potential. As early as 1950, the onset of the Korean War produced a need for a considerable increase in Western defence. At a meeting of the Council of Europe in August 1950, the British Opposition leader, Churchill, carried a motion calling for the creation of a European army. This motion was welcomed by the West German Chancellor, Adenauer. On 12 September 1950, the U.S. Secretary of State, Dean Acheson, met his British and French opposite numbers, Bevin and Schumann, in Washington and proposed that West Germany should be allowed to rearm and contribute to the common defence. At the end of September, the N.A.T.O. Council accepted the idea of establishing a mixed force in Europe with German contingents, under a Supreme Commander.

Naturally enough there was widespread opposition, just five years after the war, to the idea of Germans in uniform again, not just in the rest of Europe, but in West Germany too. However, the military necessities of the Western Alliance were overriding. To overcome the hostility to the idea of a new German army, the French National Assembly on 24 October approved a plan to create German military units while at the same time obviating the necessity of having a German army. The French Pleven Plan was to set up a European Defence Community (E.D.C.) which would have a unified European command and would incorporate contingents from N.A.T.O.'s European members. The advantages of the plan were that the German contingents would not be under the control of the West German Government which would be unable to use these forces for its own national purposes.

The U.S.S.R. found neither the Acheson nor Pleven Plans palatable. She was also faced with the prospect of an E.D.C. which could have posed an even greater threat. If the E.D.C. had been created – in fact the negotiated version of the Pleven Plan was finally rejected in the French National Assembly in 1954 – it would have been a major stage on the road to the creation of a 'United States of Europe' which by virtue of its size would have been as big as the U.S.S.R. in terms of population and much bigger in terms of industrial output. The E.D.C. offered a long-term threat to the U.S.S.R. but the question of rearming West Germany posed an immediate threat. The very idea struck a raw nerve in the Kremlin, where it was 'believed that any anti-Soviet alliance, to be really effective, had to include a revivified and rearmed West Germany. Without it, N.A.T.O. was bound to remain a cumbersome agglomeration of a few American, French, British divisions, and some stray Belgian, Norwegian, etc., brigades.'[2]

Soviet diplomacy between 1950 and 1952 was aimed at preventing the rearming of Germany and the creation of the E.D.C. As such it was aimed at governments and public opinion in Western Europe and West Germany. The West German opposition party, the S.P.D., was opposed to rearmament and disinclined to integrate further into the Western camp because this made reunification more unlikely. The Soviet Union offered unification at the price of Germany remaining unarmed and this offer found many listeners in the Federal Republic* although not in Bonn or the other Western capitals. By the spring of 1952, it was becoming apparent that even if the E.D.C. idea was rejected, West Germany would be rearmed. In 1951, the three Western Allies formally ended the state of war between themselves and West Germany and Adenauer got them to agree that if ratification of E.D.C. was delayed too long in any of the E.D.C. countries† then Britain, France and the U.S. would still sign the 'German Treaty' granting the Federal Republic full sovereignty. Soviet diplomacy took account of the prevailing realities and trimmed its sails accordingly. On 10 March 1952, Soviet Notes were received by the three major Western Allies proposing a peace treaty and a unified Germany up to the Oder–Neisse line. The Soviet plan proposed the withdrawal of all occupying forces from Germany within one year after the treaty came into force. Full democratic, civil and religious rights would be guaranteed. The new state could have the forces necessary to her own defence and

* Nearly half the West German population had a direct, personal interest in reunification. In 1961, 21–25 per cent of the Federal Republic's population consisted of refugees and expellees from the East and 44 per cent of the population had relatives or close friends in the East. The 1961 figures were little different from those of 1952.

† France, West Germany, Italy, Belgium, Luxemburg and the Netherlands.

arms industries necessary to support those forces. All organizations 'hostile to democracy' and to the 'cause of maintaining peace' would be banned from Germany and she would not be allowed to join any alliance or coalition directed against any state which had fought against her in the Second World War.

The Soviet Union proposed that the new German Government should be a coalition of the two existing German governments. But Bonn feared such a prospect. West Germany was unarmed in 1952, although she did possess police forces, whereas East Germany was armed. At the end of 1945, the U.S.S.R. had permitted the arming of the 'People's Police' (*Volkspolizei* or *Vopos*). By the end of 1946 there were 45,000 *Vopos* and two other police bodies, the Frontier Police and Railway Police. In March 1948, new police units were set up, the *Bereitschaften*, which by 1950 numbered 50,000. The *Bereitschaften* were led by former *Wehrmacht* officers with Red Army advisers. They were quartered in barracks and trained to use infantry weapons. Adenauer and his colleagues feared that if the Soviet plan was put into effect then their communist partners in a coalition government would have at their command an 'army' of more than 100,000 men. A communist take-over of the whole of Germany could have been quick and relatively unopposed.

The Soviet 'draft treaty' was not acceptable to the West, but by 1954 the international climate had changed. Stalin was dead, the Korean War had come to an end and French forces began to return from Indo-China. The E.D.C. was rejected by France and was replaced by a Western agreement that West Germany should enter N.A.T.O. with twelve divisions and should become fully independent. By 1955, East and West had become fully committed to the idea of two Germanies. On 9 May 1955, the Federal Republic formally became a member of N.A.T.O. and on 14 May the U.S.S.R. formally constituted the Warsaw Pact – East German forces were admitted the following January. On 9 September, Adenauer visited the U.S.S.R. and diplomatic relations were established between Bonn and Moscow. On 20 September a treaty was signed between the U.S.S.R. and East Germany giving the D.D.R. full sovereignty over its foreign policy. Bonn continued to claim that it was the sole legal government of Germany and the Western Allies refused to recognize the D.D.R., but nevertheless the reunification issue was now demoted as an international problem.

Berlin, however, remained. Berlin represented in one city the problems that the lack of a peace settlement presented to the Four Powers. The 'iron curtain' was complete everywhere except in Berlin and the West Berlin example came to be seen by the D.D.R. and the U.S.S.R. as a threat to the stability of the D.D.R. and therefore to the whole Soviet glacis. Initially, the three major Western Allies and the Soviet Union took care to see that they denied to their newly independent, sovereign allies control over those areas of inter-German relations which could cause most friction. Britain, France and the U.S.A. declared that they would continue to be responsible for Berlin, affairs dealing with the whole of Germany, reunification, and the question of a peace treaty. The Soviet Union gave the D.D.R. control over its own frontiers, territory and foreign affairs with one important exception. In a Note to the U.S. Government on 18 October 1955, explaining the U.S.S.R.–D.D.R. treaty of September 1955, the Soviet Government wrote:

> As for control over the movement between the German Federal Republic and West Berlin of military personnel and freight, of garrisons of the U.S.A., Great Britain and France quartered in West Berlin, in negotiations between the Governments of the U.S.S.R. and the German Democratic Republic, it was stipulated that this control would henceforth be carried out by the command of the Soviet military forces in Germany temporarily until the achievement of a suitable agreement.[3]

For the next three years, the Berlin situation remained relatively stable, but by 1958, West Germany had been accorded diplomatic recognition by most of the countries of the world, while East Germany was only recognized by other communist countries. The U.S.S.R. had hoped that her control over Eastern Europe would become widely accepted. This had not happened, as the non-recognition of the D.D.R. by the West indicated. As long as the West continued to regard the D.D.R. merely as the 'Soviet zone of Occupied Germany' then Central Europe remained a potential trouble spot. Between 1958 and 1962, the U.S.S.R. tried to force recognition of the D.D.R. upon the West, by threatening to hand over to the East German authorities responsibility for the access routes to West Berlin. If this had happened, then whether they liked it or not the Western Powers would have had to deal directly with the East Germans. This would have constituted *de facto* diplomatic recognition of the East German regime, and acceptance of the post-war division of Europe.

The new Soviet attitude to West Berlin became apparent during 1958, when D.D.R. leaders began to refer to a 'normalization' of the situation in the 'capital of the D.D.R.' In Moscow on 10 November 1958, Khrushchev declared:

> The time has evidently come for the Powers which signed the Potsdam Agreement to abandon the remnants of the occupation regime in Berlin and thus make it possible to create a normal atmosphere in the capital of the German Democratic Republic. The Soviet Union, for its part, will hand over to the sovereign German Democratic Republic those functions which are still wielded by Soviet organs. Let the United States, France and Britain form their own relations with the German Democratic Republic and come to an agreement with it, if they are interested in certain questions relating to Berlin . . .[4]

For the next two weeks, the new Soviet policy on Berlin, remained unofficial. Then, on 27 November 1958, Soviet Notes were handed to the three major Western Powers containing what amounted to an ultimatum. The Note, throwing diplomatic protocol to the winds, referred to Berlin as a 'smouldering fuse that has been connected to a powder keg. Incidents arising here . . . may, in an atmosphere of heated passions, suspicions and mutual apprehensions, cause a conflagration which will be difficult to extinguish.' The Note accused the three major Western Powers of having broken the Potsdam Agreements on Berlin and Germany and said that they used West Berlin as: 'a springboard for intensive espionage, sabotage and other activities against Socialist countries.' Then Khrushchev offered his solution: West Berlin could become a free, demilitarized city, possibly under the auspices of U.N.O. The occupying forces would have to withdraw and any countries desiring access to the free city would have to negotiate routes with the D.D.R. The Note represented a major policy change on the part of the U.S.S.R. but the important part came at the end:

> The Soviet Government proposes to make no change in the present procedure for military traffic of the U.S.A., Great Britain and France from West Berlin to the F.R.G. [Federal Republic of Germany] for half a year . . . If the above-mentioned period is not utilized to reach an adequate agreement, the Soviet Union will then carry out the planned measures through an agreement with the D.D.R.[5]

The Western Allies were prompt in their reaction to the Soviet initiative and were unanimous in their intention to preserve their rights in West Berlin. The Allies had almost total support from the West Berliners. In an election on the issue, only 2 per cent of the population voted for 'free city' status. As the Western reaction hardened and no reply to the Note was forthcoming the Soviet Government prepared another option. Potentially the most dangerous element of the Note was the six months' 'ultimatum', so the

U.S.S.R. took steps to defuse the situation. On 5 January 1959, Anastas Mikoyan – the Soviet Politburo's foreign trade expert who happened to be in the U.S.A. on holiday at the time – visited the U.S. Secretary of State and told him that the six months' deadline was only a suggestion and not an ultimatum. On 9 February, Dulles announced that the U.S.A., Britain and France had agreed on the steps they would take if they found their access to West Berlin blocked. Khrushchev was faced with an impasse. He had threatened the West and now Dulles threatened the U.S.S.R., and Dulles was known to be implacable in his opposition to the U.S.S.R. On 16 February, the West answered the Soviet Note. They rejected Khrushchev's proposals and stated that they would ensure their continued freedom of access to West Berlin. On 17 February, the Soviet Union first raised the possibility that, since the West refused to sign peace treaties with the two Germanies until after reunification, the U.S.S.R. might sign a separate treaty with the D.D.R. – therefore handing over to the D.D.R. responsibility for access routes to West Berlin.

Of the four occupying powers, the only one that wanted to change the Berlin situation was the U.S.S.R., but to change it she would have had to take provocative action, which in view of Dulles' declaration of 9 February could have resulted in war. The Western Allies were on the defensive and in this they had the advantage, as any move leading to war would have to be made by the Soviets and not by them. But the West threw Khrushchev a lifeline. They proposed a ministerial meeting to discuss Berlin and the peace treaty issue, and on 2 March Khrushchev accepted. Four Power negotiations provided Khrushchev with an honourable way out of his difficulties. On 5 March, in Leipzig, he said that the six months' deadline was not fixed, and four days later in East Berlin he removed his objections to Western troops remaining in the city. On 19 March, Khrushchev climbed down completely when he told a press conference: 'I believe that the United States, Britain and France do have lawful rights for their stay in Berlin.'[6]

Between May and August 1959, the Foreign Ministers of the four occupying powers met in conference at Geneva, but failed to come to any agreement, although the conference did agree a date for Khrushchev to visit Eisenhower in the U.S.A. In their subsequent talks the two men acknowledged their joint responsibility, as leaders of the world's two super-powers, to maintain world peace. Khrushchev appears to have been impressed with Eisenhower. On his return to Moscow he described the U.S. President as a man 'who enjoys the complete confidence of his people . . . [and who] sincerely wants, like us, to end the Cold War.'[7] But perhaps Khrushchev thought that Eisenhower might be prepared to compromise on Berlin now that Dulles was dead. At the Camp David talks in the U.S.A., Eisenhower had accepted that a solution to the Berlin problem must be found, thus implying that the U.S. might accept a change in West Berlin's status. Also Khrushchev's claim that the Berlin situation was 'abnormal' had not been rejected by the Americans.

By early 1960 Khrushchev had real hopes of a victory in Berlin. The idea of the British Premier, Macmillan, for a Four Power Summit was accepted, with Paris as the venue. The Soviet Union kept up the pressure on the West in three ways. Firstly, Khrushchev made a speech to the Supreme Soviet of the U.S.S.R. on 14 January 1960, in which he revealed that the Soviet Union would shortly possess a weapon so terrible that the risk inherent in its use would be unacceptable.* He therefore proposed not to hold nuclear tests so long as the West did the same, and to reduce the size of the Soviet armed forces by one-third. Ostensibly these moves appeared to be designed to reduce international tension but possibly Khrushchev was just trying to make capital out of the fact that the U.S.S.R. was committed to reducing conventional forces anyway. The Soviet leadership had decided, independently of what was happening in East-West relations in 1960, to increase the size of their nuclear forces at the expense of conventional forces, although this did not become apparent to the West for some time. Secondly, while Khrushchev behaved with apparent moderation, his East German clients did not. A number of incidents took place in West Berlin culminating in East German demands – for which they had full Soviet backing – that a height limit be imposed on the Allied air corridors to West Berlin.

The U.S.A. protested against the illegality of this action but nevertheless complied with it. The Americans were concerned for the outcome of the Paris Summit but their readiness to co-operate with the U.S.S.R. and to give way before the excesses of the D.D.R. regime worried the governments of Bonn and West Berlin who became afraid that the U.S.A. and Britain might be prepared to do a deal with the U.S.S.R. Thirdly, Khrushchev attempted to isolate

* Possibly Khrushchev was referring to the sixty-megaton bomb tested in 1961.

the West German Government. He knew that the support for Bonn of the French President, de Gaulle, on the peace treaty and the Berlin issue was uncompromising, and he therefore visited Paris to try to win de Gaulle over. He was unsuccessful.

Khrushchev wanted two things from the Paris Summit: an agreement on Berlin and an agreement to prohibit nuclear weapons in Germany and in the Pacific area. As the Summit approached, agreement on Berlin came no nearer and the nuclear issue began to grow in importance to the Soviet Government. By 1960 there were four nuclear powers and the prospect was beginning to emerge of more of the U.S.A.'s N.A.T.O. allies acquiring some control of N.A.T.O.'s nuclear defence. At the N.A.T.O. Council meeting of December 1960, the U.S. Secretary of State, Herter, proposed setting up a Multilateral Nuclear Force (M.L.F.) which would have given West Germany a share in a European nuclear force, but the M.L.F. never came into existence. Also, in the previous June, the U.S.S.R. had denounced its agreement to share nuclear knowledge with Peking, and Sino–Soviet relations had deteriorated rapidly. At a Warsaw Pact meeting on 4 February, the Chinese observer stated that China could not consider herself bound by any 'international disarmament agreement' or any other agreement in which China did not participate,[8] which meant that Khrushchev's Summit prospects looked bleak. Khrushchev had been the target of repeated Chinese criticism for his policy of 'peaceful coexistence', and it looked as though his policy of negotiation rather than confrontation was not going to yield the results he had hoped for – if any. Khrushchev was approaching another dilemma when the U-2 affair broke upon the world.

For some years, U.S. spy planes, U-2s, had been flying photo-reconnaissance missions over the U.S.S.R. The Soviets knew about these but it was not until 1 May 1960, that they were able to shoot down a U-2. On 4 May, Khrushchev announced that a spy plane had been shot down while violating Soviet air space, but said nothing about what had happened to the aircraft or the pilot. U-2s were fitted with a 'self-destruct' mechanism for just such an emergency and the relevant U.S. authorities probably thought that the pilot, Gary Powers, had obeyed standing orders and destroyed the complicated electronic gadgetry that the plane carried. The U.S. announced that a U-2 had been lost while studying meteorology at high altitudes. On 7 May, after the U.S. authorities had committed themselves to denying the hostile intent of the U-2 mission, Khrushchev revealed that both aircraft and pilot had been captured. If Khrushchev had wanted an excuse to call off the Paris Summit then he had found one. He had been proclaiming the virtues of peaceful coexistence and now U.S. actions in ordering U-2 overflights demonstrated to Khrushchev's domestic and Chinese critics that they had been right in their assessment of the policy objectives of the U.S.A. If Khrushchev was able to get some sort of agreement on Berlin out of the Paris Summit he could take it to Moscow and proclaim it as a triumph for the Khrushchev line over the policy favoured by the 'cold warriors' in Peking. This he would try to do, but now he had a face-saving way out if the Summit failed. Khrushchev condemned the U-2 overflight but said he was prepared to accept that it was the work of irresponsible subordinates and that the President knew nothing about it.

On 15 May, the day before the Summit Meeting was to begin, Khrushchev listed the minimum conditions he required if it was to take place: the U.S.A. must apologize for the U-2 affair, stop all such flights in future, and punish those responsible. Eisenhower cancelled future flights but found the other conditions unacceptable. The Summit failed almost as soon as it had begun. Khrushchev declared that the Summit should reconvene in six to eight months' time, and in this way delivered a personal insult to Eisenhower, for by January 1961 Eisenhower's term of office would be ended and there would be a new President in the White House. Khrushchev departed from Paris for East Berlin leaving such a tense and expectant atmosphere behind him that the Americans thought he might pre-empt the situation on the German peace treaty and Berlin, so the U.S. Secretary of Defence ordered a world-wide alert of American forces. Again the world was moving towards war, but Khrushchev did not sign a separate peace with the D.D.R.; in fact, he repeated his call for another Summit in the future and hoped that neither side would make a unilateral move on the German question. Berlin was put on ice while Khrushchev waited for the advent of a new American President from whom he might be able to obtain concessions on Germany.

During the remainder of 1960, Khrushchev hammered home his policy of 'peaceful coexistence' with the West. This was a major policy departure for the U.S.S.R. and even though it contributed so much to the Sino–Soviet split, Khrushchev was committed to it. But by 1961, Khrushchev was operating under very great pressure. Some of his domestic policies were less than successful, China no longer acknowledged Soviet predominance in the communist world and even tiny Albania was able to proclaim her independence from Moscow. In 1961 Khrushchev needed a victory to vindicate his policies and silence his critics; he was to seek such a victory again in Berlin.

In January 1961, John F. Kennedy was inaugurated as President of the U.S.A. Kennedy was young to hold such a high office, and possibly Khrushchev thought that Kennedy's inexperience was something he could take advantage of. The Soviet press reduced its anti-American outbursts when Kennedy took office, and the East Germans eased restrictions on travel to West Berlin. In April, the U.S.A. mounted the spectacularly unsuccessful Bay of Pigs landing (see Chapter 10), so when Kennedy and Khrushchev met in Vienna in June, Khrushchev was able to adopt an air of superiority as Kennedy arrived trailing his foreign policy disaster behind him. In Vienna Khrushchev issued another 'ultimatum': if no agreement were reached on Berlin by December 1961 the U.S.S.R. would sign a separate peace with the D.D.R. The Vienna Summit failed and was followed by a rapidly developing crisis over Berlin.

Not only Khrushchev but the D.D.R. leaders also needed a solution to the Berlin problem, and quickly. The very presence of Berlin was threatening the fabric of the East German state. Between 1949 and 1958, 2,189,000 East Germans 'voted with their feet' and fled to West Germany and this out of a total D.D.R. population in 1949 of 17,500,000. A high proportion of the fugitives were young, skilled or professional people without whom East Germany could not develop her economy. In addition, this loss was a persistent reminder that the communist regime was not popular in the D.D.R., no matter what the authorities claimed. By 1958, the East Germans had closed off the 850 miles of frontier between East and West Germany with wire fences backed up in places with mine fields. Those attempting to flee the D.D.R. risked being shot, blown up or captured to face a fifteen-month sentence as illegal emigrants. Between 1958 and 1961 fugitives continued to reach the West through the thirty-mile frontier between East and West Berlin. Their numbers remained high but not high enough to prevent considerable economic advances being made in the D.D.R. until the first six months of 1961, when 103,000 people fled from the D.D.R. to West Berlin. The Russians could not continue to allow their client state to be damaged in this way. Walter Ulbricht, the D.D.R. leader, kept up pressure on Khrushchev and maintained tension in Berlin. His problem was more urgent than Khrushchev's. Twice Ulbricht tried to pre-empt the West and the U.S.S.R. by closing the Berlin frontier and twice the *Vopos* were turned back by Soviet troops as they moved into position.[9] On 8 July, Khrushchev announced that Western attitudes forced the U.S.S.R. to increase the size of its military budget by 33 per cent. On 25 July, Kennedy asked Congress to increase the size of the U.S. military budget, increase the army intake of conscripts and call up reservists. He also requested a build-up of N.A.T.O.'s forces in Europe. On the same day the U.S.S.R. Foreign Minister, Gromyko, told the West German Ambassador to Moscow that if a separate peace treaty was signed Soviet troops would be deployed along the East–West German frontiers.

Threat and counter threat raised the political temperature of the Cold War and more importantly, increased the possibility that one or both sides might lose control of the escalation process upon which they had both embarked. Kennedy considered sending troops down the autobahns to Berlin if a separate peace were signed. Khrushchev told the British Ambassador just how many nuclear devices would be needed to destroy Britain. But in all the implied threats of military measures there was an undercurrent of unreality. There were only 11,000 Western troops in West Berlin to guard a West Berlin–D.D.R. frontier of 100 miles. West Berlin could not be defended by conventional means, and paradoxically this was its strength. Khrushchev could only alter the status of West Berlin by running the very real risk of nuclear war, which he did not want to do. But by August 1961 there was a marked increase in the numbers of refugees to West Berlin which exacerbated the already acute labour shortage in the D.D.R. As Philip Windsor wrote: 'The crisis which Khrushchev had conjured up could no longer be controlled; and if it entailed a rising in East Germany or the breakdown of its government, it would threaten the very purposes he had intended it to serve, and even increase the danger of war.'[10]

In the small hours of Sunday morning 13 August 1961, while Western ministries and embassies were manned by juniors, the East German *Vopos* sealed off West Berlin with wire fences. Four days later they began building a wall and the number of crossing points for the thirty-mile boundary in Berlin was reduced to four.

There were some shooting incidents between police on both sides, but the Western Powers could no nothing. The D.D.R. demanded the right to control all civilian air traffic to West Berlin and the West replied that they would hold the U.S.S.R. responsible for any interference in the air corridors. The U.S.S.R. and U.S.A. announced the resumption of nuclear tests. Both sides brought reinforcements to Berlin and there were confrontations between tank units at the crossing points in the city.

The recurring crises of 1958–61 which had largely been tests of will between the U.S.A. and the U.S.S.R. finally came to a head in the autumn of 1962 over Cuba and then passed away. After the Cuban crisis the U.S.S.R. recognized that Western resolve was too strong. The West had convinced the U.S.S.R. that the status of West Berlin could not be altered without war.

The Berlin Wall did stop the population flight to the West, thus allowing the D.D.R. economy to expand. Therefore it removed some of the urgency from the pressures upon Moscow to bring about a solution to the Berlin problem. The Russians and East Germans claimed that the Wall was built to stop Western spies and saboteurs from crossing into the East. Indeed Ulbricht was vituperative in his condemnation of West German government actions which forced the D.D.R. to erect the Wall. In a radio broadcast on 18 August he justified the building of the Wall on the grounds that: 'our dear brothers and sisters, the West German people' had allowed their government to 'fall into the hands of Fascists, Nazis, militarists, revanchists, warmongers, slave-traders and head-hunters'.[11]

But the East Berliners and the East Germans must have been as aware of the truth as were their compatriots in the West: East Germany needed to build a wall to keep its people in. Also, despite all his threats to sign a peace treaty with East Germany and hand over responsibility for access routes, Khrushchev did not do so; his diplomacy and blustering had failed. The West had been unable to prevent the building of the Wall. They had successfully defended the status of West Berlin but the Potsdam Agreement had made the three major Allies joint trustees of the whole of Berlin. Their trusteeship had failed. The building of the Wall divided a city, families and friends, brought grief to separated Berliners and a loss of face to the Allies. The Berlin Wall was a defeat for both sides in the Cold War.

*Ten*

# THE CUBAN MISSILE CRISIS

In the Western hemisphere, two potentially left-wing regimes emerged before the advent of Castro's Cuba. In British Guiana, Cheddi Jagan's People's Progressive Party won 18 out of 24 seats in the Guiana Assembly elections held in April 1953. When Jagan combined his calls for land reform and industrialization with a demand for self-government, the worried British Government accused him of intending to establish a communist regime; they suspended the constitution, despatched naval forces to the area, and arrested P.P.P. leaders. In Guatemala in 1951, Arbenz Guzman won the elections with Communist Party support and instituted a land redistribution scheme; in 1953 he began the confiscation of the assets of the massive American United Fruit Company. The Company provided arms and money and the C.I.A. provided advice to an exile force, led by the Catholic Colonel Armas, who invaded Guatemala in June 1954; the Guatemalan army refused to fight, Arbenz resigned, the illiterate peasantry were disenfranchised and the Communist Party outlawed. The neighbouring dictatorships in Nicaragua, El Salvador and Honduras breathed again – as did the United States.

But on 26 July 1953, a young lawyer, Fidel Castro, and 150 followers, attacked the army barracks at Santiago de Cuba in the Cuba of dictator General Batista. Half the rebels were killed, Castro was imprisoned and then exiled. In December 1956, Castro and eighty-two members of the '26 July Movement' returned to Cuba's Sierra Maestra Mountains. By December 1958, Castro had opened conventional war against Batista, whose regime collapsed by January 1959.

During 1959 Castro began a land reform programme, which involved the confiscation of American-owned sugar plantations and mills. While not a communist, Castro was determined to oust U.S.

'dollar imperialism': an American report for the U.S. Department of Commerce in 1953 stated, 'The only foreign investments of importance [in Cuba] are those of the U.S. American participation exceeds 90 per cent in the telephone and electric services and about 50 per cent in the public service railways and roughly 40 per cent in the raw sugar production – Cuba ranks third in Latin America in the value of U.S. direct investments.'[1] Castro's nationalization drive led him into conflict with President Eisenhower, who broke off diplomatic relations with Cuba in January 1961. During the Presidential elections of 1960, Kennedy called for American support for the 'democratic anti-Castro forces in exile and in Cuba itself, who offer eventual hope of overthrowing Castro'.[2] Kennedy inherited a C.I.A.-backed plan for logistic support for an exile-manned invasion of Cuba in the Bay of Pigs area in April 1961. The attack failed, and the invasion forces were destroyed on the beaches. U.S. involvement was obvious to the world, and Castro railed against U.S. imperialism while tightening his links with the Soviet Union, which had agreed in February 1960 to accept Cuban sugar and provide aid following the American economic boycott of Cuba. In December 1961, Castro declared 'I am a Marxist–Leninist', and in July 1962 Raul Castro and Che Guevara journeyed to Moscow to increase economic links and arrange defence aid in case of further U.S. intervention in Cuba. This was by no means impossible, for after the Bay of Pigs incident, Kennedy had declared:

> If the nations of this hemisphere should fail to meet their commitments against outside Communist intervention, then the government will not hesitate in meeting its primary obligation which is the security of this nation. Should that time ever come, we do not intend to be lectured on intervention by those whose character was stamped for all time on the bloody streets of Budapest . . . I am determined upon our system's survival and success, regardless of the cost and regardless of the price.[3]

On 4 September 1962 Kennedy warned the Soviet Union that he would not tolerate Soviet offensive missiles (i.e. ground-to-ground, as opposed to ground-to-air) being stationed on Cuba. On 11 September the U.S.S.R. issued a public announcement, stating that it had no need to place offensive missiles on Cuba. The first missile ship had arrived on the 8th and a C.I.A. agent saw missile transporters in the San Cristobal area on the 12th, but the C.I.A. discounted such 'unreliable' reports because the American Government thought that the stationing of missiles in Cuba was incompatible with Soviet foreign policy, as the Russians had never previously stationed nuclear missiles outside their own borders. There were a number of reasons why the Soviets broke this rule. In 1958 the U.S. Gaither Report had estimated that the Soviets would possess 100 I.C.B.M.s by 1959, and accordingly President Eisenhower had increased the U.S. military budget by $12 billion. But by 1962 the Soviets were estimated to possess only 50 I.C.B.M.s, 150 intercontinental bombers and 400 I.R.B.M.s. U.S. power consisted of 1,200 intercontinental bombers, nineteen Polaris submarines with 304 missiles, 1,000 carrier-based and overseas-based planes capable of dropping nuclear bombs and dozens of Minutemen I.C.B.M.s – i.e., a vastly superior force. Not surprisingly, Khrushchev was worried. Russia would be hard-pressed if she was forced to begin an expensive I.C.B.M. programme, while if she could place her existing M.R.B.M.s and I.R.B.M.s on Cuba, she would double her hitting power against the U.S. (eventually forty-two strategic missiles and forty-two strategic bombers were installed in Cuba); she would have missiles ninety miles off the U.S. coast; she would leapfrog N.A.T.O. and, moreover, face the soft under-belly of America. With missiles so placed, Soviet prestige regarding China would be increased. Moreover the Soviet Union would be in a better position to intimidate the Americans over Berlin in in any future German confrontation. Also, Khrushchev considered Kennedy to be inexperienced and weak, for he had failed to act over the Berlin Wall and had allowed the Bay of Pigs invasion to fail.

In August 1962, S.A.M. missiles and 5,000 Russian technicians arrived in Cuba, followed in September by Ilyushin bombers. On 14 October a high-flying U-2 flew over Western Cuba near San Cristobal and took photos which revealed missile sites (owing to tropical storms, no U-2 had flown over San Cristobal since mid-August). Kennedy ordered more flights, and on 16 October detailed photos revealed between sixteen and thirty-two missiles. Defence Secretary McNamara is reported to have said: 'A missile is a missile. It makes no difference whether you are killed by a missile fired from the Soviet Union or from Cuba.' But, of course, the accuracy of these missiles would be extremely high and U.S. warning time would be reduced to between 30 seconds and 2 minutes.

On 18 October a pre-arranged interview with the Soviet Foreign Minister, Gromyko, took place and he reiterated the lie that the

KEY
▲ Russian missile bases
■ American bases

SCALE
1,000 miles
2,000 km.

**THE CUBAN CRISIS (1962)**

Soviets had no offensive missiles on Cuba. Kennedy was horrified: unless the Soviets could be shown that such a threat and such deceit would not be tolerated, America could never feel safe in negotiating with Russia again. Kennedy told Dean Acheson that 'this is the week when I had better earn my salary'. The Executive Committee of the National Security Council met to discuss American options. If diplomatic channels alone – either with Khrushchev, Castro or the U.N. or a mixture of them all – were followed, the Soviets could gain the time necessary to complete the erection of the missile sites. There were a number of options: the military, including General Maxwell Taylor, preferred a 'surgical airstrike'; some preferred an invasion of Cuba. In either of these courses, Russian technicians would be killed and the volatile Khrushchev, perhaps pressurized by his ambitious subordinates in the Politburo, might be obliged to escalate the situation in Berlin, Turkey, or even towards a full Third World War.

However, Kennedy was immediately attracted by McNamara's suggestion of a 'blockade' on Cuba which Kennedy renamed a 'quarantine'. This course would allow Khrushchev time to reassess the situation, but unfortunately it would also allow time for the missiles to be deployed. Consequently, the military were ordered to arrange the planes necessary for an air strike against Cuba any time after 23 October (it was postulated that some Soviet missiles would be operational by the 28th). To keep the invasion option open, 100,000 men were to be directed to Florida, while over 100 ships, with 40,000 marines, were to be organized for the 'quarantine' of Cuba. On 19 October, Britain was informed of the American decision. On the 20th, a military clash on the Sino–Indian border (the prelude to war on that border) opened the possibility of a joint Sino–Soviet pressure on the West. Kennedy did not at that time appreciate the extent to which the Sino–Soviet split rendered such co-operation unlikely.

On 21 October Kennedy left for Illinois, to carry on with the campaign for the November Congressional elections. At this stage, therefore, America and the Soviets remained ignorant of Kennedy's knowledge of the missiles in Cuba. In his absence an aide, Sorensen, was to draft a speech which the President intended to make on radio and TV at 6 p.m. on 22 October. The telephone kept Kennedy in touch with Washington and in charge of the situation – 'Tell Sorensen he's writing a speech announcing a blockade – not Armageddon!' During the 22nd, forty-three governments, including the Soviet Union, were informed of the impending blockade. Dean Acheson was personally sent to the potentially troublesome De Gaulle, who accepted that 'in the circumstances President Kennedy has no other choice'. During the day, wives and children were evacuated from Guantánamo; B-47 bombers were diverted to forty civilian airports; B-52 bombers were put on Red Alert; and 156 I.C.B.M.s were primed ready for 'go'. At 6 p.m., Kennedy informed the U.S. public of the missiles and the blockade, and reminded them that:

The 1930s taught us a clear lesson: aggressive conduct, if allowed to go un-checked and unchallenged, ultimately leads to war ... It shall be the policy of this nation to regard any nuclear missile launched from Cuba against any nation in the Western Hemisphere as an attack by the Soviet Union on the United States requiring a full retaliatory response upon the Soviet Union ... [He called upon] Chairman Khrushchev to halt and eliminate this clandestine, reckless and provocative threat to world peace ... [and take the] opportunity to move the world back from the abyss of destruction.

On 23 October there was no reaction in either Berlin or Cuba; the Organization of American States accepted the blockade by 19 votes to 0, and by evening the Russian technicians were working by flare-light on the missile sites. Khrushchev had badly misjudged Kennedy's reaction; refusing to get bogged down in the U.N., Kennedy had startled Khrushchev with the speed of the blockade and the speed with which America consulted both N.A.T.O. and the O.A.S. Kennedy had no intention of 'negotiating under the gun' but was determined not to 'let events get out of hand'. At 800 miles, U.S. ships were outside of Cuban MiG range and U.S. warships were informed that the decision to board or fire upon a Soviet ship running the blockade must emerge direct from the President. Kennedy was desperately trying to avoid the necessity for an air strike against the sites: the best evidence was that 10 per cent (i.e. seven missiles) would survive such a strike. The alternative was to pressure Khrushchev to back down.

On Wednesday 24 October, two Soviet ships and a submerged submarine were approaching the 500-mile blockade line (which Kennedy had reduced from 800 miles to give Khrushchev more time to think) and on the previous night the Attorney General, Robert Kennedy, had informed the Soviet Ambassador, Dobrynin, that 'We will turn your ships back'. Khrushchev knew that S.A.C. was on full alert, that America had more nuclear power than the Soviet Union, and that the Soviet conventional navy was no match for the American navy. Kennedy was informed that the ships had slowed, then stopped, and finally turned back. The President immediately issued a direct order that no Soviet ship was to be harassed if it kept beyond the line. But were the Soviets simply regrouping with the six submarines estimated to be in the Caribbean area? By the 24th Kennedy had reliable estimates of over thirty missiles in Cuba (enough to kill perhaps 80 million Americans) and he ignored U Thant, Secretary General of the U.N., who called for the end of the blockade and a three-week period of negotiations.

On Thursday 25 October a communication from Khrushchev arrived. It accused Kennedy of 'recklessly playing with nuclear fire', of 'piracy' and 'aggression'. (It could, of course, be argued that blockading the high seas or boarding foreign ships did constitute 'acts of war'.) On Kennedy's order, the Russian tanker *Bucharest* was permitted to cross the line when, after being hailed, the captain replied that she carried only petrol. But the blockade was still on, and although the picture quality gave the Soviets some estimate of the capacity of the U-2s, Kennedy agreed to publish photos of the Cuban missiles. Thus, at the U.N., Adlai Stevenson was able to embarrass the Soviet Ambassador who, on Khrushchev's orders, was still refusing to admit any such Soviet offensive missiles were stationed on Cuba.

On Friday 26th, Kennedy ordered flights to be made over the missile sites every two hours at 700 feet and ordered 5 million leaflets in Spanish 'explaining' America's reasons for invading Cuba. But at 6 p.m. a new communication arrived from Khrushchev. The tense, not to say frightened, Soviet leader suggested an evacuation of Soviet missiles from Cuba in exchange for an American promise not to invade Cuba in the future. Kennedy, determined on caution, demanded an analysis by the following morning. However, since America and Russia were on different day and night times, this delay gave the Praesidium an opportunity to replace the personal initiative made by Khrushchev with a new offer, received by Kennedy on Saturday 27th.

The second missive demanded the removal of (what were in fact obsolete) Jupiter missiles in Turkey in return for the removal of Soviet missiles from Cuba. *The Times* of 29 October quoted the offer: 'Your rockets are situated in Italy and are aimed at us. Your rockets are situated in Turkey. You are worried by Cuba. You say it worries you because it is a distance of 90 miles by sea from the coast of America. But Turkey is next to us. Our sentries walk up and down and look at each other.' Kennedy was furious for a number of reasons: because he had ordered the removal of the Jupiters back in 1961, because Turkey, a stout ally, must not be let down, because there were now doubts as to who really ruled in the Soviet Union, and because an attack on Cuba would obviously risk Soviet retaliation against Turkey, thereby involving N.A.T.O. in a potential European – if not world – war.

It was a harrowing day. At 10.15 a.m. the U-2 which had taken the photographs on 14 October was shot down over Cuba, and at 2 p.m. another U-2 'strayed' over the Russian Chokut Peninsula, opposite Alaska. Both leaders were desperately trying to keep control and prevent the mistakes of their juniors from provoking irreversible catastrophe. Kennedy ordered the American missiles to be disarmed, and only to be rearmed on his specific orders, but there were rumours that the Russian Embassy personnel were burning their records – an action normally taken only when war is imminent. At about 8 p.m., Robert Kennedy persuaded the President to ignore the letter sent by the Politburo, and to reply to the proposal made by Khrushchev. President Kennedy agreed, but stated that the American response must include a demand for a Soviet reply by Sunday, 28 October. According to one American historian:

> The American Government did not fail to let the Russians know that 144 Polaris, 103 Atlas, 105 Thor and Jupiter, and 54 Titan missiles were ready to convert the U.S.S.R. into a radioactive heap of rubbish within 30 minutes. In addition, there were 600 I.R.B.M.s and 250 M.R.B.M., 1,600 long-range bombers and 37 aircraft-carriers, together three or four times as much fire-power as the Soviet Union could put into the air.[4]

If the Russians did not respond, then Cuba was to be invaded on Monday 29th and the world would be much closer to a Third World War.

At 9 a.m. on 28 October, Radio Moscow broadcast Khrushchev's reply: 'In order to liquidate with greater speed the dangerous conflict, to serve the cause of peace . . . and to calm the people of America, orders for the dismantling of the weapons you describe as "offensive", their crating and return to the Soviet Union [have been issued].' It was rumoured that General Curtis E. Le May of Strategic Air Command recommended to the President . . . 'We attack Monday in any case', but at 12 a.m. the radio Voice of America broadcast Kennedy's acceptance of Khrushchev's 'states-manlike' offer. Secretary of State Dean Rusk is reported to have said: 'We looked into the mouth of the cannon. The Russians flinched.' Within, two months no trace was left of the missiles of October, the land was ploughed over, the Cold War had lived through its 'warmest' days and a year later, in August 1963, the U.S. and the Soviets agreed to a Partial Nuclear Test Ban Treaty and to a Hot Line telephone contact between Washington and the Kremlin. The first wavering sign of *détente* was visible, but much American energy for the remainder of the 1960s was to be dissipated in a massive counter-insurgency operation in Vietnam, which sapped her strength, stained her democracy and inhibited the development of a dialogue with the Soviet Union.

# Eleven

# THE WEAPONS OF THE COLD WAR

On 16 July 1945, at Alamagordo in the New Mexican desert, the atomic age began. A plutonium bomb exploded with a blast equivalent to 14,000 tons of T.N.T. As he watched the explosion Robert Oppenheimer, a leader of the Manhattan Project that had cost $2,191 million, quoted from Sri Krishna, the Exalted One: 'I am become Death, the Shatterer of Worlds.'

The use of atomic bombs against the Japanese cities of Hiroshima and Nagasaki on 6 and 9 August were two of the last acts of the Second World War and, in some senses, some of the first acts of the Cold War. Undoubtedly, as Vannebar Bush (Chairman of the U.S. National Defence Research Committee) admitted, one reason for the speed of atomic history in the summer of 1945 was 'so that there was no necessity for any concessions to Russia at the end of the war'.

By September 1945, an A-bomb factory had begun production at Albuquerque, and German scientists such as Dr. von Braun, 'captured' in May 1945, were beginning to explain to the Americans the workings of 'confiscated' V-2 rockets. But in 1946, America was still hoping to avoid conflict with the Soviets. They offered the Baruch Plan, entailing U.N. control of atomic weapons, and U.N. supervision of potential or actual atomic powers, to ensure that no country was developing or stock-piling nuclear weapons. But the U.N. was American-dominated in 1946 and any U.N. 'supervisors' would therefore be highly suspicious in the eyes of the Soviets who, in any event, in a 'closed' society, had no wish for foreign inspection. Besides, even if the U.S. did hand over its weapons to the U.N., it could not remove or destroy the knowledge among its scientific minds of how to build such weapons. The plan failed, and henceforth its successors involved limitations on atomic and thermonuclear weapons, and their delivery systems, rather than the concept of nuclear disarmament.

The events of 1945–9 worried many Americans, including Edward Teller, an Hungarian refugee. He had worked on the A-bomb and as early as 1942 had been involved in advanced research at Los Alamos, the Manhattan Project H.Q., on the possibility of an even bigger device, based on the fusion – not fission – of atoms. In 1945, America and its scientists had not yet become sufficiently anti-Soviet to begin research on the 'super' bomb. General Groves, the military head of the Manhattan Project, had estimated that it would take twenty years for the Soviets to be able to produce an atomic device. On 20 September 1949, the U.S. discovered that Russia had exploded one, codenamed 'Joe 1' by the West.

On 29 October a committee of scientists, which included Oppenheimer, was given the task of considering the merits and demerits of an American attempt to produce the superbomb. The majority report of five scientists stated: 'We are all reluctant to see the U.S. take the initiative in precipitating this development. In determining not to proceed to develop the super bomb, we see a unique opportunity of providing by example some limitations on the totality of war and thus eliminating the fear and rousing the hopes of mankind.' Scientists like Teller were furious, believing that: 'It won't be until the bombs get so big that they can annihilate everything that people will really become terrified and begin to take a reasonable line in politics. Those who oppose the hydrogen bomb are behaving like ostriches if they think they are going to promote peace in the word.'[1] In January 1950 the Fuchs case broke in Britain. Fuchs, a nuclear physicist who had fled from Nazi Germany and joined the British and then the American atomic projects, was found guilty of spying for the Soviet Union. Truman ordered the National Security Council to reconsider the superbomb. Johnson, Secretary of Defence, and Acheson, Secretary of State – unlike Lilienthal, Chairman of the Atomic Energy Commission – recommended its development. On 31 January 1950 President Truman announced, 'It is part of my responsibility as Commander-in-Chief of the Armed Forces to see to it that our country is able to defend itself against any aggression. Accordingly, I have directed the A.E.C. to continue its work on all forms of atomic weapons, including the so-called hydrogen or "super" bomb.'[2] In March 1950, the Joint Chiefs of Staff persuaded Truman to inform the scientists that the production of an

H-bomb 'was of the highest urgency'. In June 1950 the Korean War began, and during the next two years scientists like Teller and the Pole, Stanislav Ulam, worked on the bomb while the Hungarian, Johnny von Neumann, worked on the Mathematical Analyser, Numerical Integrator and Computer (MANIAC!) – an aid essential to the speedy analysis of the complex statistical data required to produce the new device.

On 1 November 1952 at Eniwetok in the U.S. Marshall Islands, the thermonuclear age began. A sixty-five-ton device, exploding with the force of 3·5 million tons of T.N.T., all but vapourized the islet of Elugelab and produced a crater 175 feet deep and one mile wide in the ocean bed.

Research continued, for a sixty-five-ton device was hardly a viable weapon, and on 12 August 1953, a Soviet H-bomb was exploded in Siberia. But in March the following year, the Americans exploded another device in the Pacific – of weapon size, and with an explosive power of 15 million tons of T.N.T. equivalent. The world had come a long way since the 14,000 tons of uranium atomic bomb had hit Hiroshima, killing over 70,000 immediately, and from the 3,000 m.p.h. V-2 missiles that had carried in their nose-cones one ton of T.N.T.

From 1954 the race was on to stockpile atomic bombs – but B-47 long-range bombers and their Russian equivalents were not the only means of delivering nuclear payloads. America and Russia spent the 1950s working also on missiles. The first U.S. surface-to-surface ballistic missile was tested in 1947, but until 1957 it was really long-range (over 5,000 mile) Inter-Continental Ballistic Missiles that evaded both competitors. In August 1957 it was the Russians who first achieved the goal of an I.C.B.M., and in October – as if to show the world their success – they launched into space a satellite called 'Sputnik' or 'Companion' 1. In December 1957 – and in second place! – the Americans launched the 16,000 m.p.h. 5,000 mile range, $30 million (per rocket) Atlas I.C.B.M.

In January 1954, there being no Soviet missiles and there being U.S. superiority in long-range bombers, Dulles had popularized the concept of 'massive retaliation' in America, arguing that 'there is no local defense which alone will contain the mighty land power of the Communist world. Local defenses must be reinforced by the further deterrent of massive retaliatory power . . . a great capacity to retaliate instantly.'[3] The idea of countering Soviet conventional moves by the threat of massive nuclear attack became increasingly unrealistic when massive retaliation turned into a two-way street, and U.S. papers carried maps of American cities ringed by concentric circles of 'destruct' areas given a hit by a Soviet missile carrying a warhead perhaps equivalent to 5 million tons of T.N.T. In June 1959, the U.S. Congressional Committee on Atomic Energy gave a series of public hearings analysing the effects of a Soviet nuclear attack on the U.S.A. of 1,500 million tons of T.N.T. equivalent (i.e. 1,500 megatons). They admitted that this was not the maximum attack the Soviets could mount. They estimated that, given hypothetical specified weather conditions – and hypothetical specified targets and types of weapons – on a given day (taken to be 12 noon on 17 October 1958), 20 million Americans would be killed on the first day and 22 million would die during the subsequent sixty days, most of them from radiation sickness. These were some of the hard facts behind the Cold War of the late 1950s, and the arms race continued unabated.

In January 1954 the U.S.S. *Nautilus*, America's first nuclear-propelled submarine, began trials. In July 1960 the first test occurred of a missile (code-named Polaris A1) fired from a submerged submarine, the U.S.S. *George Washington*. A nuclear submarine capable of remaining submerged for over two months and of firing a 1,500 nautical mile range missile in 1960 was able to attack anywhere in the Soviet Union except a limited area of Central Russia around Omsk. Before long, the Polaris A2 emerged, with a 1,700 mile range – and nowhere in the world is more than 1,700 nautical miles from the sea. By the mid-1960s, Polaris A3 (with a warhead of 0·7 of a megaton) capable of 2,500 nautical miles (2,850 miles) was operational, as were hundreds of the new American I.C.B.M., code-named Minuteman. By 1963–4, with camera-carrying satellites like the U.S. Samos or Soviet Cosmos spying from the skies, Polaris submarines roaming the seas and I.C.B.M.s slowly disappearing into hard underground silos in Montana and Siberia, the weapons of the Cold War began to take on the appearance of modernity to the eyes of the 1980s. Nevertheless, there are at least two obvious differences: in the early 1960s, American nuclear superiority was starkly obvious, especially to the Russians; and in 1960 the still modern V-bombers gave the British independent nuclear deterrent an air of credibility.

The U.S. and U.S.S.R. had lost their atomic monopoly in 1952, when Britain exploded her first A-bomb, and their thermonuclear monopoly in 1957 when she exploded an H-bomb. Satisfied with her Victor, Valiant and Vulcan bombers in the mid-1950s, Britain turned to missile development at the end of the decade. After expensive failures (and expensive near-success like 'Blue Streak') between 1957 and 1962, Prime Minister Macmillan elicited from Kennedy at the Nassau Conference in 1962 agreement that Britain should purchase Polaris missiles from America. The V-bombers were phased out of a nuclear role in 1968 but the four Polaris submarines became part of the British contribution to N.A.T.O. Each submarine was equipped with sixteen 2,880 mile range Polaris missiles and each missile was armed with three British-designed 200 kiloton M.R.V.ed warheads.

The French nuclear deterrent, unlike the British, was not assigned to N.A.T.O.; moreover, the French force includes nuclear bombers and land-based missiles. On the Plateau d'Albion, some fifty miles north of Marseilles, the French Air Force has its first *Groupement des Missiles Stratégiques*: eighteen missiles spaced several miles apart with a 1,500 mile range and with warheads of 150 kilotons – twelve times the force of the Hiroshima bomb. The *Force de Dissuasion* also includes thirty-three Mirage IVAs – two-man, mach 2+ bombers with a 2,000-mile range (a 3,000+ mile range with in-flight refuelling), each of which can deliver one 100 kiloton bomb. The *Force de Dissuasion* also includes four nuclear submarines (to be joined by a fifth), one armed with sixteen 1,900 mile range S.L.B.M.s carrying a 500 kiloton warhead, and the other three each armed with sixteen 3,000 mile range S.L.B.M.s carrying one 1 megaton warhead. France has even created a version of America's vast and diverse arsenal of tactical nuclear weapons – thirty Pluton rockets, each with 15–25 kiloton warheads and a 75 mile range.

General de Gaulle, though not the originator of the French nuclear programme, was wholeheartedly in favour of an independent French deterrent; he described the need to continue the development of the French force in April 1964: 'For France to give up the capability of deterring an enemy from attacking her ... would mean entrusting France's defence and, therefore, her existence, to a foreign, that is to say, an unreliable, protector. No, we are worthy of better than this.'[4] The British used much the same logic for their decision to go nuclear. 'We had to hold our position *vis-à-vis* the Americans. We couldn't allow ourselves to be wholly in their hands.'[5] Critics of the British and French deterrents often point to the huge disparity between them and those of the super-powers. This is answered in Paris and London with the cry of proportional deterrence. If it were possible for the Soviet Union to conquer America, or to turn China into a subservient ally, it might take a major risk of losing a large part of the Soviet population to deter the Soviets from attempting these actions. But the risk of losing Moscow and Leningrad might deter them from attempting the conquest of a lesser country – thus, according to this logic, a small country needs less of a deterrent force than does a super-power, to give it the same degree of safety. Of course, the strongest argument against this *force de dissuasion* is that it is militarily vulnerable. The Mirages are vulnerable if an attack comes so quickly that they are caught on the ground; one estimate suggested that seventy-two Soviet I.C.B.M.s could 'take out' the Plateau d'Albion bases, and with four submarines built, the French can keep only two at sea at a time. The question would then become: would the destruction of France be worth the reception of two submarines' missiles? The Chinese, of course, con-sidered such theories irrelevant in the 1950s and 1960s, arguing that it was people, not bombs, who won wars.

However, since deploying her own strategic forces and having to come to terms with the 'unthinkable', the new Chinese view of the post-Mao leadership in Peking is much less sanguine about the pros-pects of nuclear war.

> 'The atomic bomb is a paper tiger.' This famous saying by Chairman Mao is known to all. China is developing nuclear weapons not because we believe in the omnipotence of nuclear weapons, or plan to use nuclear weapons. China's aim is to break the monopoly of the nuclear powers and to eliminate war ... We believe in the people. It is the people who decide the outcome of a war and not any weapon.[6]

# Twelve

# AMERICA AND THE VIETNAM WAR

In 1956 President Diem of South Vietnam refused to co-operate in all-Vietnam elections; by 1958 he was facing selective assassination of government village chiefs, and by 1961 a force of 20,000 Vietnamese communists (Vietcong or Vc) determined to oust him and reunify Vietnam. In 1961, there were just 685 American military advisers in the South – they were there to prevent South Vietnam from being the first 'domino' to fall under Asian communist pressure. In April 1954, Eisenhower had said, 'You have a row of dominoes set up, you knock over the first one and what will happen to the last one is a certainty that it will go over very quickly.'[1] Kennedy apparently accepted the thesis; in September 1963 he stated: 'China is so large, looms so high just beyond the frontiers, that if South Vietnam went, it would not only give them an improved geographic position for a guerrilla assault on Malaya but would give the impression that the wave of the future in South-East Asia was China and the Communists.'[2] The Americans, shorn of their Asia specialists (men who had been hounded from the State Department during the McCarthy era after the 'loss' of China) were undecided as to whether the National Liberation Front of South Vietnam founded in 1960 was directed by China, North Vietnam or the N.L.F. itself. Though General Harkins, Head of U.S. Operations there in June 1963, argued: 'The guerrillas are obviously not being reinforced or supplied systematically from North Vietnam, China or any other place. They depend primarily on what they can capture.'[3]

Vietcong identification was a difficult question: many had been north and returned – in 1954 approximately 80,000 Vietminh followed their leader, Le Duan, north of the 17th Parallel. Were they therefore southerners and part of an indigenous revolt against Diem, or were they infiltrating northerners? If they were northerners, was Vietnam two states? And therefore was crossing the 17th Parallel tantamount to invasion across an international border? Of course, even if the Vietcong were southerners engaged in a civil war with Diem's government, that government had been elected (though the elections run by Diem's brother were hardly 'fair' by Western standards), and therefore the U.S. had the right to answer a call for help from an established government.

In November 1961, after his visit to Vietnam as Kennedy's military representative, General Maxwell Taylor – later to be Chairman of the Joint Chiefs of Staff – advocated the despatch of 8,000 U.S. troops to Vietnam to aid Diem, while he built up his army (the A.R.V.N.) to 200,000 during 1962.

On 8 November Defence Secretary McNamara, reflecting the pressure from his generals, recommended even greater U.S. military commitment. George Ball, the Under-Secretary of State, had worked closely with the French during the Indo-China War and had seen the false optimism of generals, the resilience and relentlessness of the Vietminh, the communist exploitation of nationalism, and the poisonous domestic effects on France of an unpopular war. Ball told Kennedy he would have 300,000 men in Vietnam in a few short years. The President laughed and said, 'George, you're crazier than hell.'[4] By the time Kennedy was assassinated there were 16,500 advisers in South Vietnam and by escalating the military commitment Kennedy had taken America deeper into a military and political quagmire. As the commitment increased, so did American verbal rhetoric in support of Diem, while reporters and even TV men went to Vietnam and the American public had their first taste of the new Asian land war. For two and a half years prior to his dismissal, General Harkins' reports overestimated U.S. success and underplayed the 'Little Yellow Men' who refused to wear military uniform, hold terrain, 'fight in the light', or follow the Geneva Convention. During 1962, Kennedy began to see his commitment developing a momentum of its own, with the President bowing to military requests for napalm, free-fire zones and defoliants. McNamara visited Vietnam in 1963, but he preferred to think in terms of data – the percentage rise in strategic hamlets, or Vietcong body counts – rather than the nature of a political war with an enemy that anyway had a different concept of 'acceptable' losses. Men like Maxwell Taylor in the Pentagon, more deeply imbued with the Cold War rationale than some of Kennedy's civilian advisers, spent 1963 smothering information that suggested a 'client' state backed by the U.S. military machine was failing to win a war against peasant guerrillas. On 1 November 1963, Diem was assassinated and Henry Cabot Lodge, U.S. Ambassador in Saigon, left for Washington to explain to Kennedy the disastrous situation in Vietnam. He arrived to find that Kennedy himself had been assassinated and that the new President Johnson was determined not to 'lose Vietnam': 'I am not going to be the President who saw South-East Asia go the way China went.' Between November 1963 and 1965, Saigon saw twelve changes of government but the U.S. remained determined in its aims. In mid-March 1964, McNamara drew up a report stating U.S. intentions:

> We seek an independent, non-communist South Vietnam. We do not require that it serve as a Western base or as a member of a Western alliance. South Vietnam must be free, however, to accept outside assistance as required to maintain its security. Unless we can achieve this objective in South Vietnam, almost all of South-East Asia will probably fall under Communist dominance, accommodate to communism so as to remove effective U.S. and anti-communist influence (Burma), or fall under the domination of forces not now explicitly communist, but likely to become so (Indonesia). Thailand might hold for a period with our help, but would be under grave pressure. Even the Philippines would become shaky, and the threat to India to the west, Australia and New Zealand to the south, and Taiwan, Korea and Japan to the north and east would be greatly increased.[5]

This was domino logic, pure and simple. Johnson was determined to hold the line; to fulfil America's obligations; to safeguard the tin, rubber and tungsten of Indo-China; and to prove to Mao and to all would-be guerrillas around the world that the 'People's War' of insurgency could be beaten.

In August 1964, North Vietnamese P.T. boats allegedly fired on U.S. destroyers which were supposedly in international waters. According to the 'Pentagon Papers' which Daniel Ellsberg, a Defense Department analyst, leaked to the press in June 1971, Johnson had had a resolution ready and waiting for such a provocation months before, which, once Congress signed, would give him extended powers to deal with the Vietnam crisis. Thus began the first bombing attacks of North Vietnam. According to U.S. reports, regular North Vietnamese soldiers infiltrated the South in the winter of 1964, to deliver the *coup de grâce* and this provided the justification for the despatch of large numbers of U.S. ground troops to Vietnam, as well as strategic bombing of the North. The war changed: 'For two months during [the 1964 elections] the Administration line was that the war in South Vietnam was substantially self-sustaining and had to be won there ... When the bombing of North Vietnam began, information was produced overnight to prove that 'aggression from the North' is the key to everything.'[6] In March 1966, Senator Clark criticized McNamara, who talked of 15,000 North Vietnamese troops in the South compared with 220,000 Vietcong – i.e. 6·5 per cent of the total after thirteen months of heavy infiltration.[7]

Nevertheless, Johnson continued to point to the communist threat to the West. In April 1965, he argued: 'The rulers in Hanoi are urged on by Peking. This is a regime which has destroyed freedom in Tibet, attacked India, and been condemned by the U.N. for aggression in Korea. It is a nation which is helping the forces of violence in almost every continent. The contest in Vietnam is part of a world-wide pattern of aggressive purpose.' (In fact, the U.S. itself admitted that during 1965, the Chinese gave $35 million in aid to North Vietnam, as compared with $225 million from the Soviet Union.)[8]

The year 1965 proved tense for America: to prevent left-wing control, marines intervened in the Dominican Republic, a Caribbean island, while in Indonesia, the prospect of a communist-armed *coup* emerged. In 1967, Robert Kennedy stated, 'Less than two years ago we were quite prepared to accept the spread of Communism in Indonesia, a nation of 100 million people, incomparably rich in resources, standing over the critical Straits of Malacca and flanking the Philippines.'[9] Since armed invasion appeared the only way to prevent the *coup*, and America was already heavily committed in Vietnam, she stayed out of Indonesia and the Indonesian generals dealt with their own communists by massacring tens of thousands of them in a *coup*-before-a-*coup*.

In Vietnam, the increasingly frustrated Americans turned to non-lethal gas, phosphorous bombs, anti-personal devices, napalm and massive so-called 'pinpoint' bombing of the North. One U.S. Congressman in 1966 estimated that to kill one Vietcong enemy of General Thieu's regime in South Vietnam cost the Americans $400,000.[10] But at least the war was one for the relatively thinly populated countryside – until the Tet offensive of 1968, during which the Vietcong attacked major cities including Hué, where they retreated leaving 1,000 executed citizens, and Saigon, where 5,000 Vietcong infiltrated the city in January, raided the presidential palace, the radio station, the airport and even the U.S. Embassy. (In the same month the North Koreans decided to enter the anti-American fray more actively by seizing a U.S. intelligence ship, the *Pueblo*, again theoretically in international waters. Its crew were not released for thirteen months.) In Vietnam, although no general rising had been sparked off by the Tet offensive, the Americans felt increasingly insecure. In March, My Lai 4 (or 'Pinkville') hit U.S. headlines – 109 women and children had been massacred in a 'war crime' by troops of the U.S. Americal Division. The ten or twelve to one superiority of Malaya was out of the question in Vietnam, for by March 1968, 535,000 Americans, 55,000 allies, 350,000 A.R.V.N. and 40,000 militia faced 200,000 Vietcong and 60,000 North Vietnamese army (N.V.A.) regulars. Johnson, increasingly unpopular, decided not to stand for re-election in 1968, and Nixon replaced him as President in January 1969.

At Guam in July 1969, Nixon formulated a new foreign policy for Asia. While maintaining her treaty commitments, the U.S. would 'carefully weigh our interests in undertaking new commitments and shun a reflexive response to threats'. Though continuing the U.S. nuclear shield in Asia, Nixon stated his 'intention to help meet other forms of aggression by providing military and economic assistance, while looking primarily to the threatened nation to provide the manpower for its own defense.'[11] The year 1969 had been a frightening one in Vietnam: U.S. troop levels topped 549,000; deaths in 1968 had averaged 278 a week; only 40 per cent of South Vietnam's rural population was under government control; inflation in Vietnam was running at 35 per cent to 40 per cent; and 'the additional costs of the war to the U.S. had reached $22 billion a year'.[12]

From 1969 to 1972 the 'Vietnamization' policy (by which the Vietnamese government took over responsibility for the war) continued fast – by December 1972 only 25,000 U.S. troops remained in Vietnam, although there were 98,000 in Thailand and Guam, and on the Seventh Fleet. Theoretically, 80 per cent of the total Southern population was under government control by 1972; a million acres of farm land had been redistributed; and through their operation against N.V.A. concentrations in Cambodia in 1970 and Thieu's against the Ho Chi Minh trail in Laos in 1971, the Americans had helped to 'buy the time needed to make our ally self-sufficient'.[13]

In January 1973 'peace with honour' emerged, but the cost had been great. The *Strategic Survey* of 1972 stated that by December 1972, 7·8 million of the 19 million inhabitants of the South were refugees. By January 1975, the figure rose to 10 million – 55 per cent of the population: and by that month, the number of orphans had reached 900,000. By 1973, military casualties included: 180,676 South Vietnamese dead; 921,350 N.V.A./Vc dead; 56,226 U.S. dead; 4,928 South Korean dead; 492 Australian and 35 New Zealand dead. Southern civilian casualties were estimated at 415,000 dead with 935,000 injured: Northern casualties at approximately 150,000 dead between 1969 and 1972. Vietnamese casualties in total between 1961 and 1972 were thus approximately 1·8 million. The financial cost to the U.S. of the war and military aid has been estimated to have been between $108,480 million and $170,000 million.[14] The U.S. Air Force alone flew 1,899,668 sorties and dropped 6,727,084 tons of bombs on Indo-China (in comparison, only 2,700,000 tons of bombs were dropped by British and American air forces on Germany in the Second World War); 8,000 aircraft were lost.

B-52 saturation bombing reached its closest to the populated suburbs of Hanoi in December 1972, and until that time Prime Minister Pham Van Dong and Politburo member Le Duc Tho had, according to President Nixon, demanded 'a fixed date for our total and unconditional withdrawal; the removal of Thieu's government; and the installation of communist rule disguised as a so-called coalition government'.[15] However, at Paris in January 1973, the North gave up that aim as a prerequisite for a truce and the U.S. gave up their aim of obliging NVA troops to evacuate the South. President Thieu accepted the 'peace' because of the boost in armaments he received in the autumn, the bombing of Hanoi and certain assurances he received from the U.S. In February 1975 he remarked at a press conference that: 'China and the Soviet Union had told the United States that they would use their influence with North Vietnam to impose restraint on Hanoi's leaders. Dr. Kissinger promised me this before and after the signing of the agreement. He said that Russia and China promised to be co-operative with the United States.'[16] Other more secret assurances came to light when the White House was badgered by Senator Henry Jackson in April 1975. On 8 April, Presidential spokesman Ron Nessen admitted that:

'The publicly stated policy and intention of the United States Government . . . to react vigorously to major violations of the Paris Agreement' had been the subject of 'confidential exchanges between the Nixon Administration and President Thieu at the time.'[17] The Paris Agreement included clauses on the withdrawal of U.S. troops, the release of all military and political prisoners, the replacement of arms to the forces in the South only on a one-for-one basis, the appointment of neutral control commissions to inspect alleged breaches of the ceasefire in Vietnam, the 'neutrality' of Laos and Cambodia and the establishment of a National Council for Reconciliation in South Vietnam to include communists and 'third force' representatives and which would organize elections in the South and negotiate the eventual reunification of Vietnam. Both North and South Vietnam ignored these clauses. The North increased its supplies to its 180,000 troops in the South – between January and December 1973 alone, about 500 T54 and T34 tanks entered the South – built airfields and S.A.M. installations in the Central Highlands, and turned the Ho Chi Minh trail into a concreted highway. Meanwhile, Thieu showed his complete disregard for the Clause concerned with a National Council for Reconciliation, and concentrated on expanding his area of control in the South by impinging on Vc areas. In August 1974, the Senate Foreign Relatious Committee stated that Thieu had gained control of an additional 6 per cent of South Vietnam's population – numbering about 1 million people, not all of whom were refugees from Vc zones. By January 1975, after two years of the 'ceasefire' – for which Dr. Kissinger was awarded the Nobel Peace Prize – about 100,000 Vietnamese had died.[18]

During 1974, Thieu experienced problems with the soaring costs of oil and of fertilizers for the American imported high-yield rice; he also had to cope with the effects of American inflation and he had to resist Buddhist democrats who protested against government corruption. The U.S. Congress cut down his aid for the fiscal year 1974–5 to only $700 million, and ammunition and spare parts for his war machinery – and especially for his air force – became increasingly sparse. A 70 per cent inflation rate hit A.R.V.N. pay and morale, and the desertion rate soared. Of even greater importance to Thieu's regime was action taken by the U.S. Congress in August 1973. Angered by what it had come to believe was a 'staged' Tonkin Gulf Resolution, and by the 'secret' invasion of Cambodia and the bombing of Hanoi in December 1972 ordered by Presidential authority alone, Congress passed a War Powers Act. This forbade the President unilaterally to carry out acts of war 'in, over, or from the waters of Indochina'. In effect, Congress belatedly obliged the President to accept the logic enunciated by Senator J. William Fulbright in *The Arrogance of Power* (1967): 'America is now at that historical point at which a great nation is in danger of losing its perspective on what exactly is within the realm of its power and what is beyond it.'[19] Congress had, of course, also deprived President Nixon and his successor President Ford of being able to take the initiative in Vietnam, and of the possibility of their threatening the North with renewed U.S. bombing.

In January 1975, the N.V.A. attacked Phuoc Binh, 75 miles north-west of Saigon: there was no U.S. reaction. In March, the N.V.A. began to cut strategic roads in the Central Highlands. A feint attack on Pleiku drew part of the A.R.V.N. 23rd Division to reinforce it, and the town they left, Ban Me Thuot, took the real attack, falling on 10 March after three days. The 23rd Division – ordered back to Ban Me Thuot on the 7th – was routed. On 15 March, Thieu with no reserves left decided without consulting the U.S. that he could not hold the Central Highlands and would pull back his defence lines to the coast, the Delta and Saigon, rather than face situations in Kontum and Pleiku reminiscent of Dien Bien Phu. Only five operational C.130 transport planes then remained of the huge U.S. transport wing of the late 1960s. Moreover, the A.R.V.N. had little helicopter gunship support and had not secured the roads out of the Central Highlands on which they and a confused mass of civilians intended to rely in order to reach the coast. With the Highlands gone, it soon became apparent that coastal enclaves like Qui Nhon were indefensible, and the four A.R.V.N. divisions in the Hué–Danang area found themselves surrounded by five N.V.A. divisions. Thieu wavered, withdrew the airborne division to Saigon and then decided to hold. The Hué–Danang road was cut and Hué had to be abandoned by sea, amidst a chaos of disarray and indiscipline on 26 March. A chain of 'withdrawal-panic', command paralysis and officer desertion followed. By the beginning of April, the surprised General Giap and General Hoang Van Thai decided to 'go for broke' and ordered their regiments southwards. On 9 April, the awaited N.V.A. attack came – not from north-east of Saigon but around Xuan Loc. Thieu decided to attempt a 'defensive' victory

THE END OF AMERICA'S WAR IN INDO-CHINA

there, but the A.R.V.N. could not hold the road from Xuan Hoc to Bien Hoa air base, and by 18 April the end was obvious. On 21 April the defeated 18th A.R.V.N. Division fought its way out of Xuan Loc and President Thieu resigned. There was no speedy re-alignment of Saigon defences, and the N.V.A. moved in on Bien Hoa, Route 4 in the Delta, and the road between Saigon and Vung Tau. By 27 April, after eight weeks of fighting, the N.V.A. were firing on Tan Son Nhut airport just to the north of Saigon.

On 1 April there were still about 6,000 Americans left in South Vietnam and perhaps 16,000 G.I./South Vietnamese children. By mid-April, an 'orphan airlift' to America began, but by 27 April it was obvious that America could not remove all the round-eyed children or half a million Vietnamese in danger of being caught in a 'Communist bloodbath' that, in fact, never materialized. At 10.51 p.m. on 28 April, President Ford ordered Operation 'Frequent Wind', by which U.S. helicopters lifted off 1,373 American and 5,595 Vietnamese from the rooftops of Saigon in eighteen hours. Four of the Marines sent in to protect the last evacuees died. Of the $2\frac{1}{2}$ million Americans who had served in America's fourteen-year Vietnam War, 56,559 had died. Up to 127,000 Vietnamese fled to Thailand by air, or by sea to the forty ships of the U.S. Seventh Fleet off the Vietnamese coast, and the last of the U.S. Marines left the U.S. Embassy on a U.S. CH-46 Sea Knight 'chopper'. At 11.05 a.m. on 30 April, the N.V.A. tank number 879 smashed through the gates of the Presidential Palace in Saigon, and its last incumbent, General Duong Van Minh, surrendered South Vietnam. A Viet Cong News Agency dispatch declared: 'the moment marked the end of the U.S. puppet regimes in South Vietnam and also of the U.S. policy of aggression in Vietnam.'[20]

At a Press Conference on 5 May 1975, Kissinger concluded: 'We did not foresee that Watergate would sap the executive authority of the United States to such a degree that flexibility of executive action would be circumscribed. We did not foresee that Congress would pass a law which prohibited us from enforcing the Paris Agreement. I do not believe that Hanoi would have sent 19 of its 20 divisions south [against 13 A.R.V.N. divisions] if these two things had not happened.'[21]

In fact by May 1975 it was not only South Vietnam, but also Cambodia and Laos which had 'fallen' to communism. U.S. advisers had been involved in Laos since 1962 in the war between royalist forces and the Pathet Lao supported by North Vietnam. A ceasefire was signed in February 1973 and theoretically all foreign troops were to withdraw, but 50,000 N.V.A. remained to protect the Plain of Jars in the north, and the start of the Ho Chi Minh trail in southern Laos. During 1974, a royalist–communist coalition government was formed, but the royalist forces' control of strategic areas and roads such as that linking Vientiane to Luang Prabang became increasingly tenuous. The communist successes in the rest of Indo-China led to student and officer-cadet riots in May 1975, which preceded the resignation of key nationalist ministers like Defence Minister Sisouk Na Champassak. He was accused on 4 May of preparing for a *coup* against the coalition government; soon the Pathet Lao had control of all key ministries in what was effectively a communist government.

In neighbouring Cambodia, the Lon Nol regime, which had come into being when the neutralist Sihanouk was ousted by a *coup* in March 1970, fell two weeks prior to the collapse of Saigon. By January 1974 the communist Khmer Rouge and their North Vietnamese allies, no longer impeded by U.S. bombing which Congress had ended in August 1973, controlled 70 per cent of the land and 50 per cent of the population. The noose tightened on Phnom Penh which, deprived by Congress of extra funds in the spring of 1975, was finally 'liberated' on 17 April.

In a television broadcast to the American people on 27 January 1973, President Nixon had stated: 'Let us be proud that America did not settle for a peace that would have betrayed our allies . . . that would have ended the war for us but would have continued it for the 50 million people of Indochina.' Yet, of all the clauses in an Agreement that some American commentators described as a negotiated 'Dunkirk', only the section on P.O.W.s was carried out. The Americans got their 1,200 P.O.W.s back, although it took Nixon and Kissinger four years and two months to arrange the American exit from Vietnam. In the week after the Paris signing, Thieu declared on television that he had been promised that the 'U.S. would react vigorously' to any major N.V.A. action. In April 1975, the South Vietnamese government released two letters of November 1972 and November 1973, in which Nixon had promised that the U.S. would 'take swift and severe retaliatory action' if Hanoi violated the Paris Agreements. But President Ford could not act: 'I'm frustrated by the actions of Congress [and] by the limitations placed on the executive over the last two years.'[22] At Paris, Kissinger talked of a 'decent interval' for the Thieu regime. Congress decided that two years was enough, and that U.S. honour was no longer involved. The *New York Times* of 7 April declared: 'If challenged, a nation's sense of honor can never exceed its perception of its own vital interests. South-East Asia has never been an area of vital American interest. Only the gratuitous American intervention made it appear to be such an area.'

It is difficult to gauge the 'results' of Vietnam. The U.S. lost its image of military invincibility and the 'People's War of Mao' performed impressively against U.S. capital and technology (although of course the Americans did not use their nuclear, biological and chemical strategic arsenal). The money spent in Vietnam reduced that available for Johnson's Great Society reforms in health, education, civil rights and the inner cities, and the army returned from Vietnam with a drugs and race problem. Careful people worried about electronic warfare and eco-war, while Congress reacted against the build-up since 1940 of Presidential power in foreign policy. With government statements at variance with government actions, America developed its 'credibility gap' under Johnson; Watergate extended it under Nixon. Pinkville and napalm on television screens worried middle America, as did American casualty lists, while students revolted, burnt draft cards or even fled into exile. These effects will doubtless condition how a president will react to 'drawing a line of containment' in the future. Some Americans doubted whether America should ever have been *in* Vietnam: by the end, most doubted the methodology of fighting the war.

Certainly, the collapse of South Vietnam occasioned considerable reappraisal of U.S. foreign policy in the spring of 1975. Defense Secretary James Schlesinger rightly remarked: 'A consequence of the events in South-East Asia has been to shake the confidence of many countries in American power, and particularly in American steadfastness.'[23]

The South Vietnamese Ambassador to the U.S. argued that there was 'only one possible conclusion' to be drawn from events in Indo-China: 'that is, it is safer to be an ally of the Communists and it looks like it is fatal to be an ally of the United States.'[24] But, of course, Phnom Penh is not Berlin nor is Saigon Tokyo, although Taipei and Seoul needed some reassuring in April 1975 and Bangkok obliged the U.S. to remove the last of the B-52s from Utapao air base in early June.

President Ford, naturally, argued: 'We are saddened indeed by the events in Indochina. But these events, tragic as they are, portend neither the end of the world, nor of America's leadership in the world. Some seem to feel that if we do not succeed in everything, everywhere, then we have succeeded in nothing, anywhere. I reject such polarised thinking.'[25] Nevertheless, Asian leaders like Lee Kuan Yew of Singapore did regard the fall of Indo-China as an 'unmitigated disaster' and told Ford: 'If the President and Congress can speak in one voice on basic issues of foreign policy, and in clear and unmistakable terms, then friends and allies will know where they stand and others will not be able to misunderstand.'[26]

Yet some world leaders felt that the end of the Indo-China 'digression' would allow the U.S. to return with more vigour to her more real and more defensible interests, while even the twenty-year 'stalling' operation against communism in Indo-China had served to allow potential 'dominoes' of the mid-1950s – like Malaya and the Philippines – to increase their strength. Ford hoped that 'America [could] regain the sense of pride that existed before Vietnam'.[27] Brezhnev, speaking in Moscow on 8 May, remarked that 'The elimination of the hotbeds of war in Indochina creates the conditions for a further improvement of the international atmosphere.'[28] The 'limited war' in Vietnam – in which neither Soviet nor Chinese 'volunteers' fought, in which Soviet ships in Haiphong were not bombed,[29] and in which a Soviet ally was not subjected to total bombing – had ended. Of course, Kissinger had remarked: 'We shall not forget who supplied the arms which North Vietnam used to make a mockery of its signature on the Paris accords.'[30] But *détente* was to continue, for as President Ford declared: 'We must outgrow the notion that every setback is a Soviet gain or every problem is caused by Soviet action . . . In Portugal, the Middle East, even in Indochina, the difficulties resulted from local conditions or inadequate U.S. responses as much as from Soviet intervention.' Nevertheless the American leader reminded the Soviet Union that it should not try to exploit 'the weaknesses around the world'.[31]

# Thirteen

# SINO–AMERICAN RELATIONS AND THE SINO–AMERICAN *DÉTENTE*

Shortly before the establishment of the People's Republic of China, the American Secretary of State, Dean Acheson, set up a committee to assess U.S. foreign policy in Asia. The committee decided that it was a fundamental principle of U.S. policy that America should not permit further extension of communist domination in Asia or in South-East Asia. However, the U.S. did anticipate the 'liberation' or 'conquest' of Taiwan; thus, a State Department Policy Information Paper was issued to help combat the 'mistaken popular conception of . . . [Taiwan's] strategic importance to the U.S. in the Pacific'.[1] On 5 January 1950 President Truman reaffirmed the Cairo and Potsdam Declarations which cited the island as Chinese territory: 'The United States has no desire to obtain special privilege or to establish military bases on Formosa at this time. Nor does it have any intention of utilizing its armed forces to interfere in the present situation . . . The United States will not provide military aid or advice to the Chinese forces on Formosa.'[2] Although the U.S. (unlike Britain) was not as yet prepared to recognize the new Chinese regime, according to the *New York Times* of 31 May 1950 Acheson had assured the U.N. Secretary-General that the U.S. would not use its veto to help keep out China, but was prepared to abide by the majority decision of the Security Council on that issue.

The outbreak of the Korean War on 25 June 1950 and the inability of the U.S. to achieve a quick victory, however, brought about a change in U.S. foreign policy. In July 1950 the U.S. Seventh Fleet moved into the Taiwan Straits and effectively blocked any communist invasion of Taiwan: 'The mission of the

Seventh Fleet is to keep Formosa out of the conflict. Our purpose is peace, not conquest.'[3] Mao, not surprisingly, regarded this move as 'interference by the U.S. in the internal affairs of China' and Sino–American relations deteriorated. They inevitably hit rock bottom with China's entry into the Korean War and by 18 May 1951, Dean Rusk, Secretary of State for Far Eastern Affairs, was prepared to see China as simply a Soviet puppet in the Cold War: 'We do not recognise the authorities in Peiping for what they pretend to be. Peiping may be a colonial Russian government – a slavic Manchukuo on a large scale. It is not the government of China. It does not pass the first test. It is not Chinese.'[4]

By the time Korea was at peace in 1953, the United States was concerned about the war in French Indo-China (1945–54), in which again there was Chinese involvement. In December 1954 an official U.S.–Taiwanese Defence Treaty was signed and within a few months the Taiwan Straits became a 'hot spot' in the Sino–American theatre of the Cold War. By 1955, Chiang's island fortress and its 600,000-strong armed forces had become, according to President Eisenhower, essential to the U.S. strategic position in the western Pacific. When Mao ordered the shelling of the Nationalist islands of Quemoy and Matsu, Eisenhower was determined to protect those outposts of his island chain 'containing' China, especially since only in 1954 had the U.S. 'lost' the French army from Indo-China. Eisenhower thought retreat would lower the morale of the Taiwanese and affect U.S. prestige *vis-à-vis* such countries as Japan and the Philippines, but was inclined to believe that the attack on the islands might precede action against Taiwan itself. Of course, any U.S. action might provoke retaliation from China and the Soviet Union, but Eisenhower doubted this. In a letter to Churchill in February 1955 he declared: 'I do not believe that even if we became engaged in a serious fight along the coast of China, Russia would intervene with her own forces. She would, of course, pour supplies into China in an effort to exhaust us . . . But I am convinced that Russia does not want, at this moment, to experiment with means of defense against the bombing that we could conduct against her mainland.'[5] In fact, to defend Quemoy and Matsu it would have been necessary to use atomic weapons against the Chinese airfields on the mainland.[6] Eisenhower talked to the U.S. press on this subject. '"Would the United States," a reporter asked me in March in 1955, "use tactical atomic weapons in a general

war in Asia?" "Against a strictly military target," I replied, "the
answer would be 'yes'." I hoped this answer would have some effect
in persuading the Chinese Communists of the strength of our determination.'[7] At the Bandung Conference in April 1955, Premier
Chou En-lai stated, 'The Chinese people are willing to strive for
the liberation of Formosa by peaceful means, as far as this is possible.'[8]
The crisis had cooled, but was only to flare up again in 1958 when,
once more, the Chinese were threatened with the possible use of
nuclear weapons against the mainland (see Chapter 14).

Sino–American relations did not improve as the Cold War
entered the 1960s: America was continuing the trade embargo
imposed against China during the Korean War; she continued to
use her influence in the U.N. to prevent Communist China's
entrance, and she provided Taiwan with heavy economic and
military aid. Indeed, the *Peking Review* of 2 July 1965 stated that
U.S. naval and air bases on Taiwan, as well as U.S. aid to Chiang's
secret agents who infiltrated the mainland (not to mention the
U.S. 'overflights' by U-2s across China), were simply part of a
process by which 'the United States has made Taiwan a colony, and
a military base from which the Chinese mainland is threatened'.
According to China, Kennedy – who took over the Presidency in
1961 – was worse than Eisenhower, since the C.I.A. were involved
in Laos, the 'U.N. Force in the Congo was just a tool of U.S. neo-
colonialism', and the U.S. provided France during her Algerian
War with 'huge quantitites of military equipment for slaughtering
thousands upon thousands of Algerian people'.[9] The Chinese were
not inclined to accept Khrushchev's theories on coexistence with
America (see Chapter 14) but continued to hope that the American
people would overthrow their militaristic and imperialist leaders,
thereby proving that the apparently strong U.S. regime was no
more than a 'paper tiger'. Until then, it was essential to aid revolutions around the world, and to keep the U.S. off balance. America
was inclined in the mid-1960s, as in the mid-1950s, to regard
China as 'the yellow peril', initiator of all major unpleasant changes
in the *status quo*. President Kennedy in a news conference on 1 August 1963 outlined this fear: 'We find a great powerful force in China
organized and directed by the Government along Stalinist lines . . .
[she] has also called for . . . international war, in order to advance
the final success of the Communist cause . . . I would regard that
combination, if it is still in existence in the 1970s . . . potentially a

more dangerous situation than we've faced since the end of the Second World War.'[10]

Both America and China spent most of the 1960s viewing each other as abstractions: the Americans were militaristic capitalists with bases all around China and the Chinese were aggressive atheistic communists ready to export revolution around the world. America's fears were enhanced by the upsurge in the Vietnam conflict in 1964. Dean Rusk stated in Congress in April 1966:

> We do not seek the overthrow by force of the Peking regime, we do object to its attempt to overthrow other regimes by force. . . . Last fall, Lin Piao, the Chinese Communist Minister of Defence [explained] Peking's strategy of violence for achieving Communist domination of the world . . . It is true that this doctrine calls for revolution by the 'natives' of each country. In that sense it may be called a 'do-it-yourself kit'. But Peking is prepared to train and indoctrinate the leaders of these revolutions and to support them with funds, arms and propaganda as well as politically. It is even prepared to manufacture these revolutionary movements . . . Some say we should ignore what the Chinese Communist leaders say and judge them by what they do. It is true that they are more cautious in actions than in words . . . But it does not follow that we should disregard their plans for the future. To do so would be to repeat the catastrophic miscalculation that so many people made about the ambitions of Hitler.[11]

Washington anticipated the spread of Chinese communist influence, moved to contain it and thereby provoked a fear in China of attack, that led her to involve herself in the revolutions of the area, thus confirming the original American anticipation. Of course, America saw it differently. According to the U.S., the Chinese ultimately intended to lead the world's revolutionaries. Because of their fanatical communism, which is inherently aggressive, the Chinese were bound to be antagonistic to America, irrespective of any actions the U.S. might have taken. Thus, containment of China was justified because it prevented China from committing the aggression she would otherwise commit: in other words, the U.S. hostility was portrayed as reactive. China, on the other hand, argued that her military forces were trained, equipped and organized to fight a defensive war inside China; that she has offered to have negotiations with America; that Tibet was and is rightfully China's territory; that India was responsible for the border war in 1962; that it was unjustifiable for America to prevent the unification of China and Taiwan; and that 'China had no troops outside her own frontiers'. Indeed, Mao Tse-tung confirmed to Edgar Snow in 1971: 'China's armies would not go beyond her borders to fight. That was clear

enough. Only if the U.S. attacked China would the Chinese fight . . .
China was very busy with its internal affairs. Fighting beyond one's
own borders was criminal.'[12] Of course, it was argued that one should
not listen to the promises of Chinese communists, for even if it seemed
unlikely that China would invade her neighbours, perhaps she
intended to subvert them by aiding or establishing indigenous communist revolutionary movements. This theory presented the West
with difficulties, for it often happened that anti-Chinese regimes in
Asia were also corrupt, incompetent and overly dependent on Western backing.

Intervention such as in Vietnam therefore had to be on the scale
that it was bound to be opposed by the Chinese, if only because it
involved large numbers of foreign troops too close to their borders.
From the opposite angle, Prime Minister Menzies of Australia, who
sent troops to aid the U.S. in Vietnam, stated in April 1965; 'The
takeover of South Vietnam would be a direct military threat to
Australia . . . It must be seen as part of a thrust by Communist China
between the Indian and Pacific Oceans.'[13] China did, indeed, provide
weapons (though not troops) for use in Vietnam, it provided a sanctuary for Thai rebels and did have some contact with the guerrillas in
Malaya and Sarawak; however, it did not attempt to aid the Huks in
the Philippines or the Burmese rebels. The West, of course, saw any
Chinese involvement in Asian affairs as dangerous subversion and
provided support to endangered 'legitimate' regimes, the 'legitimacy'
of those regimes usually being measured solely by their existence, not
necessarily their democratic nature or even their control over most of
their territory. The Chinese, of course, argued that they did not
attempt to 'export revolution'. Vice-Premier Chen Yi said in September 1963,[14] 'The question of world revolution is one thing for the
countries concerned. If countries are not ripe for revolution, then
China can't do anything about it . . . China cannot pour revolutions
on or off when she wants to.'

Yet in February 1972, President Nixon visited Peking and in
his Report to Congress a year later he stated: 'The United States
and China seem to have no fundamental interests that need collide
in the wider sweep of history.'[15] The build-up to 1972, when in
Nixon's words, 'The leader of the most powerful nation' met 'the
leader of the most populous nation', started in 1969. During 1969
and 1970, the President gradually relaxed trade and passport
restrictions in regard to China; in April 1971 a U.S. table-tennis

team was invited to China; in June 1971 the twenty-one-year trade embargo on China was ended, and in July 1971 the U.S. Secretary of State, Dr. Kissinger, visited Peking. There are various explanations for America's change of policy towards 'Red China'. It might be argued that the U.S. recognized the ineffectiveness of its attempted 'containment' of China; or that Nixon was attempting to 'do a deal' on Vietnam. Perhaps the President wished to gain electoral popularity in America by defusing a potentially dangerous relationship. Possibly Nixon's actions were designed to worry Moscow into increasing the speed and extent of its *détente* with the U.S. Nixon himself suggested 'China, outside the world community, completely isolated, with its leaders not in communication with world leaders, would be a danger to the whole world that would be unacceptable to us and unacceptable to others.'[16] There does in fact seem little doubt that America could ill afford not to have some greater understanding of, and a 'hot line' contact to, a nuclear China with I.C.B.M. potential. Moreover, after the 1969 Guam doctrine of Vietnamization, the Americans were involved in a disengagement from the Asian mainland. In the last analysis, America (unlike the U.S.S.R., which is an Asian land power) could reduce its role on the Asian mainland, if not in Pacific Oceania. Given the American understanding of their relatively decreased power in the world (see Chapter 19), it was perhaps easier to sign the Shanghai Communiqué of 28 February 1972 which included clauses such as: 'neither [America nor China] should seek hegemony in the Asia–Pacific region and each is opposed to efforts by any other country or group of countries to establish such hegemony.'[17]

According to Nixon:

> China exemplified the great changes that had occurred in the Communist world. In the 1960s the forces of nationalism dissolved Communist unity into divergent centers of power and doctrine, and our foreign policy began to differentiate among the Communist capitals. But this process would not be truly effective as long as we were cut off from one-quarter of the globe's people. We could not effectively reduce tensions in Asia without talking to Peking . . . Furthermore, the time was past when one nation could claim to speak for a bloc of states; we would deal with countries on the basis of their actions, not abstract ideological formulas.[18]

In spite of Nixon's subsequent visit to Moscow, *Pravda* of 28 March 1972 emitted worried noises. The East Berlin newspaper *Neues Deutschland* suggested on 3 March 1972: 'The understanding between the Mao group and the American Government is

essentially directed against the Soviet Union.' But perhaps Russia took
solace from the obvious Sino–American thorn of Taiwan. At
Shanghai, the Chinese reaffirmed their position that Taiwan was a
crucial problem obstructing the normalization of Sino–American
relations, while Nixon in his 1972 Report to Congress, took up an
interesting position: 'With the Republic of China, we shall maintain
our friendship, our diplomatic ties and our defense commitments.
The ultimate relationship between Taiwan and the Mainland is
not a matter for the United States to decide.'[19] Moreover, although
Sino–American trade expanded – from $5 million in 1971 to $500
million in 1973 – the *Peking Review* and other Chinese media continued to attack U.S. policy on, for example, 'tied' aid, on U.S.
pressure to keep underdeveloped countries' raw materials prices
low, and on the U.S. 'export' of inflation.[20]

The *détente* had some interesting repercussions. Mrs. Gandhi,
the Indian Prime Minister, at a press conference on 27 October
1974, protested: 'First they [the Americans] said they were going
to save us from communism and save us from China, and then they
were the ones who became completely pro-Chinese. In the Bangla-
desh crisis [1971] we were told they did not want to spoil their
*détente* with China' (by supplying India with arms to use against
China's friend, Pakistan).[21] In July 1971 Mao graciously acceded to
Washington's request for a presidential visit to Peking. According
to Mao (in a conversation with Edgar Snow in 1970), China's
problems with America 'at present' had to be dealt with in negotiations with 'monopoly-capitalists' like Nixon. Chou En-lai, at a
banquet for Nixon in Peking, suggested that the 'Chinese and
American peoples' had demanded better relations and, of course,
the leaders had to follow the people who 'are the motive force in the
making of world history'.[22] In a speech to a Party Congress in Peking
in September 1973, Chou suggested that negotiations with America
were possible because of the decreased threat it represented to
China and the world people. The Premier stated that the U.S.
had started to go downhill after its 'defeat' in the Korean War and
'it has openly admitted that it is on the decline'.[23]

The fact that the 'leader of the capitalist world' had visited
Peking enhanced Chinese prestige. Moreover, the very announcement of the visit ensured China's entry into the U.N. The vote on
this issue on 25 October 1971 was 76 in favour, 37 against and 27
abstentions. Taiwan was expelled in spite of America's efforts to

keep her in the General Assembly, and China was allowed to take her seat on the Security Council and her place in the General Assembly. For China, these were prizes worth having, not only for the opportunity to block Soviet action through vetoes in the Security Council, but also for the new manoeuvring position *vis-à-vis* the Third World. Of course, very high among the reasons for the Sino–American *rapprochement* was China's assessment that the threat from the Soviet Union was greater than that from America. *Détente* might increase the speed of U.S. military disengagement from Asia, lessen the risk of a Soviet–American 'gang up' in the Far East, and leave the Chinese free to watch Russia in the north.

At the very least, with China presenting a new, more friendly face to the Western world, there would be more likelihood that she would be seen as a 'victim' in any future Sino–Soviet clash. It was even possible that *détente* with America might increase American unease over such a possible clash. Perhaps equally important was the possibility that *détente* could lead eventually to the peaceful liberation of Taiwan. Yet, despite numerous visits by Kissinger and the visit by President Ford in 1975, Washington appeared to be in no hurry to accord China full diplomatic recognition, nor to find a compromise over Taiwan. China was also being cautious, as her Deputy Foreign Minister, Chiao Kuan-hua, stated in the U.N. General Assembly on 3 October 1972:

> People of all countries must not be deluded by certain temporary and superficial phenomena of *détente* at the present time and develop a false sense of security. While striving for world peace and the progress of mankind, we must maintain sufficient vigilance and make necessary preparations against the danger of new wars of aggression any imperialism may launch.

In attempting to understand Maoist philosophy, it is useful to re-read Maoist tracts of the 1930s and 1940s. In *On Policy* of 1940, Mao wrote that the objective of a 'United Front' (of all anti-Japanese forces) was 'to make use of contradictions, win over the many, oppose the few and crush our enemies one by one'. This logic implies making distinctions between adversaries, determining which at a given moment is primary, or which enemy can be used against the other. It also implies making use of any shift in an enemy's policies (resulting from internal contradictions) to enhance the advantage of the revolutionary forces. Sino–American *détente*, therefore, may have uses, but not as 'collusion' or as the 'general line' of a foreign policy. The 'general line' of Chinese foreign policy remained that of rallying as much of the world as possible against imperialism and social imperialism, for if unmolested, those forces would collude to maintain the international *status quo* and prevent changes in the balance of world power that might upset one 'ally' sufficiently to threaten hostilities between them. The Chinese 'line' then remained: in the future, world revolution leading to socialism, and at present: 'We are opposed to the power policies and hegemony of big nations bullying small ones ... at no time ... will China be a super-power subjecting others to its aggression, subversion, control, interference or bullying.'[24]

# Fourteen

# SINO–SOVIET RELATIONS AND THE SINO–SOVIET SPLIT

In 1946 Liu Shao-chi (later to be President of China) told American journalist Anna Louise Strong: 'Mao has not only applied Marxism to new conditions but has given it a new development. He has created a Chinese or an Asian form of Marxism.'[1] Many historians argue that Liu's assertion and others like it between 1946 and 1950 constituted a bid for Chinese leadership of Asian communism. This assertion was apparently dismissed in the Soviet Union, where Strong's book was banned. On 1 October 1965, *Pravda* stated: 'The revolutionary movement in China . . . arose under the direct influence of the October Revolution in Russia.' The *Peking Review* of 5 November 1965 disagreed: 'The Russian October Socialist Revolution served as an example for revolution in the aggressor nations, that is, for revolution in the imperialist countries; while the Chinese Revolution set an example for revolution in the oppressed nations, that is, the colonial and semi-colonial countries.' Mao would certainly have disputed Stalin's contribution to the Chinese Revolution for Stalin had advocated a united front with Chiang Kai-shek's Kuomintang Nationalist Party in the 1920s, but Chiang turned on the unprepared communists and massacred large numbers in 1927. Stalin had also advised the Chinese Communist Party to rely on the urban proletariat to lead the revolution – an attempted urban rising in China's big southern cities like Canton in 1927, led by 'Muscovite' communists, was very efficiently crushed by Chiang's police and military.

In early 1927 Mao had visited Hunan Province to study the Peasant Associations there; he decided that the Chinese Revolution could not depend solely upon the proletariat – only 2 million – and stated: 'Without the poor peasants there would be no revolution. To deny their role is to deny the revolution.' Henceforth, according to Stalin and Stalin's understanding of Leninism, Mao was guilty of the 'peasant' heresy. Following Mao's takeover of power in 1935 from the 'Muscovite' faction, the Soviets appear to have ignored the Chinese Civil War. In May 1943 Mao stated that since 1935 the Comintern had not 'meddled in the internal affairs of the C.C.P.'.[2] Throughout the 1930s Stalin – afraid of Imperial Japan – maintained cordial relations with Chiang Kai-shek and even in 1945 signed a treaty concerning Soviet trading concessions in Manchuria which accepted Chiang as undisputed leader of China. Indeed in 1945 Stalin told the C.C.P. bluntly that 'we considered the development of the uprising in China had no prospects, that the Chinese comrades should seek a *modus vivendi* with Chiang Kai-shek, and that they should join the Chiang Kai-shek government and dissolve their army.'[3] Mao ignored this advice and also Stalin's suggestion that in 1948 the C.C.P. should stop their conquests at the Yangtse River – thus allowing the existence of a non-communist Southern China – in order not to provoke American intervention. Furthermore, Stalin's ambassador to Chiang's China remained with the Nationalists until 1949. Perhaps Stalin was uneasy about the development of a united and Titoist-like China, a communist state of huge proportions that the Red Army had not helped to emerge and therefore was in no position to control. Mao too must have been uneasy in October 1949: if he accepted political and military dependence on the Soviet Union, he would have to follow Soviet foreign policy lines, and the alternative of seeking great-power status might widen the political gap between China and the Soviet Union, though it would frighten the U.S. even more.

But China needed economic aid after a civil war that had lasted intermittently since 1927, and a Japanese War that had lasted from Manchuria in 1931 to 1945; she could hardly expect aid from the West and was, in any event, ideologically committed to the struggle against the 'haves' of the world. Mao decided to ally with the Soviet Union, for 'Internationally we belong to the anti-imperialist front headed by the Soviet Union'.[4] In 1950, for the first time, Mao left China – for Moscow – and in February signed a treaty of 'immutable, unshakeable friendship'. From the Soviet point of view, Stalin secured Russia's eastern flank by gaining China's military alliance; persuaded Mao to accept the independence of

Mongolia, once part of China, but from 1921 onwards increasingly 'independent' under Soviet tutelage; confirmed that Dairen and Port Arthur would remain Soviet bases, as they had done under Chiang, at least until 1952; and organized the foundation of joint-stock companies to exploit Chinese mineral resources. China, in return and after two months of negotiations, was to receive the equivalent of $300 million in long-term credits – far less per head of population than, for example, Stalin gave Poland in 1948. This was not an altogether auspicious new start to Sino–Soviet co-operation and understanding.

However, it would be wrong to underplay Soviet aid to China in the 1950s. The Chinese admit that by the end of 1957 the Soviets were helping in the construction of 211 major industrial enterprises, providing the industrial and technical blueprints for Chinese use; supplying between 7,000 and 10,000 experts to China; training an estimated 10,000 Chinese in the Soviet Union; and taking about 50 per cent of China's foreign trade. It is nevertheless true that China did not receive large aid grants, partly because the Russians expected China to follow an austerity programme and partly because Khrushchev increased his aid to Third World countries like India, Egypt and Iraq, particularly after the Bandung Conference of 1955. Khrushchev visited China in October 1954, and discussed new industrial credits as well as the return of Port Arthur. But tensions existed in Sino–Soviet relations even by 1954. When, according to the Communists, South Korea attacked the North, China intervened. In the 1960s the C.C.P. stated: '[We are] firmly opposed to a "head-on clash" between the Soviet Union and the United States and not in words only ... [but in] the Korean War ... and our struggle against the U.S. in the Taiwan Straits, we ourselves preferred to shoulder the heavy sacrifices necessary and stood in the first line of defence of the socialist camp so that the Soviet Union might stay in the second line.'[5] The Chinese paid dearly in Korea and, moreover, had to reimburse the U.S.S.R. for its war aid of $2,000 million.

During the 1954 visit, Mao resurrected the question of Outer Mongolia's independence and the following year China, at the Bandung Conference, greatly increased her prestige with the Third World. Russia, as a white, relatively rich power which had never been subjected to European colonization, was not present at Bandung. Khrushchev had by 1955 decided to compete with America in the neutral world rather than to risk nuclear confrontation in Europe, and it must have been inconvenient to find Moscow's claim to world communist leadership contested by Peking. But according to Chancellor Adenauer, who met Khrushchev in Moscow in September 1955, the Soviet leader was concerned about more than just competition in the Third World: '"China already has 600 million inhabitants who live on a handful of rice. Each year there are 12 million more. How is it going to end?" he added, folding his hands together . . . I beg you to help us to resolve our difficulties with China.'[6]

Those difficulties vastly increased after the Twentieth Congress of the Soviet Communist Party in February 1956. At the conference, Khrushchev advocated peaceful coexistence with the West, the achievement of socialism by relying on communist successes at the ballot box in Europe if not elsewhere, and summed up by denouncing his predecessor Stalin. The Chinese were horrified: as their later statements clarify, they disagreed with all three of Khrushchev's pronouncements:

> Khrushchev [said] that the imperialists were beginning to admit that the 'positions-of-strength' policy had failed and that 'symptoms of a certain sobering up are appearing' among them. It was as much as saying that it was possible for the U.S. government not to represent the interests of the U.S. monopoly capitalists and for them to abandon their policies of war and aggression and that they had become forces defending peace.[7]

The Chinese were prepared to accept that Lenin's thesis on the possibilities of peaceful coexistence between countries with different social systems could apply between Russia and India; they doubted that it could apply to the America of Eisenhower and Dulles, and definitely disputed that peaceful coexistence should be the 'general line of the foreign policy of the U.S.S.R.'. The Chinese also disagreed that it was possible to achieve socialism 'through the parliamentary road' and suspected that such logic was dictated by Khrushchev's desire to avoid violent conflagrations around the world which might upset an embryonic Soviet–American *détente*: 'Violent revolution is the universal principle of proletarian revolution . . . Historical experience shows that the seizure of political power by the proletariat . . . is accomplished invariably by the power of the gun.'[8]

Finally, though the Chinese agreed that 'It was necessary to criticize Stalin's mistakes', they felt Khrushchev had 'completely negated Stalin, and in doing so defamed the dictatorship of the proletariat, defamed the socialistic system, the great Communist Party of the Soviet Union, the great Soviet Union and the International Communist Movement'.[9] In short, Mao – the 'old man' of communism after Stalin's death – was angry at his 'junior's' unilateral action, felt that the cult criticism was implicit criticism of his position in China as well as of Stalin's old position in Russia, suspected that such outright condemnation of Stalin would weaken communist prestige and have unacceptable repercussions on the discipline of the communist world, and simply did not believe that 'peaceful' imperialism or 'parliamentary' communism were legitimate Marxist–Leninism. Though the Western world was not to appreciate the extent of the ideological split for four years or so, what was happening was that the communist monolith was dividing into 'revisionists' (those who revise or change Marxist–Leninism) and 'dogmatists' (a Soviet term meaning those who dogmatically adhere to communist doctrine, when circumstances warrant or demand the adaptation or revision of that doctrine).

But China waited for Soviet actions to prove or dispel its doubts on Khrushchev's new policies before embarking upon independence from Moscow. The repercussions of Stalin's denunciation in Eastern Europe were soon made obvious (see Chapter 8). Mao disapproved of the projected Soviet military intervention in Poland, but was obliged to back Khrushchev against a Hungary that threatened the stability of the Warsaw Pact. In January 1957 the Chinese Prime Minister, Chou En-lai, flew to Moscow, Prague, Budapest and Warsaw, to reinforce Khrushchev's position, but one suspects that Khrushchev's gratitude was tempered by a profound dislike of having to use Chinese aid to bolster Soviet policies in Eastern Europe, previously a Soviet preserve. However, by the autumn of 1957, with Sputnik 1 launched and Soviet leadership in rocket technology obvious, Soviet prestige needed no Chinese support.

Mao thought the time was ripe to play brinkmanship with the West and by threat of war force the U.S. to give ground in Germany, Indo-China, Taiwan and around the world. Khrushchev, who did not think the Americans were 'paper tigers', was hoping to use his temporary military advantage to persuade the Americans to grant greater respect to the Soviet Union and its position and interests in the world. Moreover, Khrushchev had a better understanding than Mao of the world-wide balance of terror, of America's huge

intercontinental bomber force, her forward tactical missiles in
Europe and her bombers on aircraft carriers in the Mediterranean
and the Far East. Besides, building a rocket capable of hitting
America from Siberia is not the same as having large numbers of
them deployed ready for use; furthermore, an American I.C.B.M.
was tested in December and anyway, in a world war in 1957–8
it was Eastern Europe and Western Russia, rather than China, that
risked being turned into uranium graveyards.

To some extent, Mao's revolutionary unease at the 'slowly,
slowly' tactics of Khrushchev was offset by the promise of Soviet
nuclear aid, which was made in December 1957. But the Soviets
had a price for providing China with a sample atomic bomb. The
*People's Daily* of 6 September 1963 recalled the negotiations thus:
'In 1958 the leadership of the C.P.S.U. put forward unreasonable
demands designed to bring China under Soviet military control.'
The Chinese rejected Soviet demands on joint control of foreign
policy and Soviet retention of control over nuclear warheads. The
Soviets responded in June 1959 by 'tearing up' the October 1957
agreements and refused to supply China with an A-bomb. It would
appear that Khrushchev did not want to trust Mao with an atomic
device. Moreover, such nuclear aid might have upset the U.S.,
who might even have granted nuclear aid to West Germany!

In July 1958, a revolution in Iraq caused a Middle East crisis.
The British and Americans were invited into Jordan and the
Lebanon to prevent the spread of revolution and the communist
world objected. The *People's Daily* of 19 July concluded that unless
'the U.S.–British aggressors withdraw from Lebanon and Jordan
. . . then the only course left to the people of the world is to hit
the aggressors on the head', but on the previous day Khrushchev
had written to Eisenhower stressing that 'We address you not from
a position of intimidation but from a position of reason'.[12] Before
the Chinese could digest this disunity on the question of force in the
Middle East, a crisis blew up in the Taiwan Straits. In August, the
Chinese began an artillery bombardment of the small Nationalist
island of Quemoy, five miles off the mainland. The U.S. Seventh
Fleet escorted the Nationalist ships to the beleaguered island, and
when China threatened to extend her territorial waters to twelve
miles, Dulles (on 4 September) not only stated that the U.S. would
ignore such a claim, but also implied that if the island was sufficiently
endangered, then the U.S. would bomb the artillery batteries on

the coast of China. China's Soviet ally was conspicuous by its silence, and on 6 September Chou En-lai proposed ambassadorial talks with America in Warsaw. The crisis having cooled, Khrushchev reminded the U.S. that an 'attack on the People's Republic of China . . . is an attack on the Soviet Union'.

The Chinese, not surprisingly, came to the conclusion that they needed a bomb of their own, since the Soviet nuclear guarantee was a dubious 'insurance'. China also decided to embark on the Great Leap Forward, which would utilize the massive Chinese population to ensure China's economic progress, and her economic self-sufficiency. Khrushchev disapproved; the Chinese were ignoring Soviet advice and if China did succeed in working economic miracles with inspiration and manpower alone, as opposed to careful planning by experts and the use of capital, science and technology, she would be calling in doubt the entire Soviet economic practice, which was at that time the model for the communist world.

On the international front, 1959 – which saw the beginning of the failure of the Great Leap Forward – also saw the Camp David talks between Khrushchev and Eisenhower. The Soviet leader, undoubtedly flattered by American recognition of his position as the spokesman of a super-power, praised Eisenhower as a 'man of peace' and a popular leader in America. Mao, on the other hand, failed to understand how the leader of the imperialists could be peaceful, much less enjoy the support of the American proletariat. The Soviet leader's remarks in America on Russian progress in consumer durables and the prospect of a four-hour working day, was also objectionable to a China suffering from droughts, floods and food rationing. To make matters worse, Khrushchev, returning to Moscow via Peking, lectured Mao and reminded the Chinese leader that 'we must not test by force the stability of the capitalist system'.[13]

In 1960, the Soviet Union began to prepare for the Paris Summit in May, which was not to include China. The shooting down of an American U-2 plane spying on Russia led to the cancellation of the Summit. but at the June Conference of the Rumanian Communist Party in Bucharest Khrushchev declared:

> We do not intend to yield to provocations and to deviate from the general line of our foreign policy . . . This is a policy of coexistence, a policy of consolidating peace, easing international tension and doing away with the cold war . . . Besides, comrades, one cannot mechanically repeat now on this question what

Vladimir Ilyich Lenin said many decades ago on imperialism, and go on asserting that imperialist wars are inevitable until socialism triumphs throughout the world. History will probably witness such a time when capitalism is preserved only in a small number of states, maybe states, for instance, such as a button on a coat. Well? And even in such conditions would one have to look up in a book what Vladimir Ilyich Lenin quite correctly said for his time; would one just have to repeat that wars are inevitable since capitalist countries still exist?[14]

The Chinese delegate P'eng Chen replied the next day stating that the lesson of the U-2 incident was that 'imperialism is, after all, imperialism, and its fine words can never be trusted'. This in turn provoked a tirade from Khrushchev on the final day of the Conference in which he raised such explosive issues as the Great Leap Forward and the Sino–Indian border dispute which had resulted in border clashes in 1959, and on which the Soviets had taken a noticeably neutral stance. Both Russia and China did, however, agree to convene a world Communist Conference in Moscow in November. Yet within a month, Russia withdrew her 1,390 industrial advisers from China; they left, carrying their industrial blueprints, theoretically because they had been subjected to anti-Russian propaganda lectures, but in practice probably because Khrushchev hoped to force the Chinese to appreciate how dependent they were on Soviet economic aid and advice. In fact, Soviet 'blackmail' increased China's drive for independence. She determined to repay the $1,562 million Soviet loans and to reduce her trading with the Soviet bloc, and by 1963 only 30 per cent of Chinese trade went to the communist world, as opposed to 70 per cent in 1955. At the Moscow Conference, some attempt was made to paper over the ideological cracks. The final Conference statement was therefore painfully inconsistent on the 'aggressive' nature of imperialism and the concept of 'peaceful transition' to socialism, but in fact the monolith had broken and the communist world began to choose sides, though the only communist state to choose China at this point was Albania (see Chapter 15).

During 1961 Sino–Soviet relations were calm, but the storm broke with border clashes in Sinkiang in the autumn of 1962 (see page 126), and with the Sino–Indian War and the Cuban missile crisis, both in October. China was furious that the Soviet Union took a pro-Indian stance in a clash almost certainly provoked by India. It was an odd situation when *Pravda*, in December 1962, could state 'there were no reasons for the border conflict between

India and China'[15] while the *Sunday Telegraph* of 21 October 1962 talked of India 'launching her offensive against the Chinese on the Himalayan border'. After the Cuban crisis, the *People's Daily* of 8 March 1963 accused the Russians of an 'adventurist' mistake in supplying rockets to Cuba and of 'capitulation to American imperialism' – by removing them under 'humiliating terms'.

During 1963 the war of words between China and the Soviet Union became unbridled and was fuelled by the U.S.–Soviet Partial Nuclear Test Ban Treaty of July. This treaty, if signed, obliged the signatory to more complex and expensive underground testing. The Chinese claimed to prefer total nuclear disarmament, the ending of all testing and manufacture, and the withdrawal of all overseas bases, for: 'Clearly, this treaty has no restraining effect on the U.S. policies of nuclear war preparation and nuclear black-mail . . . The central purpose of this treaty is . . . to prevent all the threatened peace-loving countries, including China, from increasing their defence capability so that the United States may be more unbridled in threatening and blackmailing these countries.'[16]

The year 1963 saw the beginning of the development of pro-Chinese splinter communist parties in many countries, such as Belgium, Ceylon, Australia, Peru and India, while some major parties, such as the Indonesian C.P., took up the Chinese stance in the developing new Cold War. By 1966 there were pro-Chinese groups and publications in virtually every European country, while in Latin–America pro-Soviet and pro-Chinese groups found competition from pro-Castro groups. By 1967 it seemed a long time since the days when communist orthodoxy could be defined simply by reference to Stalin's interpretation of Marxist–Leninism. By the end of 1963, propaganda normally associated with anti-communist American publications – such as suggesting that Russia was trading with South Africa, or that China was exporting opium via Macao – were being given wide circulation in Chinese and Soviet publications respectively.

During 1963 each side accused the other of various heresies. In the 1920s, traditional Marxist–Leninist doctrine had stated that the advance of communism in the world relied on the efforts of existing communist states, on the efforts of workers in advanced capital-ist countries and on the anti-colonial struggle in the underdevel-oped countries – in that order. But the Chinese came up with the 'intermediate zone' concept: Western countries (such as Japan, Canada and Australia) trying to free themselves from 'U.S. control and bullying'; and the ex-colonial countries of the Third World. The increased importance attached to the underdeveloped world in the advance of the 'Revolution' was, according to Russia, an ideological heresy. Soviet stress on European countries and Chinese stress on Asian countries also tended to foster the ideological clash over 'parliamentary' means to socialism. In France and Italy and perhaps in Portugal, there is at least a possiblity of communism coming to power by peaceful means. In most of the Third World, communists are suppressed and can only expect to come to power by force. However, the bulk of material aid to revolutionary movements still tends to come from the richer Soviet Union. The Chinese argue that the Soviets do not aid revolution (as in Greece in 1948 or Algeria in 1960) when it is against their national interests, or when they fear possible nuclear confrontation. The Sino–Soviet split strays into the realm of war from Mao's stress on force – 'any Communist must learn the truth that "the gun is the source of power"' – and Khrushchev's stress on economic competition, intended to prove the supremacy of communism, thereby attracting all the world's people to that ideology. On this question, Mao's comment to Nehru in 1955 is his most famous and most easily distortable comment: 'Let us imagine, how many people will die if war should break out? Out of the world's population of 1,700 million, one-third – or, more, half – may be lost. It is they and not we who want to fight . . . If the worst came to the worst and half of mankind died, the other half would remain while imperialism would be razed to the ground and the whole world would become social-istic.'[17] Khrushchev in his memoirs stated that 'Mao Tse-tung believes that a world war would weaken the capitalist countries and therefore lead to further gains for the proletariat. That's ridiculous. War would do as much harm to the socialist countries as it would to anyone else.'[18]

The debate continued, with the Chinese claiming the Soviets wanted peace at any price, and the Soviets claiming that the Chinese wanted war at any price, or at least that they would 'manufacture' revolutions in countries where the conditions were not ripe and where the danger of nuclear escalation existed. The U.S. appeared to accept the Soviet analysis; in 1961 Kennedy declared: 'These Chinese are tough – it isn't just what they say about us but what they say about the Russians. They are in the Stalinist phase, believe in class war and the use of force and seem prepared to sacrifice 300 million people, if necessary, to dominate Asia.'[19] Given these beliefs, it is not surprising that America greeted with foreboding the explosion of a Chinese A-bomb in October 1964, though on the following day the Chinese Government declared 'that China will never be the first to use nuclear weapons'.

The change of leadership in the Soviet Union in October 1964 brought a temporary lull in the ideological war, but soon Brezhnev and Kosygin were being accused of 'colluding' with the U.S., reintroducing 'capitalism' into the Soviet Union and using the Vietnam War for their own ends. Kosygin visited Peking in February 1965 to ask for 'unified action' in Vietnam which, according to the Chinese, meant an air corridor through China and the use of two Soviet-garrisoned airfields in South China. 'We have every reason to think you have ulterior motives in offering such assistance. Frankly speaking, we do not trust you,'[20] declared a Chinese government statement in July. Moreover, Mao was afraid that domestic 'revisionism' in Russia, by which a new highly paid privileged élite of party bureaucrats had come to power and was living 'the parasitical and decadent life of the bourgeoisie',[21] might infect China. In 1966, to prevent this and other elements of 'backsliding', Mao inaugurated the Cultural Revolution which according to the Soviets was designed to purge the C.C.P. of communists who preferred Soviet-type communism and disapproved of the Sino–Soviet split.[22] Between 1966 and 1968 China's attention was focused on the domestic crisis, though the Chinese press continued to accuse Russia of 'allying' with America, India and Japan to 'contain' China.[23] The Red Guards besieged the Soviet Embassy in Peking in January 1967, and in February 1967 the Soviet leaders were variously compared in the *People's Daily* to the old Tsars, Hitler and the Ku Klux Klan!

Chinese attention reverted to the world political scene in response to the invasion of Czechoslovakia in August 1968. As Peking saw it, the Soviet army had invaded another communist country simply because Moscow did not like the brand of communism practised there, and the Chinese knew that Moscow disliked Maoism far more than Dubček's 'Socialism with a human face'. The Brezhnev Doctrine was therefore seen as 'out-and-out gangster logic put out by the new tsars to justify their aggression'[24] and judging by

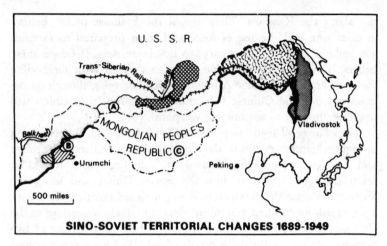

**SINO-SOVIET TERRITORIAL CHANGES 1689-1949**

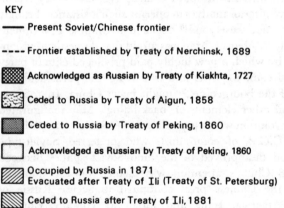

KEY

—— Present Soviet/Chinese frontier

---- Frontier established by Treaty of Nerchinsk, 1689

▓ Acknowledged as Russian by Treaty of Kiakhta, 1727

▒ Ceded to Russia by Treaty of Aigun, 1858

■ Ceded to Russia by Treaty of Peking, 1860

☐ Acknowledged as Russian by Treaty of Peking, 1860

▨ Occupied by Russia in 1871
Evacuated after Treaty of Ili (Treaty of St. Petersburg)

▧ Ceded to Russia after Treaty of Ili, 1881

Ⓐ  Occupied by USSR in 1922. Finally annexed to USSR in 1944

Ⓑ  Pro-Soviet 'East Turkestan People's Republic' 1946-49

Ⓒ  Independence from China confirmed by Soviet-Chinese Treaty, 1950

✳  Damansky or Chenpao Island region

Lenin's criticism of those who are 'socialist in word and imperialist in deed', the Soviet leaders were undoubtedly guilty of 'social imperialism'.

On 2 March 1969 the war of words turned into major physical clashes on the Sino–Soviet border. The Sino–Soviet border question has a long history. On 27 September 1920, the Soviet Acting Commission for Foreign Affairs stated that Russia 'declares void all the treaties concluded with China by the former governments of Russia, renounces all seizures of Chinese territory and all Russian concessions in China'.[25] However, this promise was never acted upon. Vast areas in the Soviet Far East, previously Chinese, Chinese-occupied or under Chinese suzerainty, had been acquired. In March 1963, the Chinese began publicly stating that these were 'unequal treaties' and should in part be renegotiated. The Foreign Minister, Ch'en Yi, claimed that in addition to the 1,540,000 square kilometres of territory annexed by Tsarist Russia, the Soviet Union had also occupied certain areas in 'violation of those treaties'.[26] In July 1964 Mao, in a conversation with visiting Japanese socialists, discussed Mongolia, the Japanese Kurile Islands occupied by Russia in 1945 and the territorial manoeuvrings in Eastern Europe in 1945. He declared: 'The Soviet Union has an area of 22 million square kilometres and its population is only 200 million people. About a hundred years ago, the area east of [Lake] Baikal became Russian territory, and since then Vladivostok, Khabarovsk, Kamchatka and other areas have become Soviet territory. We have not yet presented our account for this list.'[27] On 2 September 1964, *Pravda*'s editorial talked ominously of what happened to states which launched *Lebensraum* (living space) wars,* but events were not to erupt until 1969.

On 2 March 1969, on the disputed Damansky (or Chenpao) Island, thirty-one Russians and an unknown number of Chinese were killed in clashes between the Red Army and the People's Liberation Army. Further fighting occurred on the 14th and in April the violence spread to the Sinkiang border. The Russians argued that the Chinese were contesting the entire 1·5 million square kilometres of Tsarist-acquired territory. The Chinese argued that what they contested was the 200,000 square kilometres that Russia

---

* In approximate figures, 30 million Chinese live in Manchuria alone, whereas there are only 20 million Russians in the whole of Siberia.

had occupied in excess of the 1·5 million square kilometres. In June
1969, the Russians began to contemplate an Asian defence pact with
India, Thailand, and Indonesia – a re-hash of the Dulles S.E.A.T.O.
logic, according to China – and a Chinese language broadcast from
Moscow's 'Radio Peace and Progress' in August reminded the
Chinese that 'the Soviet Union has a full arsenal of nuclear rockets.
What have Mao Tse-tung and his lackeys to counter them?
Nothing!'[28]

On 28 August the C.C.P. Central Committee gave a 'prepare for
war' directive, and the Chinese people began to construct nuclear
shelters. Tension eased when border negotiations began in September, after Kosygin's visit to Peking, but flared up again when the
negotiations collapsed in December.

If Soviet–American *détente* had been a necessary corollary of a
nuclear world – the nuclear tail wagging the Marxist–Leninist tiger
– it became even more desirable as the Soviet Union had to redirect
some of its armed forces to counter the 'yellow peril' threat from the
East. By December 1969, 658,000 Soviet troops faced 814,000
Chinese troops on the border.[29] By July 1970 the Soviets had 6,750
T62 tanks facing 2,000 Chinese T59 tanks on the central and eastern
border zone. Moreover, the Soviets had 140 long-range bombers
available, whereas the Chinese had none, and they had 550 medium-
range bombers to China's 15. Soviet tactical nuclear missiles were
installed in Mongolia close to Chinese nuclear facilities at Haiyen,
Lanchou and Paotou while, of course, Soviet I.C.B.M.s and the
Soviet Pacific fleet's nuclear submarines could all be employed
against China if required. An authoritative survey suggested: 'In
an unrestrained nuclear conflict, the Soviets could virtually destroy
the Chinese air and naval forces and wreak widespread devastation
in cities.'[30] By 1972 the Soviets had on the Chinese border 10,000
tanks, 1,200 combat aircraft (one-quarter of her air force) and,
according to China, 'one million troops'.

The Chinese launching into earth orbit of a 380 lb. satellite
signalling 'The East is Red', in 1970, must have provoked a Russian
debate on the merits and demerits of a 'surgical strike', at least
against Chinese nuclear installations, before China could deploy
an I.C.B.M. By 1973, forty-five Russian divisions were on the
Chinese border and an authoritative analysis at that time postulated
that 250 Soviet missiles could destroy China's nuclear potential.[31]
The question at issue, therefore, is why did the Soviet Union not

conduct either a conventional invasion of Sinkiang (to destroy Lop Nor and the Chinese uranium mines) or a nuclear strike against China, as a pre-emptive measure in the early 1970s? There are a number of possible reasons. The Soviets would have had to destroy about seventy Chinese intermediate- and medium-range rockets which were on 'soft' sites (above the ground, rather than in deep steel and concrete silos) but they had a range of up to 2,000 miles, and therefore if some had escaped Soviet rocket attack major Soviet cities like Vladivostok, Khabarovsk and Irkutsk would have sustained severe casualties. The Chinese also had 150 TU-16 short-to-medium-range bombers, some of which were based near Chinese cities, and to have 'taken them out' would, through blast and radiation clouds, have caused in nuclear parlance sizeable 'collateral damage' to the Chinese civilian population. Russian propaganda would have had difficulty explaining these civilian deaths to the communist world, let alone to the Third and Western Worlds. Moreover, if such a strike had been accomplished, the Soviets could hardly have hoped to occupy China and install a docile puppet government. The alternative was a government hostile to the Soviet Union and one which might swing temporarily to an American 'alliance' of some sort. An attack on China would in effect have started a series of international events over which the Soviets would have had difficulty in maintaining control. The Americans (before and after Nixon's visit to Peking in 1972) had informed Russia of their opposition to any Sino–Soviet confrontation. No nuclear weapons have been used since August 1945 and their use by any state against another would be a highly destabilizing element in international relations. Moreover, any Sino–Soviet war would have upset the Soviet–American nuclear balance, as well as placing intolerable strains on the world and European *détente*. In short, waiting and hoping for a more amenable Chinese leadership after Mao did have its attractions.

Relations between the two countries continued to be tense in the mid-1970s. China accused the Soviets of attempting to gain military bases in the countries to whom it gives 'aid',[32] and also of plundering their natural resources and interfering in their internal affairs. In January 1974, Russia was accused of being responsible for 'dismembering' Pakistan in the Indo–Pakistan war of 1971. This period was undoubtedly tense. President Nixon, in his Foreign Policy Address to Congress of 1972 declared: 'In the 1971 crisis the Soviet Union was willing to veto U.N. action and to make military moves to deter China on India's behalf. For the U.S. to compete with the Soviet Union in fuelling an arms race, obstructing U.N. efforts to stop a war and threatening China was out of the question.'[33] In 1974 Brezhnev was accused of being a 'Confucian', afraid that the liberty China displayed during and after the Cultural Revolution might 'infect' Russia.[34] In January 1974, five Soviet Embassy personnel were expelled for spying on China[35] and the Chinese press railed against 'so-called mental hospitals' in Russia, where 'lunatics who oppose the dark rule of Soviet revisionism' are sent.[36] Even a sign of apparent moderation – the Chinese offer of a non-aggression pact with Russia in November 1974 – included a proviso that troops should withdraw a certain distance from the disputed border areas, and Russia had no intention of withdrawing from territory she did not consider anything other than 'undisputed' Soviet land.

In any event, China continued to criticize Soviet behaviour, for example in the Middle East after the October 1973 war (see Chapter 17). The Soviets were accused[37] of trying to 'dictate the destiny of the Arab peoples', of failing to supply sufficient arms to Egypt, and of supplying Israel with manpower by allowing Jews to emigrate in obvious collusion with Israeli Zionism and U.S. imperialism.[38] According to China's representative at the U.N., the Soviets arranged a 'nuclear war crisis' with America, in order to force an *in situ* peace 'thereby ensuring a situation that serves the two super-powers best in their scramble for spheres of influence, oil reserves and strategic positions in the Middle East'.[39]

In the Far East, Japan received advice in January 1975 from Chou En-lai to form closer ties with America. China preferred that Japan be linked to America than be tempted by Siberian oil into an Asian defence pact with the U.S.S.R. China therefore stressed the £1,300 million-worth of Sino–Japanese trade in 1974, and reminded Japan of the continued Soviet occupation of the Japanese Kurile Islands.

In the West, China supported the E.E.C. as a power bloc capable of standing up to the Soviets, and warned the European nations that 'While trying to create a false sense of *détente* in Europe, it [Russia] is building up its military strength to pave the way for infiltration and expansion in Western Europe'.[40]

# Fifteen

# EASTERN EUROPE AND THE BREZHNEV DOCTRINE

The Soviet attitude to the varying degrees of desire for self-determination among her allies during the 1960s has been ambiguous. Since 1960, Albanian nationalism has been successful in establishing complete independence from Moscow. Rumania maintains a foreign policy which often conflicts with that of the U.S.S.R.; Poland and Hungary have developed economic and social systems which differ considerably from those of the Soviet Union, and yet Czechoslovakia's attempt in 1968 to achieve limited independence was ruthlessly crushed by the Soviet Union. The Soviet Union has embarked upon a policy of *détente* with the West but the West measures the success of *détente* partly by the extent to which increased contacts can be made with individual East European states, independently of Moscow. Soviet policy in the last decade has tried to obtain the benefits of *détente* while at the same time ensuring the continuation of Soviet dominance in Eastern Europe. In June 1968, the Soviet Foreign Minister, Andrei Gromyko, addressed the Supreme Soviet (Parliament): 'For the Communist Party of the Soviet Union, the Central Committee, the Soviet Government, for the whole Soviet people, there is nothing more sacred in the field of foreign policy than the consolidation of the community of socialist countries.'[1] One of the principal tools used to consolidate the 'community of socialist countries' has been the Warsaw Pact.

On 9 May 1955, the leaders of the U.S.S.R., Poland, Czechoslovakia, Hungary, Rumania, Bulgaria, Albania and the D.D.R. gathered in Warsaw to sign the treaty which established the Warsaw Pact. The Warsaw Pact served to bind the East Europeans closer to the Soviet Union and has been used by the Kremlin to exert a more subtle kind of control over the East Europeans than was the case in Stalin's day. The Treaty brought benefits to the satellites, as it formalized their relationships with the U.S.S.R. and gave them a measure of control over their armed forces that Stalin had never allowed. High-ranking Soviet officers serving with the East European forces, like Rokossovsky in Poland and Panchevski in Bulgaria were replaced by nationals of the countries in question. The privileges which Soviet personnel had enjoyed in Eastern Europe were withdrawn. During the late 1950s and early 1960s, the East Europeans' forces were reduced in number, re-equipped with more modern arms and made more efficient. They assumed a more meaningful role in the defence of Eastern Europe and were prepared for the job previously done by the Red Army, of maintaining in power their own national communist parties.

The Warsaw Pact was a symbol of the increased trust accorded to the East European states by the U.S.S.R., but that trust has always been limited. The Military Commander of the Warsaw Pact has always been a Russian – N.A.T.O.'s Supreme Commander has always been an American – and the High Command of the Warsaw Pact appears to be an integral part of the Soviet Ministry of Defence. The Warsaw Pact is used by the U.S.S.R. to co-ordinate military and defence policy in Eastern Europe but also it serves as a vehicle for the transmitting of Soviet political requirements to her 'allies'. But the very creation of the Warsaw Pact and the de-Stalinization that accompanied it have raised difficulties for the U.S.S.R. in her relations with the East Europeans. Once the iron grip of Stalin was removed, nationalism in one form or another appeared in Eastern Europe. Nationalism in the East European context can only be expressed in policies and attitudes which are deviations from, and even hostile to, the U.S.S.R. and the all-pervasive Soviet influence.

Yugoslavia was the first communist country to assert her independence from the U.S.S.R. and although relations between the two countries have been restored, Belgrade has retained its sovereignty and remains a half-way house between East and West. The country that made the most complete break with Moscow is also one of the smallest and poorest countries in Europe – Albania.

After 1945 Yugoslavia with Soviet approval, planned to incorporate the tiny state into the Yugoslav federation, so when Yugoslavia was expelled from the Cominform in 1948, Albania declared her unflinching support and friendship for the Soviet Union. In this way, Albania gained a protector who was big enough to deter Yugoslavia but distant enough not to be able to do herself what the Yugoslavs had threatened. When Russo–Yugoslav relations improved in the late 1950s, the Albanian leadership was faced once more with the possible threat of annexation to Yugoslavia. Fortunately for the Albanians, the Sino–Soviet split provided another protector to replace the U.S.S.R. Four Soviet submarines had to leave their Albanian base of Valona, and in 1968 following the invasion of Czechoslovakia, Albania formally left the Warsaw Pact, although she had effectively ceased to play any part in the alliance seven years earlier. Albania's friendship for China was not the result of a search for ideological purity on the part of Enver Hoxha, the Albanian leader, but a search for a Great Power protector. In the wake of the invasion of Czechoslovakia in 1968, Albania began to mend some of her bridges with Yugoslavia and Rumania as all three states had cause to fear possible Soviet military action against them. But as the threat of Soviet invasion receded so too did Albania's desire for East European friends.

Until the late 1960s the Soviet Union did not have the naval capacity to mount an invasion of Albania and there is no shared frontier between a Warsaw Pact state and Albania. If the Soviet Union had tried to re-establish control over Albania then the Soviet–Yugoslav *détente* would have been shattered – such an example of aggression would also have complicated Soviet relations with the rest of the world, and especially China. Also, as long as Yugoslavia has wanted to keep the U.S.S.R. at arm's length Albania has been safe, because Yugoslavia's independence depends upon her good relations with the West which could be destroyed if Belgrade tried to swallow Tirana.

For none of the other East European satellites has complete independence been possible. Poland, the D.D.R. and Bulgaria all needed Soviet protection because their borders have been the subject of dispute with other countries. The artificial frontiers of Poland and the D.D.R. remained officially open to question by the West and especially by the Federal Republic of Germany until the early 1970s. Bulgaria has a dispute with Yugoslavia over Macedonia, and besides, Bulgaria is the only East European country to have benefited financially from her links with the U.S.S.R. Hungary and Poland have each introduced reforms which make their states less oppressive than the U.S.S.R. but both states have learned that the U.S.S.R. will not allow them to be anything but loyal to the Soviet Union. The two countries which attempted to take advantage of the changing circumstances of the 1960s to exert their own forms of national identity have been Rumania and Czechoslovakia.

Rumania is not in the front-line of the Soviet defensive system in Eastern Europe and she has been able to use this happy accident of geography to her advantage. In 1958, Bucharest secured the withdrawal of Soviet troops from Rumanian soil, which in itself gave the Rumanian leaders room for manoeuvre. The Sino–Soviet split gave Rumania the opportunity to assert her own economic priorities in the Comecon. As the Communist world split into two opposing camps, the U.S.S.R. attempted to secure the ideological loyalty of the East Europeans. The Comecon assigned the roles that the East Europeans were to play in the Soviet economic system in the 1960s, and Rumania was allocated the function of supplying her allies – and especially the U.S.S.R. – with raw materials such as oil, salt, chemicals, timber and grain. This plan would have resulted in Rumania having an unbalanced economy and being almost totally subordinate to the U.S.S.R. for her economic well-being. The Rumanian Communist Party leader, Gheoghiu Dej, successfully opposed the Comecon plan and as a result Rumania has been able to establish a balanced and largely self-sufficient economy based upon trade with both Western and Eastern Europe. In October 1963, a West German trade mission was opened in Bucharest and Rumania began to import machinery from the West. In the same year, Rumania embarked upon a joint hydro-electric project on the Danube with a non-Comecon partner, Yugoslavia.

In 1963 Rumania began to proclaim her adherence to the principle of non-interference in the affairs of other states, and in April 1964 declared that all communist parties were equal. These attitudes adopted by the Rumanian C.P. must have been uncomfortable to the U.S.S.R. as they implicitly denied its supremacy, but they were principles which the Soviet Union herself acknowledged and which she could ignore only at the risk of alienating much of world opinion, especially in the Third World. In November 1964 Rumania announced the reduction in the length of compulsory military service from two years to sixteen months. This decision indicated an official Rumanian attitude which contrasted markedly with the political and military readiness that Moscow required of her allies.

Rumania refused to take part in large-scale Warsaw Pact military exercises or to allow such exercises on her soil. It seems that the Soviet Union exerted a great deal of pressure against Rumania in the mid-1960s even going so far as to drop hints of possible military action against the Rumanians. In May 1965 Warsaw Pact defence ministers and military commanders took part in a meeting which was unusual in that it lasted nine days and took place in the Western Ukraine near the Rumanian border. The Rumanian leadership – from 1965 the First Secretary of the Rumanian C.P. had been Nicolai Ceausescu – benefited from having the constant support of Yugoslavia in their search for autonomy, for a Soviet invasion of Rumania could have seriously damaged relations with Belgrade.

In May 1966 after a meeting with Tito, Ceausescu made a speech in which he called for the dismantling of military alliances, foreign military bases and the withdrawal of foreign troops from other countries. This statement prompted a visit to Bucharest by the Soviet party leader, Leonid Brezhnev, but Soviet pressure failed to bring about a change in Rumanian policy. In June 1966, when the Sino–Soviet dispute was nearing its height, the Chinese Premier, Chou En-lai, made a visit to Rumania and was warmly received, to the embarrassment of the Russians. On 30 January 1967, Rumania established diplomatic relations with West Germany. The U.S.S.R. reacted against this by summoning a conference of European communist parties in Czechoslovakia in April 1967 at which it was decided that no communist state should establish diplomatic relations with West Germany without having first obtained the approval of the D.D.R. The Soviet Union could not reverse Rumanian actions but took care to see that the Rumanian example was not followed by others as this could have resulted in the isolation of the D.D.R. and the destruction of *détente* based upon the *status quo* towards which the U.S.S.R. was working. Rumania took no part in the invasion of Czechoslovakia in 1968, and indeed joined with Yugoslavia, China and Albania in condemning the affair. Since 1968, Rumania has maintained diplomatic relations with Israel, received a state visit from Presidents Nixon and Ford, continued to expand her trade with the West and remained on good terms with China.

Rumania has been able to establish a measure of autonomy from the U.S.S.R. because of her geographical position, the Sino–Soviet split, but most of all because in internal matters she remains one of

the most orthodox countries in Eastern Europe and has never threatened to leave the Warsaw Pact. There has been no danger to the
Soviet defensive system of domestic liberalism in Rumania spilling
over the frontier and contaminating her neighbours with dangerous
ideas of freedom of speech – as was the case in Czechoslovakia.

On 5 January 1968, Antonin Novotny – a Stalinist of the old
school – had to resign the First Secretaryship of the Czechoslovak
Communist Party. Economic growth in Czechoslovakia had been
small and there had actually been a decline in the standard of
living. The desire for change, very strong among people who could
remember better conditions in the past, was also echoed in many
echelons of the Party. Novotny was voted out of office by the Czechoslovak Central Committee and was replaced by Alexander Dubček.
The replacement of Novotny was well received in Moscow and at
the end of January Dubček visited the U.S.S.R. where he was
welcomed.

The 'Prague Spring' began. Greater freedom of speech and of the
press were announced, but as much of Czechoslovak society began
to be seized with an enthusiasm for the critical debate which had
been denied under Novotny's regime, other Warsaw Pact states
looked uneasily at their neighbour. In Dresden on 23 March, the
Czechoslovak leadership met their allied opposite numbers to
explain their liberalizing measures, but Rumania was not invited to
the meeting. In the same month Novotny was replaced as President
of Czechoslovakia by General Svoboda who was sympathetic to
Dubček's ideas. In April a new Prime Minister, Oldrich Cernik,
was elected; both he and the Chairman of the National Assembly,
Josef Smrkovsky, were supporters of Dubček, so when the new Czech
C.P. 'Action Programme' was announced, it had the backing of the
Czech leadership. The new programme, entitled 'The Czechoslovak
Road to Socialism', denounced the mistakes, crimes and suppression
of liberty under the Novotny regime and attacked the centralized
management of the economy which had resulted in stagnation. The
Party itself was criticized for the 'monopolistic concentration of
power in the hands of party bodies'. The programme declared that
the Party was not a 'universal caretaker of society' and guaranteed
the right to travel abroad, to freedom of speech, and to a free press.
It promised judicial reforms and the intention to curb the secret
police. Most important were the comments on the role of the Party:
'Each member of the Party and Party bodies has not only the right

but the duty to act according to his conscience. It is impermissible to restrict Communists in these rights, to create an atmosphere of distrust and suspicion of those who voice different opinions, to persecute the minority under any pretext – as has happened in the past.'[2]

In denying the primacy of the Communist Party, the Czech leadership laid themselves open to mounting criticism from the Soviet Union. Early in May Dubček and his Foreign Minister, Hajek, went to Moscow but did not succeed in quieting the fears of their Soviet hosts, although the Soviet leaders did indicate that they would not interfere in Czechoslovakia's internal affairs. It now became a matter of priority for the Czech leadership to try to explain their reforms to their East European critics and to assure them that Czechoslovakia would remain a loyal member of the socialist community and of the Warsaw Pact. On 15 May, Smrkovsky declared: 'We must understand the fears of the Soviet Union, which has in mind not only Czechoslovakia but also the security of the whole socialist camp.'[3]

Moscow began mounting an increasingly hostile propaganda campaign against the 'action programme' and on 8 May a meeting was held in Moscow of the 'loyal' Warsaw Pact countries, excluding .Rumania, Czechoslovakia and Albania. On 15 May, the Polish–Czech frontier was closed and a joint Soviet–Polish military exercise took place in Poland, near the Czech frontier, in the presence of the Russian Marshal Grechko, the Commander-in-Chief of the Warsaw Pact. As soon as the exercise was over, Grechko went to Prague to talk to the Czech Minister of Defence. He was joined by the Soviet Premier, Kosygin, who held discussions with the Czech leaders between 17–25 May. Kosygin went to Prague to discuss the strengthening of the framework of the Warsaw Pact, which can only have been an attempt to establish closer Soviet control over the Czech army. On 15 June the Czech Government proclaimed the establishment of the Czechoslovak National Front, a coalition of the communist and other socialist parties. The Front was designed to be a coalition of communist and non-communist interests, but as it effectively demoted the Czech C.P., it was bound to arouse the hostility of the U.S.S.R., so the Czechs also proclaimed the leading 'role' in the Front of the Party and stressed the importance of the Soviet alliance. On 27 June President Svoboda declared: 'The firm and invariable friendship and alliance with the Soviet Union is the guarantee of our security and independence. The importance of this alliance and of all the commitments Czechoslovakia has taken as one of the Warsaw Pact countries is unambiguous.'[4]

In mid-July, Czechoslovakia's East European critics gathered in Warsaw; they were sufficiently disturbed at events in Prague – which threatened to find followers in Poland and the D.D.R. – to send a letter to the Czechs that was openly threatening:

> The development of events in your country evokes deep anxiety in us . . . we cannot agree to have hostile forces push your country off the road to socialism as this jeopardises the interests of the entire socialist system. Anti-socialist and revisionist forces have laid hands on the press, radio and television . . . A situation has thus arisen which is entirely unacceptable for a socialist country . . . we believe that a decisive rebuff to the forces of anti-communism . . . in Czechoslovakia is not only your task but ours too.[5]

The Czech leadership met with the Soviet Politburo and the signatories of the 'Warsaw Letter' and all pledged their loyalty to the Warsaw Pact. In early August, it looked as though Dubček had received Soviet acquiescence in his 'action programme'; but all the new Czech policies remained, as did all the Soviet objections to them, and Soviet military preparations went ahead. The military exercises held around Czechoslovakia's frontiers between May and August had been interpreted by the Czechs as part of the war of nerves against them, but after 20 August, when Warsaw Pact forces under Russian command moved smoothly across the Czech frontiers, they were seen to have been careful preparations for the invasion.

The invasion did not meet with armed resistance but with a massive wave of passive hostility from the Czechoslovak people. So solid was public opinion and the Government behind Dubček, that the Russians had to release him, Cernik and Smrkovsky from arrest. The Soviet troops stayed in Czechoslovakia, the reforms were reversed and Dubček was finally dismissed from his post in March 1969. The invasion was condemned by China, Rumania, Yugoslavia and the West, but the West did nothing. Czechoslovakia in 1968 threatened to disturb the East-West balance, so while the West sympathized with Czech desires for greater freedom, Western military planners appreciated the strategic imperatives which dictated Soviet actions in crushing Czech freedom. Soviet military action in Czechoslovakia did halt the process of *détente* for a short time, but by 1969 both sides had taken up where they had left off in the summer of 1968. Czechoslovakia has been part of the price that the world has had to pay for *détente*.

The Soviet Union justified the invasion of Czechoslovakia by proclaiming what the West has called the 'Brezhnev Doctrine' or the 'Doctrine of Limited Sovereignty', which was spelt out in detail by the Soviet First Secretary, Brezhnev, in November 1968. Brezhnev declared:

> When internal and external forces hostile to Socialism attempt to turn the development of any Socialist country in the direction of the capitalist system, when a threat arises to the cause of Socialism in that country, a threat to the security of the Socialist commonwealth as a whole – it already becomes not only a problem for the people of that country but also a general problem, the concern of all Socialist countries.[6]

Since 1968, there has been considerable change in the internal affairs of the East European states. All have an increasing although small-scale private sector. In Poland in 1970, riots forced the replacement of Gomulka by Gierek who had to reverse some of the economic policies of his predecessors. This was forced upon him by strikes in Lodz in the spring of 1971 provoked by Gomulka's large-scale price increases in basic commodities. Gierek also improved relations with the Catholic Church and recognized the political power of organized labour. All these measures have been allowed by the U.S.S.R. because despite the fact that they deviate from Soviet practice they did not threaten communist supremacy in Poland. A British writer commenting upon the events of 1968 wrote:

> What Dubček had tried to do was consistent with the logic of 'liberalisation'; but it demonstrated that it is not possible to liberalise Communism. The ruling party has or has not the monopoly of power; that is the meaning of totalitarianism . . . If freedom of speech and of the press is allowed, it is meaningless unless it includes freedom of dissent, and the freedom of dissent comprises the right to say that the ruling party should move out and make way for another.[7]

Czechoslovakia demonstrated that liberalization in Eastern Europe, which the West wanted, would only be allowed in those areas which threatened neither communist supremacy in Eastern Europe nor the Soviet glacis. It would appear that the U.S.S.R. remains a believer in Eisenhower's 'Domino Theory' logic.

# Sixteen

# *DÉTENTE* IN EUROPE

The period of the late 1960s and early 1970s was one in which the static battle lines between N.A.T.O. and the Warsaw Pact began to wither away. The '*Ostpolitik*' or Eastern Policy of the West German Government has normalized relations with the countries of Eastern Europe by acknowledging the continuation of the post-war territorial division of Europe. Britain, France, the U.S.A. and the U.S.S.R., signed the Four Power Agreement on Berlin thus accepting each other's responsibilities in that city. There have been considerable increases in trade and cultural exchanges between the Soviet Union, her allies and the West. Talks on a European Security Conference (C.S.C.E.) culminated in the Helsinki Conference of August 1975.

Political and economic aspects of *détente* have been matched by negotiations on military aspects: the Strategic Arms Limitation Talks and the negotiations on Mutual and Balanced Force Reductions in Europe. To a large extent, all these negotiations have been part of the same thing, East–West *détente*, but the questions of Germany and Berlin have been fundamental to all the talks in Europe: without progress on the one, there was no agreement on the others.

Until the late 1960s, West German policy towards Eastern Europe had been dominated by the Hallstein Doctrine, according to which Bonn did not have diplomatic relations with any state which recognized East Germany except the U.S.S.R. The Doctrine, named after the then State Secretary of the West German Foreign Office, was first enunciated by Chancellor Adenauer in 1955 and was enforced twice: in 1957 when the Federal Republic broke off diplomatic relations with Yugoslavia, and in 1963 when West German–Cuban relations were severed. The Hallstein Doctrine was seen to be no longer operational on 30 January 1967 when Bonn established diplomatic relations with Bucharest, and it was finally abandoned in

January 1968 when diplomatic relations were restored between West Germany and Yugoslavia. The rejection of the Hallstein Doctrine marked a definitive break in West Germany's foreign policy. Although the idea of German reunification still had very great emotional and electoral appeal in West Germany it had become obvious to many that, given the attitude of the East Europeans and the Soviet Union, the prospects for reunification were minimal by the late 1960s. Furthermore, although West Germany's allies continued to support Bonn's desire for reunification, their attitude – never extremely enthusiastic – was undergoing a change. On 7 October 1966 President Johnson made a speech in which he said that the reunification of Germany and Europe could only be the result and not the prerequisite of *détente* between East and West. This indicated clearly to the West German Government that the United States had interests in *détente* of her own and did not intend to allow West Germany's problems to interfere with bilateral Soviet–American negotiations. Johnson's speech raised in Bonn the always present – but usually dormant – fear that the United States might be tempted to do a 'deal' with the U.S.S.R. over West Germany's head and possibly at her expense. This fear was justified to some extent, because any bilateral easing of tension between the U.S.A. and the U.S.S.R. would involve some increased, if possibly only tacit, recognition of the *status quo*.

Similarly, West Germany's major E.E.C. partner, France, was engaged in seeking a closer understanding with the Soviet Union. In 1967, then, there was a possibility that if Bonn did not try to improve her relations with Eastern Europe on her own terms, she might be outpaced by *détente* achieved by her two major allies and so might find herself diplomatically isolated, in which case the prospects of improving inter-German relations would have been further off than ever. The deciding factor in the birth of the *Ostpolitik* was the change in the West German Government in December 1966. In that month the Grand Coalition of the Christian Democratic Union and Christian Social Union (the major party of government since 1949) and the S.P.D. was formed. The S.P.D. leader Willy Brandt became Foreign Minister in the new Government. The major reason behind the S.P.D. joining the coalition was that Brandt was determined to develop an *Ostpolitik*. Although he was not prepared to admit it at the time, Brandt realized that German reunification was probably impossible in the prevailing circumstances and his foreign policy was based upon this realization.

At the N.A.T.O. Council Meeting on 14 December 1966, Brandt outlined his *Ostpolitik* ideas. He intended to pursue gradual improvements in East–West relations beginning with Poland and Czechoslovakia. In return for normalization of relations Brandt was prepared to offer Bonn's acceptance of the Oder–Neisse frontier between East Germany and Poland, and Bonn's recognition that Hitler's Munich Agreement of 1938 was invalid. However, Brandt would not make unilateral concessions to the East Europeans; they had to be part of a wider East–West European *détente* which would create a climate in which there could be *rapprochement* between East and West Germany.

As well as offering formal recognition of the frontiers of Poland and Czechoslovakia, Brandt also said that the Federal Republic would support any moves to reduce the levels of armed forces in Europe and, more importantly, would support any moves to control the spread of nuclear weapons. Bonn was aware that any *détente* with Eastern Europe would have to be approved by Moscow so this offer was intended to allay continuing Russian anxieties that West Germany might some day acquire a nuclear capability which she might threaten to use to obtain a revision of Central Europe's frontiers.

Brandt's *Ostpolitik* got off to a good start, for at the end of January 1967 diplomatic relations were established between West Germany and Rumania but Bonn's 'peace offensive' worried some of Rumania's allies. Warsaw Pact Foreign Ministers met in Warsaw within weeks of the Bonn–Bucharest agreement to decide on a common attitude towards the new West German moves. The country most concerned at the possible effects of Bonn's diplomacy was the D.D.R., which feared she might become isolated and this was indeed part of Brandt's intention. The Soviet Union was also concerned that the Federal Republic might be able to drive a wedge into her glacis, so Moscow shared some of the D.D.R.'s apprehension. Between 24–26 April a full-scale conference of European communist parties was held at Karlovy Vary in Czechoslovakia to discuss 'problems of European Security'.

The Karlovy Vary Conference agreed that none of the East European states would establish diplomatic relations with the Federal Republic without having first obtained the agreement of East Germany, and called for the setting-up of a European security conference. Also, the participants agreed that they must all try to bring about the recognition of the D.D.R. by the West. After the conference, and with the active support of the U.S.S.R., East Germany negotiated and signed 'mutual assistance' and 'friendship' treaties with Poland and Czechoslovakia, thus increasing the cohesion of those states upon which depended the security of East Germany – and the U.S.S.R.

The Soviet Union maintained a strong interest in *détente* during 1967. Apart from the negotiations with the United States on nuclear issues (see Chapter 18), she entered into a major trade agreement with Italy. A contract was signed between the U.S.S.R. and the Italian E.N.I. Company to build a pipeline between the Ukraine and Trieste which would carry a twenty-five year supply of Soviet natural gas to Italy at a cost of $413 million. Also, the U.S.S.R. placed a number of ship orders in Western European shipyards. Apart from this, however, progress on the *Ostpolitik* was slow during the rest of 1967 and early 1968, but it was given an added stimulus at the N.A.T.O. Foreign Ministers' Meeting of December 1967, when N.A.T.O. adopted the 'flexible response and conventional options' doctrine.

Flexible response was a military strategy designed to maximize N.A.T.O.'s defensive capacity in the event of a possible Soviet attack upon Western Europe. The new strategy envisaged any attack being met with the appropriate level of conventional, tactical nuclear, or even strategic nuclear response, but this raised special problems for the West German Government. If conventional defence had to be seen to be on the point of failing before nuclear weapons were used, then West Germany would stand to lose much of its territory during the early stages of a limited Soviet attack. If such territorial loss were to be avoided, then the West would have to use nuclear weapons from the outset. Either way, in the event of war, West Germany would be likely to suffer occupation by the U.S.S.R., nuclear devastation, or both. So the adoption of the 'flexible response' strategy spurred on the Federal Republic to do all she could to limit the probability of a war, in which she would be the first victim, by further pursuing the *Ostpolitik*.

In February 1968, West Germany opened a trade mission in Czechoslovakia, and in the same month the Federal Republic sent a memorandum to the Soviet Union in which Bonn expressed a desire to improve relations between 'both parts of Germany'. The invasion of Czechoslovakia in August 1968 put a temporary halt to the *Ostpolitik*, for the West German Government condemned Soviet actions and East–West relations remained strained for the rest of the year. In September 1968 Bonn lifted the ban on the West German Communist Party which had been outlawed since 1955. During 1968, the East German Government allowed more citizens of the D.D.R. to visit West Germany – about 1·5 million, nearly all old-age pensioners – and more West Germans to visit the D.D.R. than had been allowed in past years. In January 1969, Moscow and Bonn resumed their bilateral negotiations, and in May Poland proposed a treaty with West Germany in which both countries would recognize the Oder–Neisse line. The West German Chancellor, Kiesinger, replied offering to open negotiations on the frontier issue. There matters largely remained until October, when after the West German general election, the S.P.D. emerged as the major partner in a coalition with the F.D.P. (Liberal Party) and Willy Brandt became Chancellor.

In the autumn of 1969 Chancellor Brandt began a new foreign policy drive. He offered to sign treaties with Poland and the Soviet Union in which the basic interests of these countries would be catered for: both sides would renounce force as a means of settling disputes; they would respect each other's territorial integrity – this was an implicit offer to recognize the Oder–Neisse line – and they would give assurances not to try to bring about changes in the social structure or alliance relationships of the other. He offered a trade agreement to Czechoslovakia and compensation for the victims of Nazism. These offers were accepted and negotiations began, but Brandt was careful to ensure the support of his allies. He pressed the three Western Occupying Powers to negotiate with the U.S.S.R. a new Four Power Agreement on Berlin, and at the E.E.C. Summit meeting in December 1969 the West German Chancellor proposed that Britain be allowed to join the Common Market. Possibly the single most important action by the West German Government in 1969 was the signing on 28 November of the Non-Proliferation Treaty. This showed the Eastern bloc, if further proof were needed, that Bonn was serious in her new diplomacy and that her intentions were peaceful. Having signed the Non-Proliferation Treaty and thus given an earnest of her good faith, Bonn was in no hurry to ratify the treaty. The West German Government now wanted something in return so that Bonn could show the West German electorate that concessions had not all been on one side. In fact, the N.P.T. was not ratified by the West German Bundestag until 20 February 1974.

Early in December 1969 a Warsaw Pact Summit meeting was held in Moscow to decide a common attitude towards Bonn's *Ostpolitik*. It seems that Ulbricht's aim at this meeting was to try to persuade his allies that West Germany should extend diplomatic recognition to the D.D.R. before there could be any genuine *détente*. Brandt would not go so far as to exchange ambassadors with East Germany; his nearest approach was to propose the formula that Germany consisted of 'two states within one nation'. This did not satisfy Ulbricht, although it did not appear to displease the other East Europeans. In a press conference on 19 January 1970, Herr Ulbricht repeated his demands for full recognition. He described East Germany as a 'Socialist German National State', whereas West Germany was: 'A capitalist N.A.T.O. state . . . with limited sovereignty'.[1] Although his condemnation of the Federal Republic continued, Ulbricht did make a concession by confirming that the D.D.R. was prepared to start negotiations with Bonn. Possibly to show that their willingness to negotiate was not because of weakness, the East Germans introduced random road blocks on to the West Berlin access routes during the rest of January. Nevertheless on 11 February, the East German Prime Minister, Willi Stoph, invited Brandt to meet him. Only the day before, the Soviet Union had accepted Western offers to open Four Power talks on Berlin.

The historic meeting between the two German Heads of Government was held in Erfurt in the D.D.R. on 19 March. To the surprise of the West Germans and the embarrassment of their hosts, Brandt was greeted by large crowds of enthusiastically cheering East Germans, who broke the police cordon to give him an ovation. The talks were conducted in a sombre atmosphere and achieved nothing apart from an agreed date for a further meeting in Kassel in the Federal Republic on 21 May. The importance of the meetings was not in what was discussed, but in the fact that they occurred. They indicated that the East Germans were prepared to talk, although this was widely believed in the West to be the result of Soviet pressure rather than East Germany's desire. Brandt believed that the different elements of the *Ostpolitik*, the N.P.T., and the talks with Poland, the U.S.S.R. and the D.D.R., were beginning to have a snowball effect. He appears to have been right: '. . . his show of patience and goodwill in his meetings with Stoph [had not] been wasted, since Moscow and Warsaw had been impressed by it.'[2]

On 12 August 1970 the Federal Republic and the Soviet Union signed a 'non-aggression' treaty in Moscow. Secretary Brezhnev appeared to be very pleased with the treaty which opened up new avenues of trade with the West and which also cleared up some of the Kremlin's foreign policy problems in Europe at a time when Sino–Soviet difficulties in the Far East were very great. For Bonn the treaty set the seal of Soviet approval upon the *Ostpolitik.* On 7 December Chancellor Brandt visited Warsaw to sign a non-aggression treaty, in which the Federal Republic formally recognized the Oder–Neisse line. At the Warsaw Ghetto, Brandt knelt before the memorial in tribute to the victims of Hitler's Germany; the simplicity, sincerity and unexpectedness of this act was not lost on its observers.

West Germany gained little in the short term from the Polish treaty but Poland did, for with the recognition of her frontiers Poland's dependence upon the U.S.S.R. was diminished. In accepting this state of affairs, the Soviet Union showed the world that she wanted *détente* in Europe to continue, but there remained one major stumbling block. Talks with Czechoslovakia and the Four Power negotiations on Berlin were making progress, albeit slowly, but the East German leadership was proving dilatory.

It seems that by early 1971, other East European states were becoming impatient with the D.D.R. The Soviet Union wanted a European security conference to put the finishing touches to *détente* in Europe, but the West would go no further until agreement had been reached on Berlin and a treaty between the two Germanies had been negotiated. The opposition in the D.D.R. was identified with Ulbricht, the party leader, a hardliner who feared the repercussions upon the D.D.R. of *rapprochement* with Bonn. The Erfurt meeting had highlighted the disturbing fact that Willy Brandt was more popular in the D.D.R. than members of the East German Government. Also, the East Germans were not popular in Eastern Europe despite their professions of friendship with their allies. A Polish diplomat said of them: 'They are the Germans we don't like, while the West Germans are those we don't have to like.'[3] On 3 May 1971 Walter Ulbricht was replaced as First Secretary by Erich Hönecker, a man more likely to follow Moscow's wishes to the letter.

On 3 September 1971 a Four Power Agreement on Berlin was reached, in which the individual and joint rights and responsibilities of the U.S.A., U.S.S.R., Britain and France were recognized as unchanged. The links between West Berlin and the Federal Republic were to remain, and West Berliners were to have easier access to East Berlin and the D.D.R. Everything that the D.D.R. had worked for on the Berlin issue during the preceding sixteen years had come to nothing. What the East Germans regarded as a basic interest had been sacrificed by the Soviet Union in her own national interests, and when the D.D.R. finally had to accept and sign the Basic Treaty with the Federal Republic on 21 December 1972, it did not bring her the full diplomatic recognition from Bonn that Ulbricht had always declared was a prerequisite for any treaty. The Basic Treaty was a compromise. It allowed for 'good neighbourly' relations between the two Germanies, increased trade, cultural and personal contacts, respect for each other's frontiers and alliance obligations. It continued to recognize the rights and responsibilities of the Four Powers in Germany and led to the exchange of Permanent Missions, but not embassies. While Bonn hoped the treaty would inspire contact between the two states, East Germany regarded it as the acceptance of the *status quo*: two separate republics. The Basic Treaty was not a peace treaty for Germany but it was as near as Europe came to drawing a veil over the Second World War and its consequences, until the Helsinki Agreement of 1975.

The success of the bilateral negotiations in Central Europe in the 1970s opened the way for talks on issues important to both N.A.T.O. and the Warsaw Pact. As early as 1954, the U.S.S.R. had proposed a European Security Conference. Moscow hoped that a system of multilateral guarantees would replace the two blocs which faced each other across a divided Europe. The U.S.S.R. returned to the idea repeatedly in the late 1960s, no doubt hoping that its successful implementation would reduce or remove the presence and influence of the United States in Western Europe. The European security conference proposals were well received in some quarters in the West, especially in France, but the West Europeans were more interested in negotiations on East–West reduction of forces in Europe which would ensure Western Europe's security far better than paper agreements and a reduction of American forces.

In early June 1971 the N.A.T.O. Council of Ministers, meeting in Lisbon, agreed to make approaches to the Soviet Union to test the willingness of the Warsaw Pact to enter into negotiations with N.A.T.O. to reduce the level of military forces stationed on the continent of Europe. The M.B.F.R. principle had first been agreed by N.A.T.O. Ministers in Reykjavik in June 1968, but in 1971 the time seemed right. The success of West German Chancellor Willy Brandt's *Ostpolitik* appeared to indicate that the Soviet Union might be receptive to ideas of a formal agreement to limit the size of military forces in Europe. A successfully negotiated M.B.F.R. agreement would have considerable advantages for the European members of N.A.T.O. In 1970 there had been a strong movement in the United States Senate to introduce legislation to reduce drastically the size of American forces in Europe. This movement was success-fully resisted by President Nixon, but it demonstrated to the Europ-eans that there was a very strong body of opinion in the United States Congress to withdraw troops from Europe. Furthermore, N.A.T.O.'s European countries had to take into consideration the fact that, although the Mansfield Resolution had been defeated once, the support for it remained in the American Congress and it could grow to a level at which the President would unilaterally have to reduce American forces in Europe. If American force contributions to Europe had been unilaterally and significantly reduced, then the Europeans would themselves have had to increase the size of their own armed forces to make up the difference; or they would have had to accept that the capacity of N.A.T.O.'s conventional forces in Europe to deter any possible Soviet aggres-sion had diminished.

In the recent past, the West European N.A.T.O. states have been notably reluctant even to consider increasing the size of their armed forces. Such a move would be expensive and unpopular with the electorates of a number of European states – including Britain, Holland and West Germany – who do not feel particularly threat-ened by the Soviet Union and who appreciate that government budgets are limited and that more soldiers and weapons means more taxes or less spending on other more socially desirable things like hospitals and schools. This reluctance on the part of America's major European allies to increase contributions to the common defence angered a growing body of American Congressmen who justifiably felt that the U.S.A. could not reasonably be expected to go on shouldering a disproportionate amount of N.A.T.O.'s defence costs. Also, with the end of American involvement in the Vietnam War, the U.S.A. had abolished conscription so that her armed forces available for world-wide commitments were reduced. Mutual and Balanced Force Reductions in Europe offered the West Europeans a possible solution to their dilemma, for it could bring about a situation in which a reduction in American and other N.A.T.O. forces would be matched by a reduction of Soviet forces in central Europe.

While the West talked about the desirability of M.B.F.R., the Soviet Union pursued its idea of a European Security Conference (C.S.C.E.) and it was not until Chancellor Brandt's visit to the Crimea in mid-September 1971 for talks with Brezhnev that East and West agreed to each other's proposals. It was decided that:

(a) force reductions should be compatible with the vital security interests of the alliance and should not operate to the military disadvantage of either side having regard to the differences arising from geographical and other considerations.

(b) Reductions should be on a basis of reciprocity, and phased and balanced as to their scope and timing.

(c) Reductions should include stationed and indigenous forces and their weapons systems in the area concerned.

(d) There must be adequate verification and controls to ensure the observance of agreements on mutual and balanced force reductions.[4]

In the summer of 1972, the two super-powers accepted that the M.B.F.R. and C.S.C.E. negotiations were two sides of the same coin which should run roughly in parallel with each other. Exploratory talks on both topics effectively began in January 1973 and full sessions began later in the year, the C.S.C.E. in Helsinki on 3 July and the M.B.F.R. in Vienna on 30 October. The M.B.F.R. talks are extremely complicated. They involve not just troops but numbers and types of weapons. Furthermore, any straight percentage cut in the number of forces which the U.S.S.R. wants would give the Warsaw Pact an even greater military superiority over N.A.T.O. than it had previously. Both sides want to reduce their forces but maintain or improve their security *vis-à-vis* each other. The U.S.S.R. wants to maintain its hold over Eastern Europe but the West, and probably some of the Eastern bloc states, want to reduce Soviet forces in Eastern Europe to a level at which a repetition of the Czech invasion of 1968 would be much more difficult, if not impossible.

The C.S.C.E. talks were similarly complicated. During the two-year negotiations all the conference participants agreed that the talks should seek to allow freer movement of people, ideas and information throughout Europe, yet these undertakings by the U.S.S.R. were not reported in the Soviet press.[5] The Soviet Union wanted the C.S.C.E. to relax tension in Western Europe (yet the Soviet media continues to exhort its citizens to continued vigilance against the West), to make Western capital and technology available to the U.S.S.R., and to acknowledge that Soviet interests are supreme in Eastern Europe. At the Helsinki talks, delegates not only from N.A.T.O. but from the European neutrals stressed that *détente* must involve greater individual freedom if it is to be real, but individual liberty is very restricted in the Soviet Union. The information services are state-controlled and state-directed, so the Soviet people hear and learn only what their government wants them to. Few Russians are allowed to travel abroad and they even need passports to travel within the U.S.S.R. Some emigration of Jews and dissidents has been allowed in recent years, but these are exceptions. Although the U.S.S.R. had subscribed to the humanitarian principles of U.N.O., it is a police state and the continuation in power of the Communist Party depends upon the denying to Soviet citizens the rights that the U.S.S.R. proclaims for others.

Nevertheless, the talks succeeded and thirty-three European countries (excluding Albania) as well as Canada and the U.S.A. signed the Helsinki Agreement in August 1975 in which they recognized the borders of Eastern Europe and implicitly, Soviet dominance there. West Germany renounced her claim to be the sole legitimate German state. East and West agreed to have observers at each other's large military exercises and all states promised more East–West contact and guaranteed human rights.

The Helsinki Declaration was a magnificent statement of principle, but the Orlov Group in the U.S.S.R., Charter 77 in Czechoslovakia, and many other groups and individuals, would no doubt have agreed with the French Foreign Minister, M. Jobert, who said at the beginning of the C.S.C.E. talks in July 1973: 'The way to peace lies through exchange of ideas, through the free movement of individuals.' He went on to say that if the C.S.C.E. did not produce liberty for all Europeans then it would merely be 'a delusion for the masses, a manoeuvre for the wiliest, a mistake for others'.[6]

# Seventeen

# THE COLD WAR AND THE THIRD WORLD: THE MIDDLE EAST – A CASE STUDY

Immediately after the Second World War, the Soviet Union tested Western resolve in the eastern Mediterranean, Iran and Korea and in so doing aroused fears in Western governments that international communism, directed from Moscow, threatened their territorial and imperial influences throughout the world. The Cold War in the Third World has increased in scope and intensity in proportion to: the decline of Western (usually British and French) influence; the adoption by the United States of the role of 'world policeman' and promoter of 'liberty'; the increase in the U.S.S.R.'s ability materially to affect international affairs far from her borders; and the growth of local 'anti-colonialist' nationalism in the recently independent countries. Communist parties came into existence in the colonial territories of the European powers between the two world wars but they received little more than moral support from the Soviet Union. Since 1945, such Third World communist parties have received help and encouragement but the main direction of Soviet aid has not been to local communist parties but to governments, irrespective of their lack of ideological purity. Soviet generosity to national governments has been decided not by the loyalty of such governments to Marxist–Leninism, but by the extent to which their ambitions and policies led them into opposition to the West.

When the Western imperial powers disengaged from their colonies, they attempted to retain their commercial links and influence in the areas from which their military presence had been withdrawn. The U.S.A., despite the Truman Doctrine and the alliance systems constructed between 1945 and 1955, was reluctant to inherit the military obligations of Britain, France and the Netherlands, but was obliged to do so as communist influence and threats to the *Pax Americana* grew. The United States, with her traditions of liberty, usually sympathized with emergent nationalism in her allies' old colonies, but was to find that some of the territories she helped towards independence tended to gravitate to the Soviet Union rather than to the West. Some, like India, Algeria, Indonesia and Tanzania, accepted help from both East and West, refusing to choose sides in the Cold War.

The process of decolonization produced a new factor in the Cold War in the 1950s: non-alignment. In April 1955 the independent Afro–Asian countries held a conference at Bandung, Indonesia, following the recent conclusion of the S.E.A.T.O. Agreement and the Baghdad Pact. The Indian and Chinese delegates attacked the spread of Cold War confrontation to their part of the globe. Opinion at the conference was divided on the question of non-alignment; Turkey, Pakistan and the Philippines valued their political and military links with the West, but Egypt, India and others laid emphasis upon peaceful relations with East and West. Bandung did not create the phenomenon of neutrality in the Cold War, it merely formalized the existing situation. But declarations of neutrality did not help Third World states escape from entanglement in the Cold War. All the newly independent countries needed financial, military and commercial aid, and usually had to accept a degree of influence over their foreign policy attitudes from the donors of aid. The Americans regarded non-alignment with hostility during the mid-1950s. In 1956 U.S. Secretary of State Dulles said: 'except under very exceptional circumstances, neutrality is an immoral and short-sighted conception.'[1]

During Stalin's lifetime, the Soviet Union shared this attitude. In September 1947, Andrei Zhdanov addressed an international communist congress in which he declared that the world was divided into two mutually opposing and hostile camps; one, led by the American capitalists, was preparing for war and the other, led by the peace-loving U.S.S.R., was preparing to defend liberty. Both sides then objected to neutrality on ideological or moral grounds but both had to modify their positions as more countries became independent and expressed disinterest in what they saw as none of their affair. The activities and interests of the super-powers together with membership of U.N.O. has involved almost all the states of the world in the Cold War, directly or indirectly, and irrespective of their desires. The Indian subcontinent and South-East Asia have become subjects of super-power rivalry, but potentially the most explosive area of the Cold War in the Third World – apart from Vietnam – has been the Middle East.

The super-powers have been involved in the Middle East since Britain handed over responsibility for her Palestine mandate to the U.N. in April 1947, for the U.S.A. and U.S.S.R. co-operated in producing the partition plan which has led to four Middle East wars in twenty-five years. As British influence declined in the 1950s, Moscow and Washington both attempted to claim a share of the resultant power vacuum and so brought their own differences into a region which has traditionally been an area of Great Power conflict.

The central Middle East problem was the non-acceptance of the state of Israel (proclaimed on 15 May 1948) by her neighbours. The West tried to preserve the territorial *status quo* after the first Middle East war of 1948–9 by limiting arms supplies to the combatants and by trying to exclude the influence of the U.S.S.R. from the region. On 11 November 1951, the U.S.A., U.K., France and Turkey founded a Middle East Command and invited other Arab states to join. On 24 February 1955, Turkey, Iran, Britain, Pakistan and Iraq signed the Baghdad Pact. Many Arabs regarded this alliance as 'neo-colonialist' and the inclusion of Iraq as harmful to Arab unity. Further, by trying to unite Arab states in a defensive alliance against the U.S.S.R., the West apparently ignored the one cause that would unite Arabs. Israel, not the Soviet Union, was seen as the major threat by the Arabs. The Baghdad Pact virtually invited the U.S.S.R. to interfere in the area because it threatened her southern flank. From 1955 it was in Moscow's interests to attempt to remove this threat by trying to subvert the Pact or by championing the cause of those states, like Egypt and Syria, who most objected to the Pact and therefore could be relied upon to further Moscow's interests in working for their own.

Following their defeat in the first war against Israel, the Arab states imposed a blockade against her. Israeli ships were denied the use of the Suez Canal despite U.N. censure and in September 1955 Egypt closed the Straits of Tiran to Israeli shipping. Arab raids into Israel increased, as did Israeli reprisals. In the heightening tension in the Middle East, King Hussein of Jordan dismissed General Glubb, his British military adviser and the Russians offered to replace British aid and influence in Jordan.

A Middle East war was not in Moscow's interests in the mid-1950s and she participated in the U.N. Security Council decision to send the Secretary-General, Dag Hammarskjöld, to mediate between the Arabs and Israelis. Despite the U.S.S.R.'s apparent desire to de-fuse the Middle East, the Western Powers believed that communist influence in the Arab states was growing. In September 1955 Czechoslovakia agreed to supply arms to Egypt, and in May 1956 Egypt recognized Communist China and soon after announced that she could obtain arms from Peking despite the U.N. embargo.

In reaction to this, on 15 July 1956, the U.S.A. withdrew her promise of financial support for the Egyptian Aswan High Dam project, the two other major backers, Britain and the World Bank, followed suit. The Aswan Dam was of immense importance to Egypt, which needed much more fertile land for her growing population. Colonel Nasser, the Egyptian leader, took prompt retaliatory action. On 26 July he announced the nationalization of British and French investments in the Suez Canal. Although international negotiations were conducted on the question of the use of the canal, Britain and France prepared for military intervention. In the summer of 1956 the U.S.S.R. offered loans to Egypt thus confirming the West's suspicions of Moscow's true intentions. On 5 November 1956, while the U.S.S.R. was embroiled in Hungary, Anglo–French forces, in collusion with the Israelis, attacked Egypt.

American pressure and the world outcry forced the British and French to halt operations within hours of the landing, but not before Soviet Premier Bulganin had threatened them: 'What would have been the position of Britain if she had been attacked by the stronger powers with all kinds of modern weapons . . . such as rocket techniques? . . . The war in Egypt can . . . grow into a Third World War . . . We are filled with determination to use force to crush the aggressors and to restore peace in the East.'[2] Despite her bellicose language, the U.S.S.R. co-operated with the U.S.A. in bringing the war to an end, but the threats of retaliation were made and the Russians must have been aware of the dangers of debasing the nuclear currency if they circulated it too easily, too often.

Anglo–French prestige in the Middle East was in ruins after the Suez incident, but the U.S. moved to replace it on 5 January 1957, when the President presented the Eisenhower Doctrine to Congress. He attacked Soviet intentions in the Middle East and asked Congressional authority to 'give economic and military assistance to all countries . . . in that region wishing to benefit from it, it being understood that this assistance could include the use of American forces'.[3]

Egypt and Syria objected to American involvement in the Middle East and to resist it they drew nearer to the U.S.S.R., thus giving further justification to Washington. The U.S.S.R. boosted its aid to Egypt and sent Soviet officers to train the Syrian forces. This aroused Western fears that Syria might go communist and so turn the flank of the Baghdad Pact and undermine the pro-Western regimes in Jordan, Lebanon and Iraq. The U.S. stepped up arms deliveries to the three 'threatened' states and Turkey mobilized and held manoeuvres on the Syrian border. On 10 September, Moscow denounced Western provocation against Syria and threatened military action against Turkey. On 19 September Dulles stated that Turkey 'now faces growing military danger from the growing build-up of Soviet arms in Syria'.[4] On 9 October, Khrushchev warned the U.S.A.: 'If war breaks out we are near Turkey and you are not. When the guns begin to fire, the rockets can begin flying and then it will be too late to think about it.'[5] Dulles answered in a similar vein but the crisis faded away at the end of October when each side was reassured about the other's intentions with regard to Syria. The crisis increased the U.S.S.R.'s standing in the Middle East for she could claim that she had successfully defended Syria and her friendship now became sought after by those states which wished to free themselves of dependence on the West.

The Middle East nearly boiled over again in July 1958 when, following a successful revolution against the pro-Western regime in Iraq, Anglo–American forces intervened to prop up the governments of Jordan and Lebanon and in so doing alarmed Syria and the U.S.S.R. Both sides, then, were prepared to intervene in the region but the Middle East states wanted no part in the Cold War. At the U.N. on 29 August, the Arab League states and Israel voted unanimously to keep the Cold War out of the region and asked the U.N. to arrange the withdrawal of foreign troops. Dramatic superpower involvement in the area subsided after 1959, thus allowing the Arab–Israeli dispute to re-emerge as the main problem.

In the 1960s Western dependence upon Middle East oil, and

therefore upon peace in the area, grew. American cultural, commercial and military investments were high: there were American universities in Lebanon and Egypt, U.S. oil companies operated in the Persian Gulf, arms were sent to Iran, Saudi Arabia, Jordan, Lebanon and Israel, and the U.S. navy was present in the eastern Mediterranean and the Persian Gulf. Nevertheless, the American Congress and people tended to be pro-Israeli. As the U.S. stake in the region grew, so too did the U.S.S.R.'s. Moscow gave aid to Egypt, Syria and Iraq but came up against the major problem that her ideology was inapplicable to the underdeveloped Middle East states and her atheism was unwelcome. The traditionalist Arab monarchies of Jordan and Saudi Arabia feared that an extension of Soviet influence could threaten their thrones. Egypt accepted Soviet aid by default as she could not obtain from the West the offensive weapons she needed, but Nasser, the Egyptian President, was always wary of Soviet motives and the Egyptian Communist Party was banned.

The links with the U.S.S.R. failed to produce the Middle East settlement that the Arabs wanted, so in 1967 Egypt and Syria moved to break the deadlock by threatening war on Israel. The ensuing conflict in June 1967 closed the Suez Canal, increased Israel's land area and humiliated the Arabs. It also demonstrated the inability of the U.S.A. and U.S.S.R. to control their respective client states whose local wars threatened, by virtue of super-power investment of military equipment and prestige in the area, to escalate into the Third World War. It is a measure of the inherent danger of the Middle East situation that the super-powers used the 'hot-line' for the first time during the June war.

In November 1967, the U.N. accepted the British-inspired Resolution 242 which called for: an end to the fighting; Israeli withdrawal from the occupied territories; recognition of the territorial integrity of all states; freedom of navigation in international waters; settlement of the refugee problem; demilitarized zones on the frontiers; and a U.N. mission to negotiate a settlement. Neither side would accept the Resolution *in toto*; border incidents continued and an arms race began. After 1967, the U.S.A. emerged as Israel's chief arms supplier and guarantor but the war was a set-back for the U.S.S.R., for the weaponry she had supplied had failed the Arabs, and her friendship and help had not prevented the humiliating defeats and losses of territory. With her value as an ally in doubt, Moscow lost little time in replacing Egyptian and Syrian losses and in mounting a diplomatic and propaganda campaign against Israel.

Intermittent fighting along the canal continued in 1969 and 1970, prompting the U.S.S.R. to send S.A.M.s and between 15,000 to 20,000 'technicians' to Egypt. In return, the Soviets were given base facilities in Alexandria and the use of airfields from which the Russians could monitor N.A.T.O.'s presence in the Mediterranean. This increased Soviet presence worried the U.S. and possibly stimulated a peace drive by the Secretary of State, William Rogers. The Rogers Plan did produce a ceasefire but brought peace no nearer. Moreover, it resulted from super-power agreement and was in their interests and not those of the Arabs to whom a ceasefire meant the acceptance of their losses of 1967. The Rogers initiatives foundered on the mutual hostility of states who were all 'in the right'.

Both super-powers were prepared to damage relations with their clients to bring about a settlement in the early 1970s. In September 1970, the U.S.S.R. tried to limit Syrian intervention in the Jordanian civil war, and the U.S.A. tried to force concessions out of Israel by withholding deliveries of Phantoms. The U.S.A. accepted that the large Soviet presence in Egypt was, paradoxically, a stabilizing influence as it lessened Egypt's control over her own armed forces. Despite their joint efforts to reach a solution, the super-powers could not force what they agreed upon their *protégés*, and on 6 October 1973, the Arabs broke the deadlock again by attacking Israel. Super-power mediation and co-operation had failed but the failure was greater on the part of the U.S.S.R.

On 28 March 1971, Nasser's successor, President Sadat, signed a fifteen-year treaty of friendship with the U.S.S.R. hoping thereby to obtain the offensive weapons he needed. This was the watershed of Soviet influence in Egypt for, on 18 July 1972, Sadat's gambit having failed, he ordered almost all the Soviet advisers to leave Egypt. The resultant break in Soviet–Egyptian relations was patched up two months later, but Sadat had regained control over his own forces and foreign policy. Such was Moscow's involvement in the Middle East that she had to accept humiliation at the hands of Sadat and now had to supply battlefield weapons on Egypt's own terms.

When the war broke out, the U.S.S.R. did try, unsuccessfully, to press Sadat to accept a ceasefire, but there was little the super-powers could do at the beginning as they had both been taken by surprise. They mounted massive airlifts of arms supplies to their

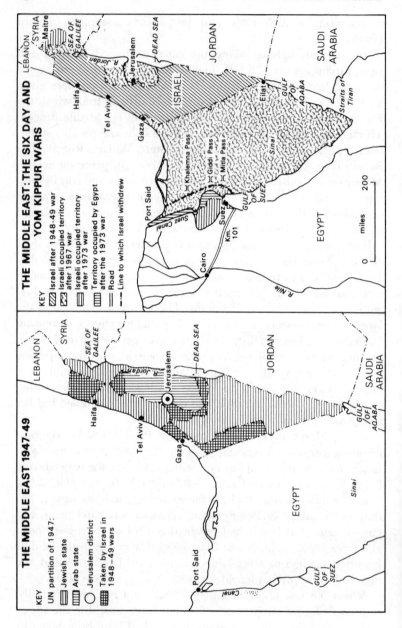

THE MIDDLE EAST: THE SIX DAY AND YOM KIPPUR WARS

KEY
Israel after 1948-49 war
Israeli occupied territory after 1967 war
Israeli occupied territory after 1973 war
Territory occupied by Egypt after the 1973 war
Road
Line to which Israel withdrew

THE MIDDLE EAST 1947-49

KEY
UN partition of 1947:
Jewish state
Arab state
Jerusalem district
Taken by Israel in 1948-49 wars

clients for although they did not want war, they could not accept defeat. As an Arab defeat approached, after Israeli forces crossed to the west bank of the Canal on 16 October, Soviet actions began to reflect their urgent need for an immediate ceasefire, and their anxiety for Egypt and Syria. The super-powers pushed a ceasefire agreement through the U.N. but as the combatants ignored it, Moscow proposed that super-power forces separate the belligerents. When the U.S.A. rejected this, the Russians appeared to prepare to send troops on their own, and on 25 October President Nixon ordered a world-wide nuclear alert of American forces. The threat was enough to produce a U.N. Security Council agreement that neither super-power would be represented in a U.N. peace-keeping force. The crisis was over but Nixon's actions warned the world that war in the Middle East actually did threaten world peace.

After the war, Egypt turned to America, not the U.S.S.R., for help towards a peace. The U.S. arranged the Israeli withdrawal from the Canal, and the Geneva peace talks. Soviet-Egyptian relations did not improve but both super-powers remained intimately involved in the Middle East and the military stalemate continued. The oil weapon has extended the impact of the Middle East conflict to much of the world (see Chapter 19) and the fact that Israel has gone nuclear and Egypt may follow, could extend it even further . . .[6]

# Eighteen

# MILITARY *DÉTENTE*

In October 1974 the Secretary General of the Pugwash Conference on Science and World Affairs stated: 'Continued development and testing of nuclear weapons have produced odds of about 3:1 on a nuclear device being used in conflict before 1984.' He suggested, moreover, that the chances of a nuclear war occurring in the remaining years of this century were even worse.[1] Ex-Premier Khrushchev was similarly pessimistic in his memoirs: 'But we've now reached the point where some people are talking about a Third World War. You can't brush such a suggestion aside by saying, "No, that's impossible now that there are nuclear weapons." World War III is possible. There are more than enough crazy people around who would like to start one.'[2]

This fear of a major war exists in spite of the spate of military agreements which began at the end of the 1960s and include the 1967 Outer Space Treaty (which banned the placing of nuclear weapons in outer space or earth orbit); the 1968 Nuclear Non-Proliferation Treaty (by which during 1968 alone the U.S., U.K., U.S.S.R. and eighty-three other countries agreed not to exchange military nuclear knowledge or hardware); the 1971 Seabed Pact (a product of the twenty-five-nation Geneva Disarmament Conference, which banned the emplacement of nuclear weapons on the seabed beyond a country's twelve-mile limit); the Biological Warfare Treaty of 1972 (which banned the development, production and stockpiling of biological weapons and their toxins); and the Strategic Arms Limitation Talks (S.A.L.T.) agreement of 1972. During 1974, the preliminary pattern of a S.A.L.T. 2 agreement was formulated, and progress occurred on a Chemical Warfare Treaty with the U.S. Senate agreeing in December to the principle of a ban on chemical weapons, including the use in war of tear gas and herbicides.

The U.S. entered the 1970s facing major changes in the nuclear balance (see Table 1). With these figures in mind, President Nixon

Table 1. The Nuclear Balance, 1964–74

| | | 1964 | 1966 | 1968 | 1970 | 1972 | 1974 |
|---|---|---|---|---|---|---|---|
| U.S.A.: | I.C.B.M.* | 834 | 904 | 1054 | 1054 | 1054 | 1054 |
| | S.L.B.M. | 416 | 592 | 656 | 656 | 656 | 656 |
| | L.R. bombers | 630 | 630 | 545 | 550 | 455 | 437 |
| U.S.S.R.: | I.C.B.M. | 200 | 300 | 800 | 1300 | 1527 | 1575 |
| | S.L.B.M. | 120 | 125 | 130 | 280 | 560 | 720 |
| | I.C. bombers | 190 | 200 | 150 | 150 | 140 | 140 |

*Note:* * An I.C.B.M. has a range of 4,000 miles plus; an I.R.B.M. about 1,500 to 4,000 miles; an M.R.B.M. 500–1,500 miles.

had by 1971 decided on a new nuclear doctrine of 'strategic sufficiency' to replace the 'assured destruction' doctrine of the 1960s. Using the new doctrine, U.S. forces were to be capable of retaliating against the Soviets even after an all-out Soviet surprise attack, and they were to be capable of offering the President a 'flexible range of strategic options' to meet all war threats. The U.S. therefore worked on a whole array of weapons: A.B.M.s, M.I.R.V.s, A.L.B.M.s, Trident submarines, B-1 bombers, Cruise Missiles, and methods of further hardening Minuteman 3 underground silos. In February 1970, Nixon asked in a policy document: 'Should a President in the event of a nuclear attack, be left with the single option of ordering the mass destruction of enemy civilians, in the face of the certainty that it would be followed by the mass slaughter of Americans?'[4] In January 1974 the 'mutually assured destruction' concept (best known by its apposite acronym MAD) was further altered. Schlesinger, the Secretary of Defence, stated that the 'eye for an eye' policy was to be partially replaced by the more complex 'tooth for a tooth' policy – that is, more American missiles than previously would be targeted on Soviet missile sites and military targets, rather than on 'soft' civilian targets. This apparently pleasing alteration does mean, however, that missile accuracy has improved and it could produce a greater risk of war: it would take a special type of mind and a special crisis to justify launching a fleet of I.C.B.M.s at Moscow or Leningrad. To give the order to launch against enemy missile batteries or bomber bases is less taxing on the mind and the situation. Moreover, if missiles do become so accurate as to be able to hit the enemy's missile silos, the temptation to launch, in a major crisis, a pre-emptive strike against the enemy's forces may be increased. In nuclear terminology, the possibility that one or both super-powers could, with a successful first strike, disarm the other, is necessarily a highly destabilizing element in the balance of terror.

Negotiations on arms limitations were to have begun in 1968, but the events in Czechoslovakia postponed the start until November 1969. The 'interim agreement' of May 1972 placed a five-year 'freeze' on I.C.B.M.s with 1,618 Soviet missiles to 1,054 American; on S.L.B.M.s with 950 Soviet ones (in 62 submarines) and 710 American (in 44 submarines); and on A.B.M.s with 100 maximum in two sites for each side. On 31 May 1972, *Pravda* welcomed the agreements in the following terms:

> [S.A.L.T.] talks show convincingly that, despite the difference in the social systems of the Soviet Union and the United States of America, despite distinctions in ideology, despite the well-known different and even opposite approach to some problems of world politics, an improvement of relations between the U.S.S.R. and U.S.A. in the interests of both the nations and the cause of promoting peace and international security, is quite possible ... The [arms] agreements signed must promote the checking of the arms drive which creates the threat of a rocket-nuclear conflict, and diverts vast means from creative objectives. These agreements are founded on the recognition of the principle of the sides' equal security and give no unilateral military advantage to either.

Nixon, however, to explain the higher Soviet figures to Congress, stated that the freeze on the Soviet heavy missiles such as the SS9 (which the Soviets were building at speed) was good for the U.S. Moreover, the agreement ignored bombers (in which the Americans have a superiority) and American tactical missiles in Europe, as well as the British and French nuclear forces. Nixon also reminded Congress that, with the American superior technology in M.I.R.V.s 'we have a 2 : 1 lead in numbers of missiles'.[5] The President stated that a 'decision of this magnitude could only have been taken by two countries which had chosen to place their relations on a new foundation of restraint, co-operation and steadily growing confidence',[6] but nevertheless reminded Congress that '*Détente* is not the same as lasting peace ... the world will hold perils for as far ahead as we can see'.[7] He emphasized that, until *détente* became far more lasting, there was no room for further unilateral military cuts in total conventional forces or forward deployment. In June 1973 the U.S. had one-third fewer combat ships than in June 1964, thirty-seven fewer aircraft squadrons and one-third fewer army divisions. Conventional forces are expensive – in 1973 they cost three times more than the strategic forces – but Nixon stressed the need to maintain the ability to act anywhere in the world with non-nuclear forces. He ended by stating: 'I am determined that our military power will remain second to none.'[8]

However, 1973 saw more military *détente*, with the agreement to reduce the A.B.M. ceiling, the ban from 1976 onwards on underground nuclear tests greater than 150 kiloton, and the joint Nixon–Brezhnev announcement that both America and the Soviet Union were pledged to 'act in such a manner as to prevent the development of situations capable of causing a dangerous exacerbation of relations, as to avoid military confrontations, and as to exclude the outbreak of nuclear war between them and between either of the parties and other countries.'

*Détente* continued under President Ford, who inherited Nixon's S.A.L.T. 2 negotiations. 'In the nuclear area, there is no rational alternative to accords of mutual restraint between the United States and the Soviet Union, two nations which have the power to destroy mankind.'[9] Agreement in principle on S.A.L.T. 2 was subsequently reached in November 1974, at a Ford–Brezhnev Summit in Vladivostok, which the U.S. Secretary of State, Dr. Kissinger, argued would mean 'that a cap has been put on the arms race for a period of ten years'.[10] The technical details of S.A.L.T. 2 were to be completed at Geneva during the spring of 1976. When and if they are signed S.A.L.T. 3 negotiations will probably begin (since the S.A.L.T. 2 agreement expires in 1982). In Ford's explanation to Congress in December 1974, he suggested that S.A.L.T. 2 would place a ceiling of 2,400 on the total number of missile launchers, including bombers, for each side: within that limit, 1,320 launchers could be fitted with M.I.R.V.s.[11]

It remains to be seen whether military *détente*, at least in strategic nuclear weapons, will lead only to a renewed arms race based on quality rather than on quantity. President Ford requested a defence budget for 1975–6 of $96 billion (an increase of $11 billion over 1974–5). Military *détente* has not therefore reduced super-power arms expenditure.

# Nineteen

# POLITICAL *DÉTENTE* AND THE MULTIPOLAR WORLD

The Parisian newspaper *Le Figaro* stated on 4 February 1972:

> Mr. Nixon believes . . . that the United States from now on will negotiate with their enemies – hence his visits to Peking and Moscow – and that they expect their friends in Europe and Asia to stand on their own feet. There is no doubt that the present stage of international relations marks the end of one period and the beginning of another. The military superiority of the United States over the Soviet Union no longer exists.

Table 2. The World Economic Balance[1] (G.N.P. in \$U.S. billion)

| *Year* | *U.S.A.* | *Japan* | *W. Germany* | *France* | *U.K.* | *U.S.S.R.* |
|---|---|---|---|---|---|---|
| 1952 | 350 | 16 | 32 | 29 | 44 | 113 |
| 1960 | 511 | 39 | 71 | 60 | 72 | 201 |
| 1966 | 748 | 102 | 123 | 108 | 107 | 288 |
| 1972 | 1,152 | 317 | 229 | 224 | 128 | 439 |

President Nixon gave changes in the world economic balance (see Table 2) as one of his reasons for the new U.S. foreign policy in his Foreign Policy Report to Congress of February 1972:

1. The recovery of economic strength and political vitality by Western Europe and Japan, with the inexorable result that both their role and ours in the world must be adjusted to reflect their regained vigour and self-assurance.
2. The increasing self-reliance of the states created by the dissolution of the colonial empires, and the growth of both their ability and determination to see to their own security and well-being.
3. The breakdown in the unity of the Communist Bloc . . . and a higher priority in at least some Communist countries to the pursuit of national interests rather than their subordination to the requirements of world revolution.
4. The end of an indisputable U.S. superiority in strategic strength, and its replacement by a strategic balance in which the U.S. and the Soviet nuclear forces are comparable.
5. The growth among the American people of the conviction that the time

had come for other nations to share a greater portion of the burden of world leadership; and its corollary that the assured continuity of our long-term involvement required a responsible but more restrained American role.

In an interview with *Time* magazine on 3 January 1972, the President spoke of the development of a new, multipolar world: 'I think it will be a safer world and a better world if we have a strong, healthy U.S., Europe, Soviet Union, China, Japan, each balancing the other, not playing one against the other.'

There are, of course, doubts as to what constituted a bipolar (American–Soviet dominated) world. Between 1945 and 1956, was the U.S. representation of the West offset by the need for her allies' resources and bases? Even when the value of those bases was lessened by I.C.B.M.s, was it bipolar when the E.E.C. (and more particularly, France) questioned U.S. predominance? Was it still bipolar when China – not to mention Yugoslavia, Albania and, to some extent, Rumania – rejected Soviet dominance after 1963? But if one does accept that the two super-powers dominated the world between 1945 and 1970, do they still not do so? Or was Kissinger perhaps more accurate when he talked of 'political multipolarity with military bipolarity', rather than Nixon's 'pentagonal balance of power'?

If the definition of a super-power is one that not only thinks in global terms but has the capacity to exert influence through formidable forces in or near all continents, then there are in fact still two super-powers. By that definition, China is only a medium power with a G.N.P. roughly comparable to that of Italy; her role outside the Far East is only symbolic (apart from her power as a member of the U.N. Security Council). She is, of course, no longer the 'sick man of Asia' and her size is a constant source of fascination to the outside world, particularly since her regime and numbers appear to be keeping the Soviet Union 'off balance'. However, although the 1970s saw much international upheaval in Asia and Africa, China's significance in global power politics remained limited.

Western Europe is economically powerful (see Table 3) and has some influence in Africa and the Middle East, but only negligible links with the Far East. The E.E.C. is the world's largest economic trading bloc, so its political and economic importance have enormous potential, but as M. Claude Cheysson of the European Commission reminded Western Europe, it is dependent on the developing world for more than just oil. Europe relies on external imports for

95 per cent of its energy needs; 65 per cent of its copper; 57 per cent of its bauxites; 99 per cent of its phosphates; virtually all its cobalt; 86 per cent of its tin ore; all of its manganese; 95 per cent of its tungsten; 92 per cent of its coffee and 100 per cent of its cocoa. The E.E.C. also imports 28 per cent of its food requirements.[2]

Table 3. The Economic Power of the E.E.C., 1973

|  | E.E.C. | U.S.A. | U.S.S.R. | Japan |
|---|---|---|---|---|
| Population '000s, mid-1973 | 256,621 | 210,400 | 247,459* | 108,350 |
| Gross National Product, £ billions, 1973 | 374·17 | 462·75 | 239·67* | 140·625 |
| Imports (external trade only) £ million, 1973 (exchange rate as at 20.8.74: $2·32 = £1) | 93,837·5 | 29,793·5 | 6,917·2* | 16,514·2 |
| Exports (external trade only) £ million, 1972 (exchange rate as at 20.8.74) | 90,712·5 | 307,402·6 | 6,621·6* | 15,918·1 |
| Average grain production, '000 tons, 1970–2 | 97,358 | 213,732 | 169,937 | 979 |
| Steel production, '000 tons, 1972 | 139,109 | 123,770 | 126,000 | 96,900 |
| Electric energy consumption, g.w.h., 1972 | 841,698 | 1,684,977 | 724,665 | 385,068 |

*Source:* C.E.W.C. February 1975 Broadsheet on Britain and the European Community.

*Note:* * 1972 figures.

Japan's G.N.P. is two and a half times that of China and she is the world's third largest industrial power. However, she imports 80 per cent of her oil from the Persian Gulf, can be isolated by the Soviet Far East Fleet, and generally maintains a low political profile. Admittedly, she has machinery and capital while China has the raw materials, but any thought of a major increase in Sino–Japanese trade following the Tanaka visit to Peking in July 1972 ignored the problems of the Japanese investments in Taiwan and the attraction of Soviet Siberian natural gas and oil, as well as China's pursuit of self-sufficiency. Nevertheless, China might be prepared to supply Japan with more raw materials if the alternative appeared to be increased Japanese dependence on the Soviet Union. However, it is self-evident that of all the 'Great Powers', Japan is the least self-sufficient in raw materials and the most dependent on foreign trade.

It could be argued that President Nixon's 'pentagonal' was in fact a 'hexagonal' world. With 139 U.N. members in 1975, about 90 of whom were non-aligned, the power of the Third World could not be disregarded. The Western Powers were particularly shocked in 1974 by U.N. support for national liberation wars, its temporary (and unconstitutional) expulsion of South Africa and the welcome it accorded to Yassir Arafat of the P.L.O. The new situation was summarized by a Chinese delegate at the end of 1974: 'Why do you Westerners talk about the so-called "tyranny of the majority"? It is only right that the majority should prevail here. By making this possible Mr. Bouteflika [the Algerian President of the U.N. in 1974] is not being partisan – he is merely being democratic.'[3] If the actions of the neutrals in the U.N. could be politically embarrassing to the West (and with China in the Security Council, the Soviet Union did not always escape unscathed from the accusations of 'colonialism'), the actions of a part of the Third World could be economically devastating on the world's energy stage. The O.P.E.C. group have been the first to translate raw material assets into economic and political muscle; other producer cartels could follow. But massive price increases (four-fold in the instance of oil between 1973 and 1975) are blunt and potentially double-edged instruments: they do not distinguish between rich and poor buyers, and they could endanger the financial solvency of the customer. The Arab oil states (especially the biggest producer, Saudi Arabia) are also susceptible to military pressure by the West, and, in the last analysis, the two powers most able to be self-sufficient and therefore most capable of resisting raw material boycotts are the U.S.A. and the U.S.S.R. America is, in fact, the greatest food and raw material producing nation, while the U.S.S.R. has the capacity to become so. From the multipolar world, we are thus led back to the enormous importance of the relationship between America and the Soviet Union – super-power *détente*.

During his visit to the U.S.A. in June 1974, Brezhnev stated; 'I am not dangerous.'[4] There is no single word for *détente* in Russian, just as there is not in English. Russians use the clumsy phrase 'the relaxation of international tension'. But *détente* had become the prerequisite for a whole host of Soviet policy goals.

It was a way of safeguarding control over defence spending and eventually, perhaps, of achieving some reduction. Over the past fifteen years, estimated Soviet defence costs rose less quickly than the country's G.N.P., but the real burden of the Soviet Union's defence is greater than the equivalent in the United States. Government-subsidized research in electronics and other advanced fields of weapons-related research has less chance of industrial application in the less sophisticated economy of the U.S.S.R. Like Western countries, the Soviet Union also wants to cut the manpower in uniform because of the country's continuing labour shortage. If Sino–Soviet tension continues, this may not be possible, in which case the Soviets would like to be able to transfer troops from a tranquil Europe to the Soviet Far East. *Détente* was also seen in Moscow as vital if the West was to be persuaded to make long-term investments in the Soviet Union. With *détente*, the Russians hoped to have the political and ideological *status quo* in Eastern Europe legitimized. They also wanted to head off efforts towards the defence integration of Western Europe, which they assumed would eventually be dominated by West Germany, the area's richest country.

The Soviet leadership has explained away its increased interest in *détente* to its own people and to the East Europeans by claiming that, firstly, the balance of power is said to have shifted towards socialism as a result of the end of the war in Vietnam, the recognition of East Germany, the strengthening of Cuba's international position and the whole system of pacts concluded between socialist and capitalist states. Secondly, the danger of nuclear world war has receded, thanks to the 1973 U.S.–Soviet pact on its prevention. Thirdly, international tension has relaxed as a result of the whole round of Summit meetings and foreign visits made not only by Mr. Brezhnev, but also by other Eastern European leaders. Finally, the idea of peaceful coexistence between states of different social systems is said to have been universally recognized.

The Russians have also expressed a new confidence about the economic and social crisis in the West. The collapse of the system has, of course, frequently been prophesied (Khrushchev once explained 'coexistence' by saying that sometimes in the West a healthy young man will marry an old, rich woman; they will live peacefully together while she sinks into decrepitude and dies). In the late 1970s the capitalist world was seen as suffering from the energy crisis, unprecedented inflation, rising unemployment, falling production in some countries and a profound crisis in the international monetary system. In this situation, Moscow wanted *détente* as a way of neutralizing the anti-Soviet card which, it complained, Western governments always played in crises. This argument lost some of its force, since Soviet trade had increased with the West to such an extent that she was beginning to be affected by the economic problems of the West. Moreover, *détente* has enabled the Soviet Union to compensate for its industrial and agricultural short-comings by importing high technology and food from the West. (In 1972 the U.S.S.R. bought – at subsidized prices! – 20 per cent of the total U.S. grain crop for that year.)

Both the U.S. and the Soviet Union would like to utilize more of their resources for domestic needs. Since the time of Khrushchev, the Soviet leadership has been under mounting pressure to satisfy the rising expectation for consumer goods of the Soviet people – and the Soviet economy is insufficiently advanced to provide 'guns and butter' on the required scale. It was no less obvious to the American leadership, which began 1975 with 7½ million unemployed (8·2 per cent of the labour force, and the highest since 1941), that there were domestic, economic and social imperatives which it was becoming increasingly difficult to ignore. Money spent on armaments in ever-enlarging amounts drained the domestic vitality of both powers. Kissinger spelt out the need for economy in September 1973:[5]

And when at the end of World War II we did conduct foreign policy on a global scale, the proportions between our resources and those of the rest of the world were so great, we could overwhelm every problem and we could always substitute resources for thought. But now we are in a situation where we have to conduct foreign policy the way many other nations have had to conduct it throughout their history.

In any event, President Nixon stated in May 1973: 'Each of us had the capacity to destroy mankind; this and the global interests of both sides, created a certain common outlook, a kind of interdependence for survival.'[6]

Bilateral co-operative ventures included the successful 1975 docking of Apollo and Soyuz spacecraft; joint work on environmental pollution; joint cancer and heart research; trade agreements which anticipated a total exchange of goods worth over $1·5 billion between 1973 and 1976; agreements on joint credit facilities; low sea freight rates; access to each other's ports; and trade complexes in each other's capitals. All stem from the talks of 1972. The United States has the capital and the high technology; the U.S.S.R. has the consumer market and vast untapped resources. Their economies could become complementary to the advantage of both. In 1973,

President Nixon argued that *détente* might be self-generating if '. . . an ever-widening circle of people in various professions and government bureaus in both countries . . . develop a fabric of relationships supplementing those at the higher levels of political leadership.'[7] However, it is necessary to point out that the Soviet Government has always restricted personal contacts, because such an exposure to Western ideas involved the risk of 'contamination' of the Soviet people.

According to the Chinese, of course, Soviet–American *détente* was largely a fiction: 'under the signboard of "European collective security talks" the Soviet Union is trying hard to consolidate its hegemony in Eastern Europe, extend its sphere of influence to Western Europe and elbow out U.S. influence there.'[8] Indeed, Premier Chou En-lai – reporting to the Chinese National People's Congress in January 1975 – declared 'There is no *détente*, let alone lasting peace in this world; . . . [the U.S. and the Soviet Union] . . . are the biggest international oppressors and exploiters today . . . [and] . . . their fierce competition is bound to lead the world to war some day.'[9]

In fact, January 1975 did witness a setback in *détente* with the Soviet rejection of the December 1974 Trade Agreement. The original concept had involved giving Russia access to unlimited American credit through the U.S. Export–Import Bank, and tariff-free entry to the American market for Soviet exports. Russia in turn would pay back part of the $11,000 million Lend–Lease debt, and allow American companies to set up offices in the Soviet Union. The Russians recanted on their original acceptance of this deal for two apparent reasons. Firstly, Senator Jackson (at one time a contender for the 1976 Presidential elections) secured the passage through Congress of an amendment to the Trade Bill which required Soviet easing of Jewish emigration and their promise of a certain number of exit permits each year. This amendment, which Kissinger nearly succeeded in persuading the Soviets to accept, was given far too much publicity, and if the Soviets had accepted under those conditions, they would have been seen to have given in to U.S. pressure on a question of Soviet internal policy. Secondly, the U.S. Congress decided in December 1974 to place a $300 million credit maximum (over four years) on the Export–Import Bank's allocation to Russia. The deal was thus less attractive: Russia possibly decided that French, German, Japanese and British credits provided an alternative, and in any event the general increase in raw material prices during 1974 meant that Soviet export earnings were greater and the Russians were in less need of credit. Under those circumstances, perhaps it was time to remind the Americans that tough methods and the use of blackmail in their relations with Russia would be counter-productive (Kissinger was always aware of this but was obviously unable to persuade Jackson). Furthermore, the introduction of an element of unease into *détente* might persuade the Americans to return to courtship methods. On this point, it is interesting to note that whereas the Soviet press remained noticeably quiescent in regard to Watergate and the C.I.A. 'destabilizing' Allende's Chile in 1973, it did condemn Kissinger's statement of December 1974 on the possible use of force by America against the Middle East oil producers in the event of their attempting to 'strangle' the West by imposing an oil boycott.

Kissinger and the Americans spent January 1975 worrying that either the Soviet Communist Party's First Secretary, Mr. Brezhnev, was angry at America's failure to deliver the goods on the trade deal, or that the sixty-eight year-old Brezhnev was ill and losing his grip on the Kremlin. When Brezhnev replaced Khrushchev, there was a temporary hardening of Soviet attitudes but, although Western opinion often assumed that Soviet *détente* was Brezhnev's creation and that it could suffer at the hands of his successors, it is worth noting that the reverse happened after the death of Mao in China.

Certainly there built up in Russia and America, in East and West, important pressure groups committed to *détente* and certainly as the web of East–West contacts grew and the volume of trade increased, the economic consequences of an end of *détente* could have become very serious for the eastern bloc especially. But the American argument that increasing Soviet trade with the West made war less likely was always a dubious one; after all, in early 1914 Britain and Germany were each other's most important trading partners. Despite the recognized benefits of *détente*, the political and socio-economic characteristics of the U.S.A. and U.S.S.R. did not change, and there remained hardliners in the Kremlin and the Pentagon who retained deep suspicions of arms agreements in particular and of *détente* in general.

# Twenty

# BEYOND *DÉTENTE* — 1975 *on*

By the time Gerald Ford and his Secretary of State Kissinger left office in January 1977, *détente* had already failed to live up to the hopes engendered by Nixon's promise of 'a new era of peace'. Yet, in one area at least, *détente* had made apparently tangible progress.

In August 1975, thirty-three European states (excluding Albania), the U.S.A. and Canada, signed the Final Act of the C.S.C.E. at Helsinki which had begun two years earlier. The treaty recognized the frontiers of Europe. West Germany renounced its claim to be the only legitimate German state. Europe finally had what amounted to a Second World War peace treaty and Moscow had won a formal recognition of the territorial *status quo*. In return, all countries agreed to give neighbours twenty-one days notice of military exercises near their borders and the West won Soviet and Eastern block acceptance of the 'basket three' provisions which guaranteed greater freedom of movement of people, ideas and the press. A section of the Final Act stipulated that 'The participating States will respect human rights and fundamental freedoms, including the freedom of thought, conscience, religion or belief for all without distinction as to race, sex, language or religion.' The Helsinki Agreement came closer than anything else to encapsulating what Western opinion – and some governments – thought *détente* was, but its effects in 'liberalizing' the Soviet regime were still-born.

Helsinki monitoring groups were set up in the U.S.S.R., the D.D.R., Poland and Czechoslovakia, but by the end of the decade the internal repression which had been a Soviet prerequisite for *détente* had gradually silenced almost all those who raised their voices in protest. In the winter of 1977–8, the Belgrade Review Conference of the C.S.C.E. achieved nothing and neither did its military parallel in Europe, the Vienna talks on M.B.F.R. which continued in a desultory fashion into the 1980s.

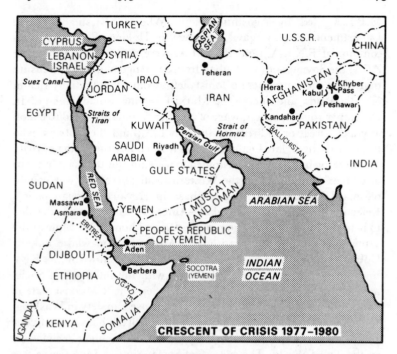

**CRESCENT OF CRISIS 1977–1980**

Neither could the Ford administration land a S.A.L.T. 2 agreement. In 1967, under President Johnson, the U.S. had ceased to expand the number of its missiles, and concentrated instead on qualitative improvements in nuclear weaponry. (Under Nixon, for example, multiple warheaded missiles – M.I.R.V.s – new long-range bombers like the B1, and cheap highly accurate Cruise missiles – updated successors to the German V1s of the 1940s – were developed). But by 1976 the Soviets had tested a M.I.R.V.ed missile, launched a new bomber, the 'Backfire', and deployed their first aircraft carrier, the *Kiev*. Although Soviet supremacy in battle tanks in central Europe and in numbers and 'throw-weight' (megatonnage) of I.C.B.M.s, was countered by American supremacy in numbers of warheads and accuracy of delivery systems, the U.S.A. began to wonder both whether its technological lead over Soviet armaments could be maintained, and how it could counter the expanding naval reach of the Soviet Union.

That reach was nowhere better exemplified than in the Soviet support of the Angolan communist liberation movement, the

M.P.L.A., led by Agosthino Neto. Whereas Kissinger's State Department secretly gave funding to Holden Roberto's non-communist F.N.L.A., and the C.I.A. were active in neighbouring Zaire, the Soviets shipped Cuban troops to Angola in order to ensure that when the Portuguese colonists left a country potentially rich in oil, diamonds and metals, a Marxist regime would emerge. In December 1975 Congress, wary of another 'Vietnam', voted to cut off any aid, direct or indirect, to the F.N.L.A.; and the Cubans, who began arriving in late October, totalled 20,000 by the spring of 1976. Washington had grown accustomed to watching for the machinations of Cuban communists in the Western hemisphere, but was caught off-guard by this new African phase in Havana's foreign policy. Rejecting the possibility of Cuban–American *détente*, Castro decided to help the forces of liberation in the African 'homeland' while at the same time earning the gratitude of Moscow upon whose aid the Cuban economy was so dependent. Soviet 'adventurism', as Kissinger termed it, in Angola, combined with the influence of Soviet advisers in Somalia and in the newly independent Marxist state of Mozambique (formerly Portuguese), all caused anxiety in Washington. Moreover, the American Government still felt hamstrung by the public unease at the prospect of any further involvement in civil wars in the Third World. The success of Soviet aims in Indo-China was confirmed by the reunification of Vietnam in 1976, followed by a Moscow–Hanoi defence treaty signed in the autumn of 1978 – a treaty that doubtless caused as much, if not more, consternation in Peking as in Washington.

In January 1977, the Democrat Jimmy Carter took over the presidency of the U.S.A. and, with Secretary of State Cyrus Vance and National Security Adviser Zbigniew Brzezinski, he began a new chapter in foreign policy. In March, to his surprise, he succeeded in antagonizing the Russians by offering them a revised set of Vladivostok S.A.L.T. 2 accords with a reduction in I.C.B.M. and M.I.R.V.ed missile numbers. The package also proposed a reduction of the number of the new Soviet 'Euro-strategic' or European-range mobile SS20 missile, but suggested the deferment of any decision both on the Backfire bomber and on the Cruise missile. The Soviets were unprepared to rush into a remodelled S.A.L.T. 2 and were also resentful of Carter's stance on human rights issues in the U.S.S.R. – particularly his open support of Andrei Sakharov, Nobel Prize physicist and monitor of the Helsinki Agreement.

The new President, a devout Baptist, clearly hoped to raise the moral level of America's international dealings by establishing the fact that U.S. foreign relations with any state would be in part conditioned by that state's approach to basic rights for its citizens such as free elections, freedom of speech, assembly and movement, and the provision of a just and equitable legal system. Irrespective of the apparent surprise in Washington at hostile reactions from allies such as the Philippines, and at the difficulty of implementing these principles with key strategic allies such as Iran and South Korea, the Soviet reaction should at least have been predictable. Moscow regarded Carter's attempt to 'link' inter-state relations to the Soviet regime's treatment of its own citizens as gross interference in Soviet domestic affairs.

Moscow became increasingly anxious at the erratic tone of the decisions emanating from the Carter White House. In May 1977, Carter prevailed upon N.A.T.O. to raise defence expenditure by 3 per cent *per annum*. But he cancelled the B1 bomber programme the next month, and neither decision involved the kind of trade-off that Kissinger or Nixon would have attempted.

Moreover, in April 1978 Carter postponed deployment of a new weapon designed for the European battlefront – the Enhanced Radiation Weapon (ERW) or neutron bomb. This low heat and blast, but high short-range neutron radiation weapon, was particularly designed to deal with large armoured formations or other military targets in the kind of heavily-populated, built-up battlefield likely to be found in West Germany, where it would be desirable to limit collateral damage to civilian targets. By the time the British and West German Governments had agreed to the deployment of this weapon, the Soviets had mounted an orchestrated campaign of denunciation based on the thesis that the ERW destroyed people but left property intact and was thus the ultimate 'capitalist' weapon. Carter's decision not to go ahead with the ERW was taken without thorough consultation with America's allies – particularly with West Germany which, after being persuaded by Secretary Vance to give public support to the controversial weapon, was displeased by Carter's unilateral decision to defer its deployment.

It must be presumed that Carter's moves were designed to smooth the way towards a S.A.L.T. 2 agreement which the Soviets still desired, partly as a result of their fears concerning the American Cruise missile, and partly because of Pentagon research on a new generation of mobile I.B.C.M.s – the MX series – which were to be mounted on underground rail tracks. Yet, as S.A.L.T. negotiations continued, America became anxious about what appeared to be a fresh phase of expansionism in Soviet foreign policy.

The Cubans in Angola were implicated in rebel action in the neighbouring state of Zaire in 1978. Meanwhile, to the south of Angola, Namibia was occupied by South Africa and was the scene of left-wing guerrilla activity organized by S.W.A.P.O. (the South-West African People's Organization). To the north, the Soviets and Cubans became involved in Ethiopia which politically had swung to the left after the fall of Emperor Haile Selassie in 1974. In 1978 Cuban soldiers helped the Ethiopian Government in a war with neighbour-ing Somalia (which had armed native Somali insurgents in Ethiopia's Ogaden province); the Cubans then embarked upon helping Addis Ababa against Eritrean insurgents on the Red Sea coast.

On the other side of the Red Sea was the Marxist state of the People's Republic of the Yemen (formerly British Aden). The pres-ence of Russian warships (which on occasion actually shelled Eritrean positions) in a key region for sea-borne trade was disconcerting to the West. (The warships were on the Red Sea–Suez Canal trade route and near the Persian Gulf–African coastline route of giant oil tankers bound for Europe via the Cape.) The Soviet fleet in 1980 possessed naval facilities at Massawa in Ethiopia as well as in Aden and on the Yemeni island of Socotra. Further, revolutionary Yemen started in late 1979 to menace non-communist North Yemen about whose security the Saudi Arabians were deeply concerned. Thus, by 1978 America had become sensitized to the strategic dangers in the Horn of Africa. With Washington's attention so focused, a Marxist *coup* took place in Afghanistan in April 1978 and created a growing unease in Washington. Messages of 'thus far and no further' began to emerge from the White House in 1978, for example, in relation to the terri-torial integrity of Somalia. During the 1976 elections, Carter had promised to withdraw the 40,000 or so American troops from South Korea but by 1978 he no longer deemed this a wise move. Back in the early 1960s, John F. Kennedy had quipped about Khrushchev's attitude: 'what's mine is mine and what's yours is negotiable'. With the Russians heavily committed in Ethiopia and Angola, with their East German proxies in South Yemen, and with their Cuban proxies involved in eleven African countries, Carter came to accept Kennedy's analysis.

After the Yom Kippur War America did succeed in freezing the Soviets out of involvement in Egyptian–Israeli negotiations. At the Camp David summit in September 1978, Sadat of Egypt and Begin of Israel agreed to a peace treaty which was to return most of the Sinai peninsula to Egypt by 1980 and the remainder by 1982. In February 1980 the two countries formally exchanged ambassadors though the contentious problems of Israeli settlements in the occupied territories, and autonomy for the Palestinians in Gaza and in the occupied West Bank, remained to be settled.

A further success for Carter occurred when, in January 1979, the U.S. formally recognized the People's Republic of China and exchanged ambassadors. Chairman Hua Kuo-feng and Deng Xiaoping (the successors to Mao Tse-tung who had died in September 1976) continued Mao's policy of hostility to what were considered to be the expansionist or 'hegemonist' policies of Soviet imperialism and its surrogate forces. In February 1979 China attacked Moscow's ally Vietnam – partly because in December 1978 Vietnam had overthrown China's protégé, Pol Pot's Khmer Rouge regime in Kampuchea (Cambodia), and partly because of worsening relations caused by border disputes and the attitude of Hanoi to ethnic Chinese within Vietnam. Between 1975 and the end of 1979, approximately 900,000 refugees left Vietnam and Kampuchea. China took 250,000 ethnic Chinese from Vietnam while the U.S. accepted over 210,000 Vietnamese 'boat people' (refugees from Indo-China who fled from the area by boat via the South China Sea).[1] Other 'boat people' arrived in Malaya, Indonesia, Hong Kong and even Australia, and some were relocated in Western Europe. Stories of the horrors committed by the Khmer Rouge in Kampuchea, combined with Vietnam's intervention there and the flight of so many Vietnamese into the open sea off South-East Asia, by which they risked death from drowning and piracy, confirmed – at least in part – American propaganda against Hanoi and the Khmer Rouge in the 1960s and early 1970s.

However, any satisfaction Washington might have experienced from witnessing communist disarray in Indo-China was offset by the developing crisis in South-West Asia – in Afghanistan and Iran.

The Shah of Iran had been a loyal ally of the U.S.A. for thirty-seven years, supported by presidents from Roosevelt onwards, and in 1953 the C.I.A. had organized a *coup* to re-instate him in power after a six-day exile. In 1972 Nixon had declared that the Shah would replace Britain as the 'policeman' of the Persian Gulf and had begun to supply sophisticated armaments to Iran. Although Iran supplied only 5 per cent of U.S. oil, she produced 6 million barrels a day in 1978 and was thus considered an important ally of the West within the O.P.E.C. bloc. But in 1978 Islamic fervour against the Shah's Western-oriented and dictatorial rule mounted and Washington found itself unable to help. Even if it had been prepared to risk defending a weakened dictator against massive popular discontent, neither the C.I.A. – emasculated by Congressional controls after the investigations by Senate committees in 1975 – nor the U.S. armed forces, which were incapable of rapid deployment of ground forces in the region, could have intervened effectively.

In January 1979 the Shah fled abroad and in October was eventually allowed to enter a New York hospital for treatment for cancer. Many Iranians were infuriated by Carter's humanitarian action – they considered it as a slight to their revolution and feared that it would be followed by the granting of full political asylum to a ruler they regarded as a tyrant and war criminal. They even believed – or purported to believe – that America might contemplate reinstating the Shah or his son if the C.I.A. and embassy 'spies' succeeded in their alleged task of subverting the new regime. In November 1979 the American embassy in Teheran and sixty hostages were seized by revolutionary students with the *post facto* support of the government of the Islamic mullah, Ayatollah Khomeini. Some hostages (blacks and women – the representatives of 'oppressed minorities' in America) were later released, but about forty-nine Americans were still imprisoned in April 1980 when an abortive American rescue attempt took place. The Iranians demanded the extradition of the Shah (who had been given asylum first in Panama and then in Egypt), the return of his overseas fortune and a U.N. investigation into the alleged tortures conducted by SAVAK, the Shah's secret police, during his rule. Although the Iranian Communist Party, the Tudeh, were not immediate beneficiaries of the Shah's overthrow, the emergence of a virulently Islamic, anti-American and unstable Iran inevitably weakened America's position in the Middle East. Moreover, Saudi Arabia's fears were compounded not only by what it saw as a string of defeats for its Western protector, but also by the upsurge of Shi'ite fundamentalism in the Moslem world – a temporary take-over of the Grand Mosque in Mecca by extremists in October 1979 heightened the tension felt in Riyadh. Some Saudis felt that their oil production – at 9 million barrels per day, the highest in O.P.E.C. – was sucking too much money into the desert kingdom, and that the pace of change this triggered might destabilize the autocratic rule of the house of Ibn-Saud.

There was another element which affected the balance between the super-powers. The abandonment by Moscow of Salvador Allende in Chile and President Siad Barre in Somalia had not called into question the U.S.S.R.'s commitment to her friends. But 1979 had seen America turn her back on two of her staunchest allies. By recognizing the People's Republic of China she cast Taiwan adrift and by not helping the Shah – irrespective of whether or not it was possible to help him – she was seen to bow to popular *force majeure* of the kind that unseated Somoza, the Nicaraguan dictator in July 1979, nearly unseated General Mobutu in Zaire and was a serious potential threat to a number of America's autocratic allies and clients in both hemispheres.

In September 1979 another mini-crisis damaged *détente* when Washington complained vehemently at the existence of what it described as a brigade of 3,000 Soviet combat troops in Cuba (as opposed to the 6,000 or so 'advisers' which it was prepared to tolerate). However, it soon became clear that U.S. intelligence services did not know how long the combat troops had been in Cuba, which threw doubts on the effectiveness of their surveillance and verification techniques in general – and, of course, satellite spy verification was a key element in any new S.A.L.T. 2 agreement. Though the storm blew over, it did so without any Soviet climb-down (and this in spite of the fact that Carter had in the early stages categorically stated that the removal of the brigade was essential). Soviet 'intransigence' was seized upon by the critics of the S.A.L.T. 2 accords in Congress and the passage of that treaty through its ratification process in the Senate was blocked.

The treaty placed a maximum limit of 2,250 launchers for each super-power (fewer than the 2,400 agreed at Vladivostok) as well as a maximum of 1,320 on all types of M.I.R.V.-carrying missiles. It also placed a ceiling of 300 on heavy missiles such as the Soviet SS18 (the U.S. had no such giant missiles, preferring to specialize in smaller and more accurate weapons). Theoretically, such provisions put an upper limit of about 9,000 on the land-based warheads that the Soviets could use against America's Minuteman force. This opened up the prospect of Minuteman vulnerability, though deterrence theory argues that any Soviet attack would provoke retaliation from American submarines and strategic bombers, as well as bombers and missiles based in Europe and on aircraft carriers. A Soviet attack would also presume that America would not launch her land-based missiles on warning of an incoming nuclear strike. In any event, the U.S. intended to deploy the mobile and thus less vulnerable MX missile in the 1980s. A protocol (operative until 1982) to the S.A.L.T. 2 Treaty prohibited the deployment of ground and sea-launched Cruise missiles with ranges exceeding 370 miles, and this upset the West Europeans who felt they had thus no effective counter to the SS20. Ironically, at the time of S.A.L.T. 1 it had been the Americans and the Europeans who had been concerned to prevent European-range weapons (as well as the British and French deterrents) from being included in S.A.L.T. negotiations. S.A.L.T. 2 did not, of course, prevent either power from increasing spending on the quality of its weapons systems – on, for example, missile accuracy – or on new types of fuel, engines or metal alloys.

While senators were discussing the over-all strategic balance in December 1979, the N.A.T.O. Council decided that the Soviet deployment of approximately 50 Backfire bombers and over 150 SS20 missiles required a response. In order to upgrade N.A.T.O.'s 'theatre' nuclear weapons, it was recommended that by 1983 approximately 572 Pershing IIs and land-based Cruise missiles would be placed in Europe. The total programme was to cost America $5 billion and the missiles, though American-operated, were to be deployed in West Germany, Britain, Italy and possibly Belgium. The two missiles, with ranges of 1,000 and 1,500 miles respectively, were designed to fill the gap between short-range missiles, like the Lance, and intercontinental missiles like Minuteman. In other words, they were to offer a credible deterrent to Soviet conventional or nuclear attack on Western Europe without N.A.T.O. being obliged to raise the nuclear stakes by threatening or launching a strategic attack from the U.S. heartland. Of course from the Soviet viewpoint, whereas SS20 missiles could hit Britain but not America, long-range Cruise missiles fired from the U.K. could reach European Russia.

The N.A.T.O. move was remarkable, coming as it did on top of the commitment given in 1977 to raise defence spending by 3 per cent per annum in real terms (that is, over and above inflation). The fact that such a group of independent nations accepted the need to take the expensive and potentially politically unpopular decision to re-equip their forces pointed clearly to the common perception of a real threat.

Such action would have been inconceivable only five years earlier, but by 1979 the Soviet Union was reaping the benefits of more than a decade of raising defence expenditure by 3–5 per cent in real terms every year. She had a long-range nuclear strike force on the verge of surpassing America's, a short-range nuclear armoury threatening to dominate Europe and conventional forces which outnumbered, and were becoming better armed, than N.A.T.O.'s European forces.

A 'window of opportunity' had arguably appeared: this was the four years or so in the mid 1980s when, it was estimated, Soviet military supremacy would be at its greatest before new Western systems like the MX missile and the Trident submarine were deployed in sufficient numbers to counter the threat. In early September 1979, ex-Secretary of State Kissinger warned: 'If present trends continue the 1980s will be a period of massive crisis for all of us … Never in history has it happened that a nation achieved superiority, in all significant weapons categories without seeking to translate it at some point into some foreign policy benefit.'[2] Russia's conventional dominance in Europe (by $2\frac{3}{4}$:1 in artillery, $2\frac{1}{2}$:1 in tanks and $2\frac{1}{2}$:1 in tactical aircraft), growing dominance in the 'grey area' of medium and intermediate range weapons, with the possibility of strategic superiority in the near future, radically altered the balance of power and was the major factor in the Senate's refusal to accept S.A.L.T. 2.

The N.A.T.O. decision occurred in spite of a major Soviet propaganda campaign against it, including the highly publicized gradual withdrawal of 20,000 Soviet troops and their tanks from East Germany to western Russia. Within weeks the West was given a fresh impetus to look to its defences. In the early morning of 25 December 1979, the situation in Afghanistan erupted as a world issue – for the first time since the nineteenth century when British imperial forces in India had attempted to intervene there to fill a vacuum they believed was too tempting for tsarist Russia. The British had felt then that Russia might intend to annex Afghanistan both with the aim of threatening imperial India and of moving towards the warm waters of the Arabian Sea. Successive tsars had attempted to overcome the problem of Russia's very limited access to ice-free seas. Solutions had included, for example, the annexation of the Chinese areas around Vladivostok in the nineteenth century.

Afghanistan had been one of the first countries to receive Soviet aid after the Second World War and Moscow's influence remained strong in Kabul throughout the period before the 1973 *coup* in which the monarchy was overthrown and a left-wing regime was formed by Mohammed Daoud. But Afghanistan remained neutralist or more accurately 'Finlandized' by its proximity to the U.S.S.R. In April 1978 the Marxist Nur Mohammed Taraki carried out a successful *coup* and Afghanistan leaned towards the Soviet camp. A Moslem insurrection followed, in which possibly up to 1,000 Soviet advisers were killed and in September 1979 Taraki was overthrown by another Marxist, Hafizullah Amin. By December the government had lost control of 80 per cent of the country and desertions had halved its army of 150,000. Soviet paratroops and armoured columns entered the country on the 25 December (according to Moscow, at Amin's request). However, Amin – along with members of his family and close supporters – was murdered on the night of the 26th and replaced by Babrak Karmal, who had been an exile in Eastern Europe for the previous year and was flown into Kabul some time after the Soviet invasion had begun. The Russians later laid the blame for the failure of the Afghan revolution on Amin's terroristic regime (which was hardly in accordance with their story that they had responded to his appeals for intervention). Meanwhile, by the spring of 1980 over 80,000 Soviet troops were required just to hold the major towns and roads and bolster up the Afghan army which in theory continued to carry the brunt of the fighting against the rebels. In January 1980 hundreds of Farsi-speaking Russians arrived to take over the central administration of Afghanistan and a number of senior Afghan civil servants were dismissed. The Western and Muslim worlds feared that Afghanistan might disappear behind the Iron Curtain.

Moscow's explanation of events did not satisfy the United Nations, where her actions were censured by 104 to 18 votes, with 30 abstentions or absences. Then in January 1980 thirty-five Moslem nations, meeting in Islamabad, Pakistan, demanded that Soviet troops leave the country. Afghanistan – unlike Hungary in 1956 or Czechoslovakia in 1968, which had both been integral parts of the Soviet bloc since the late 1940s and were members of the Warsaw Pact – was regarded as a non-aligned country whose territorial integrity and national sovereignty were the intimate concern of the Third World. Despite the U.S.S.R.'s pretence of answering the calls of a friendly government trying to fend off insurgents helped and armed by America, China, Pakistan and Britain, she was not able to obscure the fact that she had flouted the principle of non-intervention – a principle to which Moscow had solemnly subscribed in the U.N. Charter, the

Bandung Declaration and the Helsinki Agreement. For the first time since 1945, the Red Army had pushed out the frontiers of the Soviet empire into 'neutral' territory.

The Soviet Union paid a high price for its Afghan adventure but Brezhnev and his Politburo colleagues must have known that this would be the case. Perhaps the Kremlin invoked the Brezhnev Doctrine out of concern that the overthrow of a Marxist government would reflect badly upon Moscow's capacity to protect its friends. Afghanistan was, of course, directly on the U.S.S.R.'s southern border and sandwiched between Khomeini's Iran and an Islamic Pakistan already providing sanctuary for refugees from Amin's rule who had crossed the Khyber Pass. Some of those refugees were insurgents in search of arms to further the *jihad* (holy war) declared against the godless regime of Kabul. The Afghan Government controlled only the towns and roads by the end of 1979, but there was no united 'national liberation movement', and the 'holy warriors' fought as much out of tradition and opportunism as religion or ideology. Besides, if Moscow was afraid of Moslem fundamentalism and revolution contaminating its own Moslem citizens, then Iran was the country to invade, not Afghanistan. Also, the Russians sent under 100,000 troops, enough to police key areas but not enough to conquer a mountainous country with few highways inhabited by fiercely independent peoples. If fear of Russia's own 35 million Moslems was one reason for the move, then an invasion which overestimated the popularity and ability of the hard-line Marxist Karmal and underestimated the xenophobia of Afghans, the global revulsion and the new-found resolve of the U.S. President, was patently not the way to head off future difficulties from Soviet Islam.

Possibly Moscow correctly estimated world response but reckoned that the Western alliance would not be able to maintain a united front for very long, that a Russian peace offensive in the summer of 1980 would calm world tempers, that business pressure would eventually force Washington to relax any trade or grain embargoes, that she could satisfy her technological needs from Europe and Japan anyway, or that commercial links with the West had gone far enough. Brezhnev had much to lose in Afghanistan but much was already lost: S.A.L.T. 2 was stalled in the Senate, probably doomed by the Cuban 'crisis'. China had been given 'most-favoured nation' status by the E.E.C. and N.A.T.O. was rearming. *Détente* had not solved Moscow's economic problems, had helped to introduce inflation to Eastern

Europe and had weakened Moscow's economic hold over her satellites. Moreover, it had not prevented a *rapprochement* between China and the U.S.A. Here, probably, was the heart of the issue. Afghanistan was a warning to Soviet citizens, her neighbouring states and the West, but it can also be seen as part of a policy which supported Vietnam's invasion of China's ally Kampuchea, and which sought friendship with India in an effort to 'encircle' China. Finally, clinging to the Marxist tenet that communism was the 'wave of the future', no Soviet government could allow the overthrow of a communist-inspired regime without calling into question the doctrines of historic inevitability and the irreversibility of the communist revolution.

Clearly, the repercussions upon *détente* were considerable from the viewpoint of either super-power. Not only did Moscow find itself being openly criticized by Yugoslavia, but Romania refused to voice support for the Soviet move and Poland was obviously worried by the turn of events. Carter, who had assumed power in 1977 after stating that he wanted defence reductions, immediately increased the 1981 defence budget by 5 per cent in real terms. He had promised during the 1976 elections that he would never use food as a weapon, but he promptly embargoed grain deliveries in excess of the 8 million tons per annum which it had been agreed in the treaty of 1975 would be sold to the U.S.S.R. Moscow had anticipated purchasing about 17 million tons in excess of that minimum. Additionally, Carter asked Congress to defer any decisions on S.A.L.T. 2, restricted Soviet access to U.S. fishing waters, limited Soviet purchases of high technology goods (such as computers and silicon or microchip technology), and in February 1980 recommended that Americans did not compete in the Olympic Games in Moscow in July 1980. In a rather ill-co-ordinated way, other allies fell in line behind the U.S.A. – Australia, Kenya, Norway and West Germany announced Olympic boycotts while Canada embargoed grain to the Soviets, but the Argentinian junta – smarting from State Department criticism of its human rights record – did not. Meanwhile, Washington's perceptions of Pakistan's importance altered overnight.

President Zia – a military autocrat who had come to power in 1977 and executed his predecessor Prime Minister Bhutto – had been unpopular with Washington. Zia had been thought to have been slow in sending rescue forces to the U.S. embassy in Islamabad in November 1979 when two Americans were killed by a Moslem mob. Carter feared that Zia was about to threaten further nuclear proliferation by building an atomic bomb. On top of this, his refusal to hold elections and the dissatisfaction of minority groups in the country – especially the Baluchis in the south-west – rendered his government both decidedly unstable and hardly in accord with Carter's stance on human rights. Nevertheless, as Afghan insurgents began seeking arms in Peshawar, America offered somewhat tentatively to provide defensive weapons for Zia's regime. The Khyber Pass was visited by Brzezinski, Deng Xiaoping and Britain's Lord Carrington. Russia thus faced a mountainous Afghan-Pakistan border which could not be sealed, and the prospect of increasing military links between Washington and Peking. Carter – who had originally hoped for the demilitarization of the Indian Ocean – decided to spend $10 billion by 1984 on outfitting the ships, planes and supplies necessary for a 100,000 strong Rapid Deployment Force in the Persian Gulf–Red Sea zone. Prospects of new U.S. military bases in Oman, Somalia and Kenya were seriously investigated. Carter also made it clear that the Gulf was a vital American interest which would be defended by American military force if necessary.

It was an uncomfortable fact of life for the West that its dependency on Gulf oil meant that its economic security was vitally tied to an unstable area close to the Soviet border. It was not, after all, Moscow that engineered the fall of the Shah. Some commentators in the West feared that Afghanistan signalled the beginning of a Soviet drive to the Gulf – though Afghanistan was rather a circuitous route for such a destination. Admittedly, if Pakistan were to go the way of Afghanistan, then the U.S.S.R. would have immediate access to the Indian Ocean. But the Afghan crisis worried India even though Indira Gandhi's return to power at the beginning of 1980 gave the Kremlin a friend in the sub-continent. Pakistan had been a *de facto* Chinese ally since the early 1970s and in 1980 America re-established a defence link with Pakistan that began in 1959 but had been allowed to lapse.

The West Europeans were also dependent on the economic life-lines to the Gulf though, in the early stages at least, their reactions to the invasion lacked coherence. Only Margaret Thatcher's Government in Britain rallied immediately to the American stance on trade and credit restrictions and the Olympic boycott. West German Chancellor Helmut Schmidt, and France's Valéry Giscard d'Estaing, were slower to respond to Washington's requests for Western solidarity. Of course, N.A.T.O. is concerned specifically with the defence of the North Atlantic region and the Western allies in the past had often been prepared to allow America alone to defend the West's interests around the world – in Indo-China and the Egyptian–Israeli crises, for example. This is not to say that the European democracies did not play a role beyond Europe: the British concentrated in 1980 on solving a Rhodesian problem which threatened had to develop an east–west dimension and to invite Cuban involvement; the French and Belgians intervened in Zaire in 1978 to support the Mobutu regime against rebels and France also assisted the governments of Chad and Mauritania, and in January 1979 helped defend Tunisia against troubles sponsored by the radical regime of Gadaffi in Libya. The West Germans concentrated on Europe – for example, by providing economic aid to their N.A.T.O. ally Turkey and in leading the E.E.C. early in 1980 towards closer economic ties with a Yugoslavia bereft of Tito's leadership. Nevertheless, the Afghan issue presented a number of problems for Western Europe. It was a crisis uncomfortably close to a region of strategic importance to the economies of many European countries, but it was a crisis in south-central Asia and not central Europe. Afghanistan posed most forcibly the question of whether *détente* is divisible – whether a European *détente* could or should survive Soviet adventures in other regions of the world.

The Western European governments had never fully accepted the Nixon–Kissinger theory of 'linkage'. (This was that East–West agreements on arms limitations, trade, investments and cultural contacts were linked in some ill-defined way to Soviet world behaviour and that the agreements could not survive in an atmosphere damaged by any major forceful (or series of forceful) alterations in the global *status quo* carried out by the Soviet Union or its allies. In reality, certain areas such as Latin America and the Near/Middle East were – and are – regarded as particularly sensitive regions.) The West Europeans, by and large, had not seen Vietnam as a vital Western interest and had always tried to draw a distinction between Western and purely American interests. The unco-ordinated reaction of N.A.T.O. to Afghanistan was not just a European commentary on perceptions of the poor quality of American leadership on this as on other issues, but it was also indicative of other differences in attitude between America and her allies. America had profited from *détente* in terms of a more congenial international climate, some increased trade and some arms control deals, but only part of this was tangible whereas *détente's* achievements in Western Europe had been concrete. This was especially so in West Germany where the reopened links with Eastern

Europe, and the ability to negotiate the re-settlement in West Germany of so many ethnic Germans from the D.D.R., Poland and the U.S.S.R., had helped immeasurably in restoring West German self-esteem and political confidence. West Europeans were in the front line and they had no wish to put *détente* irretrievably at risk. It should also be mentioned that the bulk of Eastern bloc trade and credit arrangements with the West were not with the U.S.A. but with Europe. By 1979 the E.E.C. exported to the U.S.S.R. alone goods worth $12 billion compared with the U.S.A.'s $3.4 billion.[3] Many East European countries were also tied to Western credits – for example, in February 1980 Poland owed $17.5 billion in hard currency. Clearly, some at least of Western Europe's prosperity resulted from its sales to Eastern bloc consumers while part of the energy requirements of West Germany and France have since 1973 and April 1980 respectively been satisfied by purchases of Soviet natural gas originating from vast reserves in Siberia.

The judgement of President Carter, which had been questioned over the 'combat brigade' in the Cuba affair, was challenged by those Europeans who argued that if the collapse of Afghanistan into the arms of the 'Russian bear' was indeed a threat to world peace, then that threat had emerged with the coming to power of Mohammed Taraki in April 1978: the advent of Russian troops on Christmas Day 1979 merely formalized something that had in essence already happened.

On the other hand, the anxiety of the French and the West Germans was exacerbated in February 1980 when Soviet dissident Andrei Sakharov was exiled to the closed city of Gorky for speaking out against the Afghan invasion, and in favour of a world boycott of the Olympics. At a Franco–German summit soon after, Giscard d'Estaing and Schmidt issued a terse communiqué stating in relation to Afghanistan that '*détente* will not survive another shock of this order'. But the Europeans were still inclined to search for ways to persuade Soviet troops to leave Afghanistan as opposed to punishing the U.S.S.R. for its actions, which was the Carter response. Potential solutions like the neutralization of Afghanistan were offered as avenues allowing for a face-saving exit for the Soviets. The Germans and French also believed in holding back some punitive measures – such as European credit embargoes on the U.S.S.R. – in case of future need, lest the West be deprived of all but sabre-rattling as a means of influencing future Politburo action. Of course, the counter arguments to *détente* were increasingly being heard in 1980: that to provide the Soviets with grain, high technology and credits – thus limiting the amounts they needed to spend on agriculture and industry, thereby freeing more funds for defence spending – was both appeasing and aiding the capabilities of an inherently expansionist power. Yet, Europeans had appreciated the degree to which the Soviets were prepared to moderate their behaviour, at least in Europe, by not provoking troubles in West Berlin, or during the Portuguese revolution of 1974, or in a Turkey rent by civil disorders and with a tottering economy. Maintaining the balance between *détente* in Europe and the strength of N.A.T.O. – between the degree to which Soviet behaviour can be moderated by the advantages it gains from good relations with the West, and the extent to which the final moderator of Soviet ambitions remains the military might of the Western Alliance – continued to be a key problem for the Europeans.

The debate as to whether after a decade of *détente* the West was stronger or weaker, in relation to the Soviet bloc, was a central issue as the 1980s began. The Soviet camp had expanded during the decade but, on the other hand, its expansion had not necessarily resulted in an undiluted extension of Soviet power. In 1976, Angola became Marxist, but some 20,000 Cuban advisers, technicians and troops were still required in 1980 to support the government against the non-communist, nationalist guerrilla movement of Jonas Savimbi's U.N.I.T.A. forces active in the south of the country. Mozambique had become Marxist the previous year though its economy desperately needed Soviet economic aid, having been weakened by its own war of liberation, involvement in Rhodesia's war and the exodus of its whites. The Cuban economy also required more aid in 1980 than it had a decade earlier. The unification of Vietnam in 1976 appeared to add strength to the Soviet bloc, but by the end of the decade one of the West's major apprehensions about that region proved unjustified: the Soviet navy had not taken over the huge ex-American base at Cam Ranh Bay in Vietnam, which would have had a revolutionary effect upon geopolitics in South-East Asia. Also, the wars in the region between Vietnam and Cambodia, and Vietnam and China, weakened the economy of all of Indo-China and provoked increasing unity in the neighbouring Asian countries of Singapore, Malaysia, Thailand, the Philippines and Indonesia. (These countries formed the Association of South-East Asian Nations (A.S.E.A.N.) in the wake of the demise of S.E.A.T.O. in 1977. Originally designed as a forum for policy debates on trade, aid and refugees, etc., it reacted to events by taking on an increasingly military character, including joint military action in 1979 by Thailand and Malaysia against the remnants of the Malaysian Communist Party which, though largely a spent force since the late 1950s, were still active along the common border.)

Ethiopia, faced by the skilled and determined Eritrean guerrillas, and Afghanistan with its Moslem insurgents, provided the Soviets with potential crises for the future. The Soviets also failed on occasions during the 1970s, for example in the collapse of Marxist Chile in 1973 and the expulsion of Soviet 'advisers' from Egypt in 1972 and Somalia in 1977. Closer to home the Kremlin was troubled by a Romania continuing to demonstrate its independence in foreign policy and a Poland at least temporarily affected by the religious fervour and re-fired nationalism provoked by the election in 1978 of the Polish Pope, John Paul II, and his subsequent visit to Poland in 1979.

The Soviet agricultural system, which in 1980 required one worker to feed 10 people (compared with 1:75 in the U.S.) remained a weak point in the armoury of the U.S.S.R. Finally, although in 1970 the Soviets had a China problem, there at least had been no question at that time of close military links with Western Europe and the U.S. or sales of military equipment to Peking.

In many ways, the weaknesses and losses that accrued to the Western Alliance after 1970 were mirror images of the strengths and gains of the Soviet bloc. The Portuguese and Spanish empires and their relative stability had gone. The Shah had been overthrown, a few radical regimes had emerged in Central America and the Caribbean, and U.S. policy throughout the world still rested frequently upon narrow bases or even individuals (for example, Sultan Qaboos bin Said in Oman). But there had been successes too for the West. Eurocommunism had turned out not to be the massively destabilizing element in East–West relations that it had threatened to become in 1975 and 1976. Portugal, Spain and Greece divested themselves of right-wing regimes but avoided communism and became pluralist democracies. An Egyptian–Israeli peace treaty had been signed which, if it left Egypt an outcast in the Moslem world, had the virtue in American eyes of sharply reducing the risks of a fourth Arab–Israeli war.

Yet the decade had witnessed some self-induced weaknesses in the Western camp. The U.S.A. suffered a leadership crisis as a result of

the Watergate scandal, which led to the resignation of President
Nixon in August 1974. Conversely, some of the strength of the
U.S.S.R. derived from the continuum of leadership since the fall of
Khrushchev in 1964. The reverberations from Watergate and
America's failure in Vietnam resulted, amongst other things, in a
Congress more difficult to manage and a people less willing to police
the world. But there was the possibility that the Teheran hostages
affair and Afghanistan might restore to the American presidency an
authority lost since 1973. As America began in 1980 to take up the
position held in the Persian Gulf by Britain up to the late 1960s it
seemed a long time since Nixon had talked of retreating from over-
extended commitments. Moreover, as links between Western Europe,
America, China and Japan tightened, Nixon's concept of a balanced
pentapolar world became increasingly seen as an aberration in post-
war American foreign policy.

A further weakness of the West's leading nation stemmed from its
growing need to import strategically important raw materials.
American vulnerability in strategic materials was frequently seen
only in terms of oil, but in reality there were other vital supplies, some
of which originated in potentially unstable areas, and all of which had
to be transported by sea, despite Soviet naval power.

For example, 65 per cent of the non-communist world's reserves of
cobalt, used in jet engines, exists in Zaïre, a country also rich in
high-grade copper and uranium ores. South Africa was a major
supplier of manganese (essential in steel production) as well as being
the major source of gold and industrial diamonds in non-communist
areas. America's deficiency in chromium was almost total and it was
imported by her from what became in March 1980 – after British-
administered elections – Robert Mugabe's Zimbabwe.

In 1970 oil was $1.80 per barrel and the U.S.A. imported little, but
by 1980 it was more than $34 per barrel and America consumed a
great deal of the world's exportable surplus. In 1978 America needed
to import 47 per cent of her oil at a net cost of $39.2 billion. In
comparison, Japan imported 92 per cent of her oil at a cost in excess of
$24 billion, while West Germany and France imported 97 per cent at
costs of $13.2 and $10.7 billion respectively. The estimated cost of
U.S. imported oil in the year ending December 1979 exceeded $65
billion. Dependence on oil helped explain Western fears during the
Iranian and Afghan crises. In 1978 Saudi Arabia, Iran, Iraq, the
United Arab Emirates and Kuwait exported oil worth $35, $21, $11,

$9 and $8 billion respectively. Of course American sources of oil included Nigeria, for example, which exported $9.5 billion worth of oil in 1978, 35 per cent of which was destined for the U.S. market.[4] The fact that the United Kingdom, Mexico, Venezuela and possibly Brazil could increase exports during the 1980s did widen the sources of this life-blood of the Western economy – though of necessity, the three Latin American sources will provoke both changes in U.S. foreign relations and the necessity for increased vigilance to the south. It was fortunate for Washington that the revolutions that occurred south of the Rio Grande in the 1970s involved non-oil-producing countries – for example, the overthrow of Nicaragua's dictator Anastasio Somoza by left-wing Sandinista guerrillas.

In 1970 the dollar was still regarded as the 'imperial currency': devaluations in 1971 and 1973 and its continuous float downwards throughout the decade, particularly against the mark and the yen, weakened the economic confidence – if not the military strength – of the West. Nevertheless, America's economy in 1980 remained the most powerful in the world. Her budget for the fiscal year 1980 was $531 billion out of a G.N.P. of $2.6 trillion, a budget greater than the G.N.P. of all except three countries in the world – West Germany ($650 billion), Japan ($900 billion) and the U.S.S.R. ($1.26 trillion).[5] Despite America's economic ills, with 7 per cent of the world's population, she still enjoyed over 30 per cent of the world's G.N.P. The budget for the fiscal year 1981 (commencing 1 October 1980 and announced after the invasion of Afghanistan) rose to $615.8 billion and included a defence allocation of $142.7 billion (an increase of $15.3 billion on the previous year).

A decade of *détente* had not reduced defence spending, but the West had not accorded such a high priority to it as the Russians. Whereas the U.S. and the U.S.S.R. probably spent about the same on defence in the decade 1967–77, the Russians spent more at the end of this period and continued to widen the gap. In 1978, the Soviet Union allocated $148 billion or 11–14 per cent of her G.N.P. on defence, whereas the U.S.A. allocated $105 billion or 5 per cent of hers. However, the Russians saw such arguments as spurious and used different sets of figures to argue their case. While the Warsaw Pact countries spent some $160.4 billion in 1978 ($161.4 if Cuba is included), N.A.T.O. spent $179.9 billion. Indeed, if Japan's $8.5 billion and China's $40 billion are added, then the U.S.S.R.'s most immediate potential enemies spent $67 billion more on defence than she did and that figure ignores all the other countries that America could call on in the event of a protracted war.[7]

Nevertheless, the balance of military power between East and West had changed in the 1970s, although not as much as some alarmist voices in the West claimed.

By 1980 the Russians had a 'blue water' navy capable of carrying the Soviet flag to all corners of the globe, but it was not quite the malevolent leviathan of some Western commentators. Soviet ships tended to be smaller than Western vessels because the prime task of the Soviet navy was coastal defence. Beyond that, it had a strategic nuclear task with its missile submarines and it also developed a sea-denial role in the 1960s and 1970s, but the Red Fleet remained outnumbered and outgunned. In 1978 one authority wrote: 'The U.S. navy has outbuilt the Soviet navy by 3.3 million tons to 2.6 million tons since 1958. In the *détente* period (since 1969) the Americans outbuilt the Russians by 12 per cent in ship numbers as well as by 71 per cent in tonnage.'[7]

Table 20.1    Relative strengths of Eastern and Western navies.

|  | Major Surface Ships | Attack and patrol submarines | Nuclear missiles submarines |
|---|---|---|---|
| U.S.S.R. | 275 | 248 | 90 |
| Total Warsaw Pact | 280 | 256 | 90 |
| U.S.A. | 180 | 80 | 41 |
| Total N.A.T.O. (excluding France) | 389 | 192 | 45 |
| Total N.A.T.O. (including France) | 437 | 215 | 49 |

Source: The Military Balance 1979–80, op cit.

Table 20.1 shows the extent to which the Soviet navy remained inferior to the combined surface fleet strength of N.A.T.O. Besides, the Soviet navy had four distinct fleets with different roles which could not immediately support each other. With a ship 'life' of about twenty years, the large number of Soviet ships which were laid down in the late 1950s were all needing replacement at about the same time around 1980, whereas America had experienced 'block obsolescence' in the mid 1960s and already had her new ships.

The balance in numbers of conventional troops remained much the same at the end of the 1970s. Ex-Commander-in-Chief, Allied

Forces Central Europe, General Count von Kielmansegg, suggested in May 1973 that, if the Russians rolled west, they could with some luck and despite N.A.T.O.'s selective use of nuclear weapons, reach the Rhine in four days. This remained the case but what had changed was Soviet military reach. In the past N.A.T.O. had argued that the Red Army's supremacy in Europe would be limited by its lack of sophisticated logistic and support facilities. But by 1980 the West had been presented with three recent case studies of Soviet military capacity whose lessons were chilling. In 1975–6 the Russians lifted by air and sea some 20,000 Cuban troops and their equipment into distant Angola, thus tipping the scales in favour of their M.P.L.A. clients. In autumn 1977 the Soviets launched an awesomely efficient and massive combined air and sea-lift operation to pour arms and equipment into Ethiopia in support of the revolutionary Dergue regime against Somalia, formerly Moscow's ally. Most impressive of all was the way in which in December 1979 the U.S.S.R. mobilized reservists to bring up to full strength divisions already based in central Asia, and then moved between 80,000 and 100,000 men smoothly into Afghanistan without apparently denuding their defences elsewhere.

If a 'window of opportunity' was about to open in the new decade the Russians were better equipped than ever before to try to climb through it: but the West was probably better motivated to try to stop them than at any time since the Cuban missile crisis of 1962. Both Washington and Moscow still held a common perception of the mutually suicidal effects of East–West confrontation, and both feared the dangers inherent in the increased hostility caused by the events and misunderstandings of the late 1970s. Herein lay the paradox, for it was just such a fear that had led to the first *détente*.

Arguably, neither of the world's superpowers gained much advantage over the other between 1980 and early 1984. In the Middle East the Israelis completed their withdrawal from Sinai in April 1982, but in June their invasion of Lebanon, though initially declared to be in defence of northern Israeli settlements, turned into a full-scale intervention in the Lebanese civil war. Despite President Reagan's remonstrations the Israelis drove on to Beirut. The U.S. was further embarrassed when Israel's allies the Phalangists massacred hundreds of Palestinian dependants in the refugee camps of Sabra and Shatila in September, shortly after Arafat and his P.L.O. fighters had been evacuated by sea from Beirut. During 1983 internecine strife broke out within the P.L.O., and Arafat and his loyalists – who had returned to Tripoli – were obliged to flee Lebanon again in December 1983 after defeats by Syrian-backed dissidents. On both occasions the U.S.S.R. seemed incapable of helping its Palestinian friends. The U.S.A., though it finally persuaded Israel to move to a buffer zone in south Lebanon, then found itself caught up in Beirut as part of a multinational force conspicuously failing to sponsor civil accord between Lebanese Christians, Muslims and Druze, while suffering over 260 Marine fatalities in the process in the autumn of 1983. Washington was also no nearer a solution to the Israeli-occupied West Bank, where perplexed Palestinians were contemplating autonomy within Israel or federation with Jordan or a Palestinian part-state (all of these options were preferred to Israeli absorption of the West Bank). The Shamir government of Israel refused to consider either of the latter options, though the inclusion of over 1 million Palestinians into a Jewish state of $3\frac{1}{4}$ million (with the Israeli government sponsoring new Jewish settlements on the West Bank or 'Judaea and Samaria') hardly seemed in U.S. eyes a viable long-term solution. The near collapse of Gemayel's Lebanon in February 1984 after the exit of the multinational force increased the likelihood of the U.S.S.R.'s protégé Syria dominating the Lebanese vacuum, thereby raising the risks of a conflict between Syria and Israel.

The Iran–Iraq border war, which began in September 1980, see-sawed on throughout this period. Perhaps because the strife was close to Soviet borders and Gulf oil, the superpowers maintained their distance from the conflict. Both had the forward-based power to intervene if the war threatened Gulf oil routes – the U.S.S.R. via Afghan bases like Baghram and the U.S. via Rapid Deployment forces, which had carried out major exercises in the area (for example, in Egypt and Oman) since November 1981. By 1983 the Iraqis were in the most trouble, but it was left to Saudi Arabia and Egypt to support their Arab ally, though the French, under Mitterand's socialist government, supplied Super-Etendard planes and Exocet missiles to Iraq, one of their best overseas arms purchasers.

In 1984 the U.S.S.R. entered its fifth year of trying to subdue the Mujaheddin guerrillas in Afghanistan (the guerrilla base areas were in north-west Pakistan – which was also home for 3 million Afghan refugees). Forced to retain over 105,000 troops in the country, its unpalatable proxy regime in Kabul had to cede up to 80 per cent of the country to a determined foe driven by both nationalistic and religious passions. The Soviets had to accept over 18,000 dead and wounded, a loss of prestige in the Third World, and the pronounced tilt of Pakistan towards the United States. Moreover, 62 out of an eligible 143 countries had refused to attend the Moscow Olympics in July 1980.

Unfortunately for Washington, it could take little solace from Moscow's trials in south-west Asia, and its enforced impotence in what purported to be the continuing peace process in the Middle East.

The United States, following Reagan taking office in January 1981, had considerable trouble in its own hemisphere. Admittedly, right-wing governments had come to power in, for example, Barbados and Jamaica. Moreover, when the U.S. decided that Grenada was about to become a military outpost of Cuba, it was able to gain help in October 1983 from Barbados, Jamaica, Dominica, Antigua and St Lucia, in subduing the Marxist regime and expelling nearly 900 Cuban personnel at the cost of 24 Cuban dead. The British, under Margaret Thatcher, disapproved of military intervention, and stood by as the U.S. 're-established democracy' in Commonwealth Grenada and simultaneously re-affirmed the Munro doctrine.

During 1982, its British ally had posed a major conundrum to Washington. Though the Soviets at least failed dismally in their opportunist attempt to improve relations with the Argentine junta during the British–Argentine conflict in April–June, this was probably the only silver lining in view to Reagan. When the U.K. despatched a task force to defend the 1,800 Falkland islanders (mostly of British stock) from General Galtieri's anti-colonial 'liberation', the U.S., in spite of its obligations to prevent foreign intervention against a Latin American state under the Rio Treaty of 1947, decided to stand by its European ally. Though U.S.–Latin American relations were damaged and part of the U.K.'s naval force was diverted from N.A.T.O. duties to an imperial outpost for an indeterminate period, the United States was even more distressed by events closer to home.

The Reagan administration decided that the Carter government had underestimated the challenge to U.S. security that was developing in Central America. In June 1979 Nicaragua's dictator Anastasio Somoza fled the country in the face of the successes of the Sandinista guerrillas. His corruption was as legion as Cuba's Batista, and Carter had regarded him as a human rights disaster zone. However, the Sandinista regime provided for the first time a mainland sanctuary for neighbouring revolutionary movements. The regime played host to 2,000 Cuban advisers and, according to the State Department, funnelled arms, particularly to the revolutionaries challenging the right-wing military regime in El Salvador. Washington's answer was to deny Nicaragua access to Western aid and investment, and to provide military funding and training to the armed forces of El Salvador and Guatemala. Congress remained unconvinced of the desirability of concentrating on military – rather than economic – aid, and was highly sensitive about the activities of the 'death-squads' of off-duty right-wing soldiers in El Salvador, a country that had suffered up to 1984 an estimated 30,000 deaths in the civil war which began in 1977. The 23,000-strong army suffered from low morale and poor training, with the result that 6,000 guerrillas dominated a third of the countryside. Reagan decided that one route to victory was to de-stabilize Nicaragua. Since mid-1982, about 4,000 armed exiles (the Contras) had been attacking Nicaragua on a 'hit and run' basis from across the border in Honduras, where the strong-man General Alvarez was a fervent anti-communist. The Contras were a combination of ex-Somozan forces, Miskito Indians persecuted by the Sandistas and the democratic elements of the original Sandistan United Front-men, such as Alfonso Robela (who fled the country following the state of emergency in May 1982, which removed the last vestiges of political and press liberty). In spite of Congressional disquiet, military advisers and the C.I.A. were actively training the Contras. To the north of Honduras, a further civil conflict has been raging in Guatemala since 1979. Carter cut off aid to the Guatemalan military in 1977 and the conflict was exacerbated in 1982, when the regime of General Garcia massacred 200 Christian Democrat politicians and then proceeded to slaughter more than 13,000 of the Indian population. In March 1982 a coup instated General Montt. He called off the death squads, in the hope that Reagan would provide aid as a reward for human rights 'improvements'. Immediately south of the Rio Grande, Mexico's oil-based boom collapsed in 1982, and it was forced to reschedule $77 billion debts in an I.M.F. package which included government spending retrenchment. (Between 1979 and 1982, the Western banking system appeared threatened by the potential default of major debtors such as Brazil, Poland and Argentina, as well as Mexico.) Though this imposed a diminution in real living standards in Mexico's explosively growing cities, the presidential elections of 1982 foreshadowed no threat to U.S. interests. Mexico's perennial Revolutionary Party coasted to power and President Madrid promptly installed a moderate team of economic ministers. Moreover, in 1983 Washington's victory in Granada caused much unease in Nicaragua, where the regime – fearful of a U.S.-sponsored invasion – requested that Havana recall many of its advisers. Of course, Nicaragua and the U.S.S.R., well aware of the United States's regional military preponderance in Central America and the Caribbean, had to walk a careful tightrope between merely embarrassing and actually threatening the interests of the Western superpower. Even if the Soviets did not hope that the 'crisis' in Central America would affect the geopolitical strategic balance, they probably hoped that an exaggerated, hysterical or merely poorly planned U.S. response would affect European perceptions of the reliability and judgement of U.S. policymakers.

It would be erroneous to suggest that the focus of East–West relations in the early 1980s was anything other than the inter-related issues of the opposing European alliances, C.S.C.E., Strategic Arms Reduction Talks – and Poland.

In 1956, 1970 and 1976, the government of the Polish United Workers Party (P.U.W.P.) had been shaken by disturbances. By 1980, Poland carried the largest foreign debt ($17 billion) of any Eastern bloc country. Proposed food-price increases sparked off a nation-wide wave of strikes in August 1980. Surprised by the strength of the protest, the P.U.W.P. capitulated on 31 August and signed the Gdansk agreement guaranteeing the right to strike, free trade unions, the lifting of censorship, greater religious freedom and pay increases. These were momentous concessions and led directly both to the replacement of party chief Edouard Gierek by Stanislaw Kania and the emergence of the $9\frac{1}{2}$ million strong Solidarity trade union, led by Catholic electrician Lech Walesa. The Kremlin feared the end of P.U.W.P. dominance in Poland, and unusually large Soviet military exercises took place on Poland's borders in the autumn. Yet, Red Army intervention may have been stoutly resisted, and the Politburo feared the repercussions on European *détente* of another adventure so soon after Afghanistan. But Soviet political pressure continued, and in October 1981 Kania was replaced by Defence Minister General Wojciech Jaruzelski. Labour unrest and political tension burgeoned during 1981; national income dropped 14 per cent and many basic foodstuffs were rationed. In December, Jaruzelski responded to a Solidarity call for a national referendum on whether Poles supported the P.U.W.P. or the union, by introducing martial law. Walesa was put under house arrest, Solidarity banned, censorship re-introduced and 10,000 dissidents were interned. The clampdown succeeded, and by November 1982 Jaruzelski could afford to release Walesa and in July 1983 to lift martial law. Western governments duly reopened negotiations on debt rescheduling, and Poland ceased to be a potential international flashpoint. Poland's version of the 'Prague Spring' had, apparently, ended.

The U.S.S.R. found a number of friends or allies on the defensive in the early 1980s; contrarily, America's 'friends' had some successes. South Africa's support of the Mozambique Resistance Front helped to de-stabilize Marxist Mozambique; while South African forces and U.N.I.T.A. guerrillas were very active in Marxist Angola in 1983–4. Over 2,000 French 'paras' intervened in Chad from August 1983 to hinder rebellion and limit the intrigue of the rebels' Libyan backers. Somalia provided defence bases for the U.S. in 1980 and even the Eritrean guerrillas managed, in 1983, to rekindle their campaign against their Marxist masters in Ethiopia. Thus, some of the Soviet 'victories' of the 1970s – in Southern Africa, the Horn and Afghanistan – may prove pyrrhic.

In 1956, B-52 and Bear bombers would have taken over $2\frac{1}{2}$ hours to reach their destinations, by October 1962, Titans and SS-6s had a travelling time of 25 minutes. In 1984, Washington was 5 minutes' flying time from depressed-trajectory Soviet S.L.B.M.s, and Moscow 12 minutes away from European Pershing 11 sites. S.A.L.T 1 had frozen missiles, not warhead numbers – both superpowers had increased these from 2,000 to 7,500 by 1984. S.A.L.T. 2, never ratified by the U.S., set warhead limits – but very high ones – and did not deal with medium-range missiles. In December 1981, Intermediate Nuclear Force (I.N.F.) Talks, and in June 1982 Strategic Arms Reduction (not just 'limitation') Talks (S.T.A.R.T.) began at Geneva.

Unfortunately, the I.N.F. talks bogged down over the SS-20 issue, and the linking of the U.K. and French deterrents to the American total, and S.T.A.R.T. got lost in the Soviet unease about reducing land-based missile numbers when proportionately more of the U.S. deterrent was at sea. Neither superpower seemed capable of the quantum leap in trust required to reduce warhead numbers – and unless numbers came down the only result, in Churchill's phrase, would be to decide 'how high the rubble will bounce'. The sole successful negotiations of 1983–4 led to the upgrading of the 'hot-line' satellite link to facilitate the transmission of documents, maps and pictures.

In December 1983, Cruise and Pershing 11 missiles arrived in the Federal Republic of Germany and the U.K.; the U.S.S.R. promptly left the talks. The atmosphere had already been soured by Reagan's invective against the Soviet's when they shot down a Korean civil airliner, with 269 passengers and crew, over the Sea of Okhotsk in September. In January 1984, the 35-nation C.S.C.E. round, which began at Stockholm, was the only East–West negotiation continuing. There was no sign of a superpower summit between the ailing 70-year-old ex-K.G.B. chief Andropov (who succeeded Brezhnev on his death in November 1982) and his 73-year-old counterpart, Reagan.

The arrival of the missiles, despite an orchestrated European peace movement campaign (particularly in West Germany) belied the strains in the Atlantic Alliances. Europeans placed more significance on the fact that it was the Polish military – not the Red Army – that cracked down on Solidarity, than did the Americans, whose allies refused to support fully the sanctions on Poland and the U.S.S.R. announced in December 1981. The British and Germans were particularly resentful about unilateral sanctions imposed by Washington on European companies who in 1983 proceeded to fulfil their contracts to the U.S.S.R. by exporting components for the installation of the Soviet gas pipeline to the West. But the greater furore ensued from Reagan's ill-considered public theorizing in October 1981 about the possibility that a limited nuclear exchange in Europe would not necessarily lead to an all-out strategic nuclear conflict. Limited nuclear war in Europe was hardly a concept likely to endear itself to Europeans. It also made it more difficult for Margaret Thatcher, Helmut Kohl and Italy's Bettino Craxi to persuade their peoples of the necessity for Cruise sites at places like Britain's Greenham Common. As American strategists discussed the possibility of pre-delegating nuclear trigger rights to on-the-spot commanders, and how the vulnerability of land-based missiles might enhance the risk of pre-emptive war on the logic of 'use them or lose them', the Western public looked on with increasing horror. Undoubtedly, public unease about nuclear weapons escalated significantly between 1979 and 1984, and the hopes engendered by Nixon's 'era of peace' were dismally unfulfilled.

Indeed, by 1984 the Western consensus – a prerequisite of N.A.T.O. cohesion – was in some disarray. European confidence in the U.S. as a reliable and predictable ally had ebbed and disagreements – over Afghanistan, over Poland, sanctions against Warsaw and Moscow, weapons deployment and nuclear strategy in Europe,

Grenada and the Soviet gas pipeline – had come thick and fast. Conversely, European criticism weakened American public support for U.S. conventional troop presence in Western Europe and angered Americans who had long argued that post-war Europe had under-spent on its own conventional defence capabilities.

Despite public clamour in the West, no dramatic or sustained peace initiatives emanated from the White House or the Kremlin in the early 1980s. The public's perception of inertia or drift was fed by the fact that Reagan held summit meetings with neither Brezhnev nor Andropov. Moreover, both superpowers were led by septuagenarians: Reagan was reported to do only '3 hours' real work' a day, and for the six months prior to his death in February 1984, Andropov was so ill that he made no public appearances. Public unease about a leader-ship vacuum was not helped when in January 1984 the 73-year-old Reagan announced that he would seek another 4-year-term of office from January 1985, and in February, when the Secretary-Generalship of the C.P.S.U. fell to the 72-year-old Konstantin Chernenko. (Neither of these leaders radiated the apparent energy of the octo-genarian Deng Xiaoping of China!)

Relative to Soviet politics, Andropov had been imaginative. He had been subtle in his foreign policy – exemplified by the way in which he conducted a propaganda 'peace offensive' against N.A.T.O. defence policy – and reformist in domestic affairs, as his campaign to rout out corruption and inefficiency from the Soviet economy dis-played. Chernenko – the archetypal apparatchik – was an obvious compromise candidate on the part of a Politburo which desired a return to the caution and myopia of the later Brezhnev years. A party functionary, Chernenko had held no important managerial post in the armed forces, government or party; he rode to power on Brezhnev's coat tails as his subordinate in Moldavia in the early 1950s and later as his chief of personal staff. Western leaders – used to seeing Chernenko at Brezhnev's elbow, topping up his glass and doling out the ailing leader's rationed cigarettes – had difficulty imagining the new Soviet leader as a man of destiny, willing and capable of re-thinking Soviet foreign policy. Meanwhile, the Soviet leadership ap-parently abandoned hope of Reagan turning into another Nixon.

During 1984 Soviet–American relations continued to be more ice-bound than they had been for two decades. The bitterness following the collapse of the I.N.F. and S.T.A.R.T. negotiations, combined with the exchange of angry rhetoric over Afghanistan and Nicaragua and the withering of cultural and scientific ties, as well as Washington's restrictions on the sale of high-tech goods to Moscow, led to an overall deterioration in superpower relations. Nevertheless, in January 1984, Reagan, on nation-wide television, reassured his audience that the U.S. military build-up since 1981 had reached a stage where – with renewed confidence in her strength – the U.S.A. could recommence 'serious and constructive dialogue' with the U.S.S.R. In his view, the political and military weakness that had sapped American strength since 1973, thus emboldening the Kremlin and raising the risk of conflict, had been halted, and 1984 was a 'year of opportunities for peace'. However, the response from Chernenko was largely negative. The disclosure in April 1984 that the C.I.A. had mined Nicaragua's three main harbours produced uproar in both Moscow and Congress. In May, the U.S.S.R. withdrew from the Los Angeles Olympic Games. However, some dialogue between the superpowers did continue – for example, on Soviet grain purchases – and by the end of the year both sides appeared to have genuinely decided that the downturn in relations had gone far enough.

In January 1985 the Soviets accepted that their five-year campaign to prevent the deployment of American Euro-missiles had failed, and Foreign Minister Gromyko announced that the U.S.S.R. would re-enter the S.T.A.R.T. negotiations, without preconditions, in March. The U.S.S.R. was especially concerned about the gathering research and development of Reagan's Strategic Defense Initiative.

• In March 1983, in what became known as his 'Star Wars' speech Reagan challenged the U.S. scientific community to achieve a collection of many technologies which, when brought together, could, at best, be able to identify, track, intercept and destroy incoming ballistic missiles. Such technologies would include: 'Kill Mechanisms' ranging from earth/satellite-launched nuclear interceptor missiles to satellites armed with lasers, particle beams or other exotica; 'Surveillance and Tracking' techniques involving an array of land, air and space based emitters and receivers; and 'Battle Management' systems for computer analysis of command, control, communications and intelligence variables. Until 1988 the U.S. had allocated $26 billion for 'Star Wars' research – thereafter estimates for deployment range up to $1 trillion. American scientists and strategists have been polarized by this issue; some believe that, at maximum, the defensive screen could only damage-limit and not defeat a Soviet attack, which would necessarily attempt to circumvent 'Star Wars' technology, while others argue that the research is itself de-stabilizing the balance of terror and/or that the cost would be prohibitive. The Kremlin, however, clearly fears that the Reagan gauntlet may be picked up by American scientists, computer specialists and technologists in a way similar to the response to Kennedy's arms and space race demands made in the early 1960s.

In March 1985 the 73-year-old Chernenko died and the reins of Soviet leadership passed to the 54-year-old Mikhail Gorbachev. Gorbachev was born in Stavropol, studied law at Moscow State University and spent 23 years in various regional Communist Party posts. Until 1978 he was largely unknown, even to Soviet citizens. An intelligent and effective apparatchik, he caught the eye of two patrons – the ideologist Mikhail Suslov and the K.G.B. head Yuri Andropov. In 1978 he was summoned to Moscow and joined the Communist Party Secretariat – a group of approximately ten men responsible for the day-to-day running of Soviet affairs. Gorbachev was made responsible for agriculture. It was as if a little-known Governor of a small U.S. State was catapaulted into the Presidential inner Cabinet and made Secretary of Agriculture. In 1980 he joined the Politburo and thereafter became a key Andropov aide. Although Chernenko became General Secretary in February 1984, his health was such that by the year's end Gorbachev effectively governed in his stead. When Chernenko died the Politburo took only five hours to replace him with Gorbachev. By September 1985, twenty-two of the 121 Soviet regional Communist Party First Secretaries had been fired, so had Grigory Romanov (considered Gorbachev's sole rival for high office • in March), and the thirteen-man Politburo had witnessed the arrival of four key Gorbachev men. Moreover, by artful stratagam the 76-year-old Gromyko – 28 years Foreign Minister – had been nudged upstairs to the prestigious, but largely ceremonial post, of Soviet President. His replacement was 57-year-old party boss of Georgia, Eduard Shevardnadzek, a man totally untried in foreign affairs.

When Gorbachev visited Britain in December 1984 – already heir apparent – Thatcher decided she 'could do business with this man'. Gromyko has, however, delivered the classic one-liner on his new boss: 'This man has a nice smile, but he has got iron teeth.' Gorbachev is clearly an authoritarian. He has already cracked down on lethargic bureaucrats and alcoholism. But he is proving the most charismatic Soviet leader since Khrushchev. Moreover, he was born long after the Russian Revolution, has no adult memories of the

Second World War, no involvement in Stalin's bloody purges, no strong ties to the Soviet military, and is a youthful and fit Bolshevik technocrat, who can realistically plan to lead his 278 million fellow citizens into the twenty-first century. Clearly, Reagan and the American leadership faced a new Soviet leadership era after March 1985.

During his visit to Europe in May to celebrate the fortieth anniversary of V.E. Day, Reagan discussed both 'Star Wars' and Gorbachev with his European allies. During August–September Shevardnadzek and Secretary of State George Shultz held further arms talks, in an atmosphere conditioned by Gorbachev's declaration that 'we firmly believe that the process of *détente* should be revived'. Also in August, the representatives of thirty-five states met at Helsinki in the tenth anniversary of the C.S.C.E. talks. Although the West contends that there are up to 10,000 Soviet political prisoners, including the dissident physicist and Nobel Peace Prize Laureate Andrei Sakharov, there remained, in spite of this, the belief that the Helsinki Accords had proved a qualified success. Before 1975 the U.S.S.R. had rejected outright the desire of the West to discuss human rights issues in the East, while in the last decade continuing C.S.C.E. discussions have facilitated the exit of Jews from the Eastern bloc and the reunification of families across the East/West divide. The Helsinki clauses on the notification of military manoeuvres has proved a confidence-building measure, and generally C.S.C.E. has proved a helpful blanket under which increased trade and aid contracts have been made between the F.D.R. and D.D.R. Of course, the Soviets remain uneasy about the scale of German *détente*, as witnessed in September 1984 when Herr Honecker of the D.D.R. had to cancel an agreed visit to Bonn as a result of pressure from Moscow. As arms discussions moved into October 1985, the Soviets offered massive (50 per cent +) joint superpower reductions in strategic nuclear stockpiles, providing a deal could be struck in relation to the downgrading of 'Star Wars' research or alternatively its continuation on a theoretical basis only, with no set timetable for practical deployment. Soon after gaining office Gorbachev accepted Reagan's offer of a superpower summit – to be held on neutral territory – Geneva – for 19–20 November 1985. It remains to be seen whether this summit, the first since 1979, can produce the political will necessary to achieve a S.A.L.T. III, and the lessening of military tension, which remains the yardstick by which *détente* is measured.

The Geneva Summit, however, proved more of a media event than a constructive dialogue. Both leaders professed the importance of face-to-face discussions and provisionally agreed to another summit in the summer of 1986 in the U.S.A. Nevertheless, Gorbachev could not deflect Reagan from the continued development of 'Star Wars' and nothing of substance emerged from the meeting. Of course, Reagan avoided the distinction of being (as he had been until then) the only postwar President who had not met his Soviet counterpart. Gorbachev did not achieve much success either in the spring of 1986, when he failed to manoeuvre the U.S. into a joint moratorium on below-ground nuclear testing (which might have inhibited 'Star Wars' research). Moreover, in the first four months of 1986, a fall in the price of oil from $30 to $12 a barrel had major repercussions for the U.S.S.R., which is the world's largest exporter. The Soviets needed the hard-currency earnings, not only for grain purchases, but more importantly for the import of high-technology goods in the areas of computer hardware and digital and micro-electronics. Soviet inferiority in such fields fuels her fears that Reagan's America has begun a new nuclear race centred on exactly those facets of Soviet knowledge and technology where her infrastructure is at its weakest.

# CHRONOLOGY

| 1943 | 25 April | Discovery of Katyn Woods massacre. |
| | 22 May | Comintern dissolved. |
| | 28 November/ | Big Three at Teheran. |
| | 2 December | |
| | | |
| 1944 | 23 July | U.S.S.R. sets up Lublin Committee. |
| | 9 October | Churchill in Moscow; Balkan Deal. |
| | 3 December | Fighting between Greek Communists and U.K. forces. Start of Greek Civil War. |
| | | |
| 1945 | 4 February | Yalta. |
| | 12 April | Roosevelt dies. |
| | 8 May | Germany surrenders. |
| | 26 June | U.N. Charter signed. |
| | 16 July | First test of U.S. A-bomb. |
| | 17 July–2 August | Potsdam Conference. |
| | 6 August | Hiroshima (9 August, Nagasaki). |
| | 15 August | Japan surrenders. |
| | 26 September | France returns to Vietnam. |
| | 18 November | Red Army occupies Iranian Azerbaijan. |
| | | |
| 1946 | 5 March | Churchill's Fulton speech. |
| | 16 June | U.S. puts forward Baruch Plan. |
| | 16 September | Byrne's Stuttgart speech. |
| | 23 November | French bomb Haiphong harbour, Indo-Chinese war begins. |
| | | |
| 1947 | 1 January | U.K. and U.S.A. set up Bizonia in Germany. |
| | 12 March | Truman Doctrine announced. |
| | 5 June | Marshall's Harvard speech. |
| | 5 October | Creation of Cominform. |
| | | |
| 1948 | 22 February | *Coup* by Czechoslovakian Communist Party. |
| | 20 March | Last meeting of Allied Control Council. |
| | 31 March | Partial Blockade of Berlin begins. |
| | 17 May | Proclamation of the state of Israel. |
| | 24 June | Berlin Blockade. |
| | 25 June | Berlin Airlift begins. |
| | 28 June | Yugoslavia ousted from Cominform. |

| | | |
|---|---|---|
| 1949 | 25 January | Comecon founded. |
| | 4 April | North Atlantic Treaty signed in Washington. |
| | 14 July | U.S.S.R. explodes its first A-bomb. |
| | 21 September | Federal Republic comes into existence. |
| | 1 October | Proclamation of People's Republic of China. |
| | 7 October | Proclamation of D.D.R. |
| 1950 | 31 January | Truman decides to build H-bomb. |
| | 25 June | Start of Korean War. |
| | 2 October | U.N. forces cross 38th Parallel in Korea. |
| | 7 October | P.L.A. invades Tibet. |
| | 15 October | People's Republic of China intervenes in Korea. |
| | 19 December | Eisenhower appointed Supreme Allied Commander, Europe. |
| 1951 | 11 April | MacArthur's dismissal. |
| | 9 July | Three Western Powers terminate state of war with Germany. |
| | 10 July | Korean armistice talks begin. |
| | 8 September | Western Peace Treaty with Japan. |
| 1952 | February | Greece and Turkey join N.A.T.O. |
| | 1 November | First U.S. H-bomb exploded. |
| | 4 November | Eisenhower elected President of U.S. |
| 1953 | 5 March | Death of Stalin. |
| | 16 June | East Berlin uprising. |
| | 27 July | Armistice in Korea. |
| | 20 August | First Soviet H-bomb tested. |
| | 12 September | Khrushchev becomes First Secretary of Soviet Communist Party. |
| 1954 | 25 February | Nasser assumes power in Cairo. |
| | 23 April | Opening of Geneva Conference on Korea and Indo-China. |
| | 13 May | Fall of Dien Bien Phu. |
| | June–July | Crisis in Guatemala. |
| | 5 September | Start of People's Republic of China bombardment of Quemoy and Matsu. |
| | 8 September | Signing of Manila Pact (later S.E.A.T.O.). |
| 1955 | 24 February | Baghdad Pact agreed. |
| | 17–24 April | Bandung Conference. |
| | 9 May | Federal Republic admitted to N.A.T.O. |
| | 14 May | Warsaw Pact signed. |
| | 15 May | Austrian State Treaty signed. Austria neutralized. |
| | 26 May–2 June | Khrushchev in Belgrade. |
| | 9 September | U.S.S.R.–West Germany diplomatic relations established. |
| | 27 September | Czech arms deal with Egypt. |
| 1956 | 14–25 February | Twentieth Congress of Soviet Communist Party. Khrushchev denounces Stalin. |

|          | 28 June      | Poznan uprising. |
|----------|--------------|------------------|
|          | 19 July      | U.S. withdraws offer to finance Aswan Dam. |
|          | 26 July      | Nationalization of Suez Canal. |
|          | 23 October   | Start of Hungarian uprising. |
|          | 29 October   | Israel attacks Egypt. Anglo–French ultimatum to Egypt and Israel. |
|          | 4 November   | U.S.S.R. intervenes in Budapest. |
|          | 5 November   | Britain and France land in Egypt. |
| 1957     | 5 January    | Announcement of Eisenhower Doctrine. |
|          | 27 February  | Mao's first 'Hundred Flowers' Speech. |
|          | 10–17 April  | Crisis in Jordan. |
|          | 26 August    | Launching of first Soviet I.C.B.M. |
|          | September    | Syrian–Turkish crisis. |
|          | 4 October    | First Sputnik launched. |
| 1958     | February     | U.S. launches first satellite, 'Explorer'. |
|          | March        | Khrushchev becomes Premier as well as First Secretary in U.S.S.R. |
|          | 3 May        | Chinese 'Great Leap Forward' begins. |
|          | 14 July      | U.S. intervention in Lebanon and U.K. inervention in Jordan. |
|          | 22 August    | People's Republic of China bombards Quemoy. |
|          | 27 November  | Soviet Note on future status of Berlin. |
| 1959     | 1 January    | Victory of Fidel Castro in Cuba. |
|          |              | E.E.C. comes into existence. |
|          | 24 May       | Death of Dulles. |
|          | 15 June      | Moscow secretly denounces atomic agreement with Peking. |
|          | 15 September | Khrushchev visits U.S.A. |
| 1960     | 13 February  | First French A-bomb test in Sahara. |
|          | 5 May        | U-2 shot down. |
|          | 16 May       | Paris Summit fails. |
|          | July         | U.N. Security Council decides to send U.N. forces to Congo. |
|          | 20 July      | U.S. successfully launches first Polaris missile. |
|          | August       | Recall of Soviet technicians from China. |
|          | 7 November   | Kennedy elected President. |
| 1961     | 17 April     | Bay of Pigs landing. |
|          | 16 May       | Start of Geneva Conference on Laos. |
|          | 3 June       | Khrushchev meets Kennedy in Vienna. |
|          | 13–19 August | Building of Berlin Wall. |
|          | 23 October   | Incidents at Checkpoint Charlie in Berlin. Tension increases. |
|          | 10 December  | Albania severs relations with U.S.S.R. |
|          | December     | Kennedy increases U.S. 'advisers' in Vietnam to 15,000. |
| 1962     | 4 May        | U.S. puts forward 'Flexible Response' doctrine. |
|          | 2 September  | U.S.S.R. announces increase of military and economic aid to Cuba. |

|   | 18 October | U-2 reports presence of Soviet missiles in Cuba. |
|---|---|---|
|   | 20 October | Chinese offensive in Himalayas. |
|   | 22 October | U.S. 'quarantines' Cuba. |
|   | 28 October | Khrushchev announces withdrawal of missiles from Cuba. |
|   | 20 November | U.S.S.R. removes bombers from Cuba. Quarantine lifted. |
|   | 21 December | Nassau agreement between London and Washington on nuclear weapons. |
| 1963 | 14 June | People's Republic of China indicts U.S.S.R. 'The Twenty Five Points'. |
|   | 20 June | U.S.–U.S.S.R. 'Hot-Line' agreement. |
|   | 14 July | U.S.S.R. replies to Chinese charges. |
|   | 15 July | Start of U.S., U.K., U.S.S.R. talks on cessation of nuclear tests. |
|   | 5 August | U.S., U.K. and U.S.S.R. sign Partial Test Ban Treaty. |
|   | 17 October | Rumania and West Germany agree to establish trade mission in Bucharest. |
|   | 22 November | Kennedy assassinated. Johnson becomes President. |
| 1964 | 27 January | France recognizes Red China. |
|   | 15 July | Federal Republic opens trade mission in Budapest. |
|   | 15 October | Khrushchev sacked. Replaced by Brezhnev and Kosygin. |
|   | 16 October | People's Republic of China explodes its first nuclear bomb. |
|   | 19 October | Federal Republic opens trade mission in Bulgaria. |
| 1965 | 7 February | U.S. begin raids on North Vietnam. |
|   | 24 April | Large-scale U.S. intervention in Dominica. |
|   | 25 August | Indo–Pakistan war in Kashmir. |
| 1966 | 7 March | France announces her withdrawal from N.A.T.O. |
|   | 18 April | Start of People's Republic of China Cultural Revolution. |
| 1967 | 27 January | Signing of Treaty on Demilitarization of Space. |
|   | 30 January | West Germany–Rumania establish diplomatic relations. |
|   | 5–9 June | Six Day War. |
|   | 17 June | People's Republic of China tests its first H-bomb. |
|   | 23 June | Johnson and Kosygin meet in Glassboro, New Jersey. |
|   | 24 August | First French H-bomb at Mururoa Atoll in the Pacific. |
|   | 18 September | U.S.A. decides to erect a billion-dollar 'thin' A.B.M. system. |
| 1968 | January | Beginning of 'Prague Spring'. |
|   | 2 July | Signing of Non-Proliferation Treaty. |
|   | 21 August | U.S.S.R. invades Czechoslovakia. |
|   | 1 November | U.S. halts bombing of North Vietnam. |
|   | 5. November | R. M. Nixon elected President of U.S.A. |
| 1969 | 1–2 February | Tito and Ceausescu denounce the 'Brezhnev Doctrine'. |
|   | 2 March | China and Russia border clashes on the Amur–Ussuri River. |

|            | July            | Nixon's 'Guam' Doctrine. |
|            | 2–3 August      | Nixon visits Rumania. |
|            | 28 September    | Brandt becomes Chancellor of West Germany. |
|            | 28 November     | West Germany signs Nuclear Non-Proliferation Treaty. |

**1970**

|            | 19 March        | Chancellor Brandt meets D.D.R. Premier Stoph, in Erfurt. |
|            | 16 April        | S.A.L.T. talks begin at Vienna. |
|            | 21 May          | Second meeting of Brandt and Stoph at Kassel. |
|            | 27 May          | N.A.T.O. suggests M.B.F.R. negotiations with Warsaw Pact. |
|            | 12 August       | West Germany–Soviet 'Non-Aggression' Treaty signed in Moscow. |
|            | 7 December      | Brandt in Warsaw, signs Poland–West Germany Treaty. |

**1971**

| 1971 | April           | A U.S. table-tennis team is invited to China. |
|      | 3 May           | Hönecker replaces Ulbricht as East German Communist Party First Secretary. |
|      | July            | Dr. Kissinger visits China. |
|      | 3 September     | Four Power Agreement on Berlin. |
|      | 16–18 September | Brandt meets Brezhnev in Crimea – agree to work for C.S.C.E. |
|      | 29 September/   | Chinese trade delegation to France. First official People's |
|      | 11 October      | Republic of China mission to the West since the Cultural Revolution. |
|      | 25 October      | China vote in U.N.O. |
|      | 17–20 December  | East and West Germany sign agreement on transit between West Berlin and West Germany. |

| 1972 | 21–28 February  | Nixon visit to China. |
|      | April           | Biological Warfare Treaty agreed. |
|      | 8 May           | North Vietnamese ports mined. |
|      | 17 May          | West German Bundestag approves 1970 treaties with Poland and U.S.S.R. |
|      | 26 May          | S.A.L.T. 1 Agreement. |
|      | 22–29 May       | Nixon visits U.S.S.R. |
|      | 15 September    | U.S.S.R./Spain trade agreement signed. First formal agreement for thirty-five years. |
|      | 25–29 September | Japanese Prime Minister, Mr. Tanaka, visits China. |
|      | 21 December     | Basic Treaty signed between East and West Germany. |
|      | 18–29 December  | Last round of full-scale bombing of North Vietnam. |

| 1973 | 15 January      | Preparatory talks for C.S.C.E. open in Helsinki. |
|      | 27 January      | U.S.–North Vietnamese Armistice Agreement on South Vietnam signed at Paris. |
|      | 9 February      | U.K. and France establish diplomatic relations with D.D.R. |
|      | 22 June         | Brezhnev in Washington – joint declaration made on avoidance of nuclear war. |
|      | 27 June         | 2–3 megaton Chinese H-bomb test at Lop Nor – fifteenth test since 1964. |
|      | 18 September    | U.N.O. admits both Germanies. |

| | | |
|---|---|---|
| | October | Yom Kippur War. |
| | 25 October | U.S. orders nuclear alert, stage 3. |
| | 30 October | M.B.F.R. talks open in Vienna. |
| | 11 December | West Germany–Czechoslovakia Treaty normalizes relations, annuls Munich Agreement, 1938. |
| | 12–20 December | West Germany establishes diplomatic ties with Bulgaria and Hungary. |
| 1974 | 25 April | Military *coup* in Portugal, Premier Caetano overthrown. |
| | 18 May | India announces underground test of first nuclear device. |
| | 28–30 June | Nixon in Moscow. |
| | 1–3 July | U.S. and U.S.S.R. agree to restrict A.B.M.s to one site each and to limit underground nuclear tests. |
| | 11 July | U.S.S.R. and Somalia sign treaty of friendship and cooperation. |
| | 9 August | Nixon resigns. Vice-President Ford sworn in as 38th President. |
| | 14 August | Turkish forces invade Cyprus. Greece withdraws from military structures of N.A.T.O. |
| | 4 Sept. | U.S. and D.D.R. establish diplomatic relations. |
| | 23 November | Ford and Brezhnev sign S.A.L.T. Interim Agreement in Vladivostok. |
| 1975 | 14 January | U.S.S.R. rejects trade/credit agreement with U.S. because of the 'Jackson amendment'. |
| | 22 January | Ford signs Geneva Convention banning manufacture, stock-piling and use of biological weapons. |
| | 5 February | U.S. Congress votes to cut off military aid to Turkey. |
| | 17 April | Phnom Penh falls to Khmer Rouge. |
| | 30 April | Saigon falls to Vietcong and North Vietnamese. |
| | 28 July | C.S.C.E. Summit in Helsinki. |
| | 23 August | Non-communist administration disbanded in Laos. Pathet Lao takes over. |
| | 20 October | U.S. and U.S.S.R. agree to five-year grain deal. |
| | 23 October | Cuban advisers and regular troops reported in Angola. |
| | 19 December | U.S. Senate votes to cut off military aid to Western-backed forces in Angola. |
| 1976 | 15 February | C.I.A. revises estimates of Soviet defence spending; military share of G.N.P. (at 11–13 per cent) is twice earlier projections. |
| | 25 April | North and South Vietnam vote to unify. |
| | 9 September | Death of Mao Tse-tung (Hua Kuo-feng becomes Chairman, 12 October 1976). |
| | 8 October | U.S.S.R. and Angola sign treaty of friendship and cooperation. |
| | 2 November | Jimmy Carter elected 39th President of the U.S.A. |
| 1977 | 23 January | Guyana applies for 'a formal association' with COMECON. |
| | 31 March | U.S.S.R. and Mozambique sign friendship treaty. |
| | 12 May | U.S. and Spain agree on a combined military planning staff. |
| | 17 May | N.A.T.O. ministers at Brussels agree to 3 per cent real rise in defence spending. |
| | 18 May | U.S. and U.S.S.R. sign 'weather-warfare' ban. |

211

|  |  |  |
|---|---|---|
| | 30 June | S.E.A.T.O. Treaty dissolved. |
| | 25 July | Albania begins to expel Chinese advisers. |
| | 25 October | Thirty-five-nation Belgrade Conference to review Helsinki Agreement. |
| | 13 November | Somalia renounces 1974 friendship treaty with U.S.S.R. Ejects Russians and Cubans. U.S.S.R. denied use of military facilities. |
| 1978 | 3 April | E.E.C. signs five-year trade agreement with China and gives her 'most-favoured nation' status. |
| | 25 April | U.S.S.R. signs Tlatelolco Treaty of 1968, banning nuclear weapons in Latin America. |
| | 27 April | Pro-Soviet military *coup* in Afghanistan. |
| | 29 June | Vietnam becomes full member of COMECON. |
| | 5 July | U.S.A. awards 'most-favoured-nation' trading status to Hungary. |
| | 11 July | China recalls technicians and cuts off aid to Albania. |
| | 12 August | Japan and China sign treaty of peace and friendship. |
| | 5–17 Sept. | Begin, Sadat and Carter at Camp David produce 'framework for peace in the Middle East'. |
| | 3 October | U.S.S.R. agrees to supply Libya with nuclear power complex. |
| | 3 November | Vietnam and U.S.S.R. sign treaty of friendship and co-operation. |
| | 20 November | Ethiopia and U.S.S.R. sign treaty of friendship and co-operation. |
| | 6 December | Afghanistan and U.S.S.R. sign treaty of friendship. |
| | 27 December | Vietnam invades Kampuchea. |
| 1979 | 1 January | U.S.A. and China exchange formal recognition. |
| | 1–10 January | Pope John Paul II visits his native Poland. |
| | 16 January | Shah Reza Pahlavi leaves Iran and goes into exile. |
| | End January to early February | Vice-Premier Deng Xiaoping in U.S.A. |
| | 1 February | Ayatollah Khomeini returns to Iran. |
| | 17 February | China attacks Vietnam in retaliation for 'Vietnamese attacks on China' and Vietnamese invasion of Kampuchea. |
| | 31 August | U.S.A. protests at presence of a 'Soviet combat brigade' in Cuba. |
| | 17 October | 1800 U.S. Marines exercise assault on Guantánamo base in Cuba. |
| | End October | South Yemen signs twenty-year treaty of friendship with U.S.S.R. |
| | 4 November | Iranian students seize hostages in U.S. embassy in Teheran. |
| | 12 December | N.A.T.O. approves increases in nuclear strength in Europe. |
| | 24 December | First wave of up to 100,000 Soviet troops begins to arrive in Afghanistan. |
| 1980 | 27–29 January | Islamic Conference Organization meets in Islamabad, Pakistan. Thirty-five nations denounce Moscow's 'military aggression' against Afghanistan. |
| | 14 February | U.N. General Assembly votes by 104 to 18 (with 30 abstentions or absences) to censure U.S.S.R.'s invasion of Afghanistan. |

|              | 26 February       | Egypt and Israel exchange formal diplomatic recognition. |
|              | 4 May             | Yugoslav leader Tito dies; 'collective' leadership follows. |
|              | 14 August         | Strikes and riots in Gdansk, Poland. |
|              | 23 September      | Iraq invades Iran: outbreak of Gulf War. |

1981  20 January      Ronald Reagan becomes 40th President of the U.S.A.
      7 June          Israelis bomb and destroy Iraq's Osirak nuclear reactor.
      13 July         Mozambique applies to join COMECON.
      2 October       Reagan authorizes building of 100 MX ICBMs and B1 bombers.
      6 October       President Sadat of Egypt assassinated.
      27 October      Soviet submarine grounded inside Sweden's territorial waters.
      30 November     U.S.–U.S.S.R. I.N.F. talks in Geneva on European nuclear balance.

1982  2 April–14 June U.K. and Argentina in Falklands War.
      6 June          Israeli invasion of Lebanon.
      29 June         S.T.A.R.T. begins in Geneva.
      10 November     Leonid Brezhnev dies; succeeded by Yuri Andropov.

1983  August          French forces intervene in Chad against Libyan supported rebels.
      1 September     U.S.S.R. shoots down South Korean Airlines flight 007.
      6 October       Lech Walesa awarded Nobel Peace Prize.
      26 October      U.S. troops land in Grenada.
      23 November     U.S.S.R. walks out of I.N.F. talks.

1984  January         South African forces strike deep into Angola both to destroy S.W.A.P.O. bases and to support U.N.I.T.A.'s rebellion.
      17 January      Opening of Stockholm Review Conference of the C.S.C.E.
      1 February      Reagan puts to Congress $313 billion defence budget for fiscal 1985 (an increase of 18 per cent and the largest, in inflation-adjusted terms, since the height of the Vietnam War).
      9 February      Death of Yuri Andropov whose health had begun failing in July 1983; replaced by Konstantin Chernenko.
      April           C.I.A. mines Nicaragua's three main harbours.
      8 May           U.S.S.R. withdraws from Los Angeles Olympics.
      October         U.S. defense budget of $292b. – a 5·4 per cent increase over 1984.
      6 November      Reagan re-elected President for second term with 59 per cent of total vote, winning 49 of 50 states.

1985  March           Geneva S.T.A.R.T. talks re-commence.
      10 March        Death of Chernenko; replaced by Mikhail Gorbachev.
      May             Rajiv Gandhi visits Moscow and obtains $1·2b credits.
      August          Helsinki: 10th Anniversary of C.S.C.E. Accords.
      1 October       Formal Soviet offer in Geneva of massive joint nuclear stockpile reduction linked to a drop-off in 'Star Wars' research.
      19–20 November  Superpower Summit Reagan/Gorbachev at Geneva.

# NOTES AND BIBLIOGRAPHY

**Chapter 1**

1. Karl Marx and Friedrich Engels, *Manifesto of the Communist Party*, edited by H. J. Laski (Allen & Unwin, 1948).
2. E. H. Carr, *The Bolshevik Revolution* (Penguin, 1966) vol 3, p. 123.
3. Alan Bullock, *Hitler* (Pelican, 1962) p. 762.
4. Edmund Ions, *The Politics of John F. Kennedy* (Routledge, 1967) p. 50.
5. Richard M. Nixon, 'United States Foreign Policy for the 1970s: Shaping a Durable Peace' (Report to Congress, May 1973) U.S. Government, p. 17.

**Chapter 2**

1. Milovan Djilas, *Conversations with Stalin* (Pelican, 1969) pp. 67–8.
2. Harry S. Truman, *Memoirs* (Doubleday, New York, 1955) vol 1, pp. 77–82.
3. Alfred Grosser, *Germany in our Time* (Pall Mall Press, 1971) p. 30.
4. Truman letter to Secretary of State Byrnes, 5 January 1946, quoted in Roger Morgan, *The Unsettled Peace* (B.B.C. Publications, 1974) p. 67.

**Chapter 3**

1. Djilas, op. cit., p. 68.
2. Robert E. Sherwood, *Roosevelt and Hopkins* (Harper and Bros., 1950) pp. 893–4.
3. Ian Grey, *The First Fifty Years: Soviet Russia 1917–67* (Hodder and Stoughton, 1967) p. 409.
4. Truman letter to Byrnes, 5 January 1946, Morgan, op. cit., p. 67.
5. Walter Bedell Smith, *My Three Years in Moscow* (Lippincott, Philadelphia, 1950) p. 53.
6. Truman, op. cit., vol. 2, p. 106.
7. Churchill telegram to Truman, 12 May 1945, in Morgan, op. cit., pp. 61–2.
8. Churchill, Fulton speech, 5 March 1946, ibid., pp. 67–8.
9. Brian Crozier, *The Future of Communist Power* (Eyre and Spottiswoode, 1970) p. 66.
10. ibid., p. 36.
11. Simon Serfaty, *France, de Gaulle and Europe* (Johns Hopkins U.P., 1968) p. 35.

**Chapter 4**

1. Keesing's Research Report No. 8, *Germany and Eastern Europe Since 1945* (Scribner's, New York, 1973) pp. 3–4.

2. Aiden Crawley, *The Rise of West Germany 1945–72* (Collins, 1973) pp. 43–4.
3. Lucius D. Clay, *Decision in Germany* (Heinemann, 1950) pp. 120.
4. ibid., p. 320.
5. Keesing's, op. cit., p. 12.
6. Terence Prittie, *Willy Brandt* (Weidenfeld and Nicolson, 1974) p. 75.
7. Clay, op. cit., p. 158.
8. Alfred Grosser, *Germany in Our Time* (Pall Mall Press, 1971) p. 65.
9. Walt. Rostow, *The United States and the World Arena* (Harper, New York, 1960) pp. 208–10.
10. Philip Windsor, *City on Leave: History of Berlin 1945–1962* (Chatto and Windus, 1963) p. 98.
11. Bedell Smith, op. cit., p. 241.
12. Clay, op cit., p. 367.
13. Hannes Adomeit, 'Soviet Risk-Taking and Crisis Behaviour', Adelphi Papers No. 101 (I.I.S.S. 1973) p. 9.
14. Acheson, in Morgan, op. cit., p. 72.

## Chapter 5

1. G. F. Hudson, *The Hard and Bitter Peace* (Pall Mall Press, 1966) p. 78.
2. L. M. Chassin, *The Communist Conquest of China* (Weidenfeld and Nicolson, 1966) *passim*.
3. Mme. Chiang Kai-shek, *Letters and Speeches of Madame Chiang Kai-shek* (Taipei Press, Taiwan, 1966) p. 144.
4. R. North, *Chinese Communism* (Weidenfeld and Nicolson, 1966) p. 95.
5. See J. Melby, *The Mandate of Heaven* (Chatto and Windus, 1969) *passim*.
6. C. J. Bown, *Revolution in China 1911–49* (Heinemann Educational Books, 1974) Broadsheet 16, p. 4.
7. ibid.

## Chapter 6

1. Harry S. Truman, Department of State Bulletin XXIII, No. 574, July 1950.
2. S. E. Morison and H. S. Commager, *The Growth of the American Republic* (O.U.P. 6th ed., 1969) vol. 2, p. 667.
3. Department of State Bulletin XXIII.
4. David Horowitz, *From Yalta to Vietnam* (Pelican, 1969) p. 129.
5. Edmund Traverso, *Korea and the Limits of Limited War* (Addison-Wesley, Reading, Mass., 1970) p. 27.
6. ibid., p. 30.
7. ibid., p. 29.
8. Horowitz, op. cit., p. 131, Toronto *Globe and Mail*, 22 February 1961.
9. Felix Greene, *Curtain of Ignorance* (Cape, 1968) p. 88.
10. Traverso, op. cit., p. 35.
11. ibid. (24 March 1951) p. 43.
12. Hudson, op. cit., p. 92.
13. Traverso, op. cit., p. 56.
14. David Rees, *Korea: The Limited War* (St. Martin's Press, New York, 1964) p. 41.
15. Dwight D. Eisenhower, *Mandate for Change 1953–56* (Heinemann, 1963) p. 180.

See also:
H. Halperin, *Limited War in the Nuclear Age* (John Wiley, New York, 1963).
Edgar O' Ballance, *Korea 1950–53* (Faber and Faber, 1969).

## Chapter 7

1. Milton Osborne, *Region of Revolt* (Pelican, 1971) p. 115.
2. Bernard Fall, *Vietnam Witness* (Pall Mall Press, 1966) p. 70.
3. Eisenhower, op. cit., p. 372.
4. Jean Lacouture, *Ho Chi Minh* (Allen Lane, 1968).
5. Eisenhower, op. cit., p. 333.

See also:
Robert Taber, *The War of the Flea* (Paladin Books, 1970).

## Chapter 8

1. John Foster Dulles, 'Policy for Security and Peace', Foreign Affairs XXXII, April 1954, p. 358.
2. André Fontaine, *History of the Cold War: Korea to the Present* (Secker and Warburg, 1970) p. 131.
3. ibid., p. 220.
4. ibid., p. 227.

See also:
Robert Hunter, *Security in Europe* (Elek Books, 1972).

## Chapter 9

1. Roscoe Drummond and Gaston Coblenz, *Duel at the Brink* (Weidenfeld and Nicolson, 1961) p. 89.
2. Adam B. Ulam, *Expansion and Coexistence: The History of Soviet Foreign Policy from 1917–1967* (Secker and Warburg, 1968) p. 504.
3. Wolfgang Heidelmeyer and Guenther Hindrichs, *Documents on Berlin 1943–63* (R. Oldenbourg Verlag, Munich, 1963) p. 177.
4. From the D.D.R. newspaper *Tagesspiegel*, 11 November 1958, quoted in Fontaine, op. cit., pp. 313–14.
5. Heidelmeyer, op. cit., pp. 180–96.
6. Louis J. Halle, *The Cold War as History* (Chatto and Windus, 1967) p. 361.
7. Fontaine, op. cit., p. 326.
8. Ulam, op. cit., p. 631.
9. Windsor, op. cit., p. 223.
10. ibid., p. 237.
11. Halle, op. cit., p. 397.

## Chapter 10

1. Robert Scheer and Maurice Zeitlin, *Cuba: an American Tragedy* (Penguin Special, 1964) p. 31.
2. ibid., p. 202.
3. ibid., p. 218.
4. Henry Pachter, *Collision Course: the Cuban Missile Crisis and Coexistence* (Pall Mall Press, 1963) p. 57.

See also:
Robert Kennedy, *The Thirteen Days* (Norton, 1969).

Elie Abel, *The Misssiles of October* (MacGibbon and Kee, 1966).
Robert Beggs, *The Cuban Missile Crisis* (Longman, 1971).

**Chapter 11**

1. Robert Jungt, *Brighter Than a Thousand Suns* (Pelican, 1964) p. 266.
2. *The Times*, 1 February 1950.
3. Department of State Bulletin XXX, No. 761, p. 108.
4. *Daily Telegraph*, 24 August 1973.
5. Elizabeth Barber, *The Cold War* (Wayland, 1972).
6. Chinese Government Statement (F.L.P., Peking) 15 September 1964.

See also:
Herman Kahn, *Thinking About the Unthinkable* (Weidenfeld and Nicolson, 1962).
Ronald Clarke, *The Science of War and Peace* (Cape, 1971).
Norman Moss, *Men Who Play God* (Penguin, 1970).

**Chapter 12**

1. Theodore Draper, *Abuse of Power* (Pelican, 1969) p. 36.
2. ibid., p. 117.
3. See David Halberstam, *The Best and the Brightest* (Barrie and Jenkins, 1972).
4. ibid.
5. ibid.
6. *New York Times*, 30 April 1965.
7. Felix Greene, *Vietnam, Vietnam* (Cape, 1967) p. 146.
8. Draper, op. cit., p. 142.
9. ibid., p. 123.
10. *New York Times*, 5 July 1966.
11. Richard M. Nixon, 'The Emerging Structure of World Peace' (Report to Congress 1972) U.S. Government, p. 32.
12. ibid., p. 39.
13. Nixon, Report to Congress 1973, op. cit., p. 20.
14. *The Strategic Survey*, 1972 (I.I.S.S., 1973) and *The Times*, 25 April 1975.
15. Nixon, Report to Congress 1973, p. 21.
16. *The Sunday Times*, 13 April 1975.
17. ibid.
18. *The Guardian*, 13 January 1975.
19. Senator J. William Fulbright, *The Arrogance of Power* (Cape, 1967) p. 3.
20. Quoted in *Newsweek* (U.S.A.), 12 May 1975.
21. *The Guardian*, 6 May 1975.
22. U.S. Television Broadcast, 3 April 1975.
23. *Newsweek*, 12 May 1975.
24. *New York Times*, 7 April 1975.
25. *The Guardian*, 24 April 1975.
26. *The Times*, 10 May 1975.
27. *The Guardian*, 24 April 1975.
28. *The Guardian*, 9 May 1975.
29. Except by accident as when, on 8 May 1972, five North Vietnamese ports were mined from the air and some Soviet ships were damaged.
30. *The Guardian*, 18 April 1975.
31. *The Guardian*, 13 May 1975.

See also:
Robert Thompson, *No Exit from Vietnam* (Chatto and Windus, 1968).
William J. Lederer, *The Anguished American* (Gollanz, 1969).
Malcolm Browne, *The New Face of War* (Cassell, 1965).

**Chapter 13**

1. State Department Information Paper No. 28, Formosa, 23 December 1949.
2. Department of State Bulletin, vol. 22, 16 January 1950.
3. Traverso, op. cit., p. 27.
4. Department of State Bulletin, vol. 24, 28 May 1951.
5. Eisenhower, op. cit., p. 471.
6. ibid., p. 476.
7. ibid., p. 477.
8. ibid., p. 482.
9. *People's Daily*, Peking, 8 May 1961.
10. *New York Times*, 2 August 1963.
11. Franz Schurmann and Orville Schell (eds.), *Communist China: China Readings* vol. 3 (Penguin, 1968) p. 497.
12. Edgar Snow, *The Long Revolution* (Hutchinson, 1973) p. 216.
13. Gregory Clark, *In Fear of China* (Barrie and Rockliffe, The Cresset Press, 1968) p. 171.
14. A. Huck, *The Security of China* (Chatto and Windus, 1970) p. 51.
15. Nixon, Report to Congress 1973, op. cit., p. 7.
16. Kansas Press Conference, 7 July 1971, quoted in The *Observer*, 16 July 1971.
17. Nixon, Report to Congress 1973, op. cit., p. 7.
18. ibid., p. 7.
19. Nixon, Report to Congress 1972, op. cit., p. 17.
20. *Peking Review*, 13 May 1973.
21. The *Guardian*, 28 October 1974.
22. *Peking Review*, 25 February 1972.
23. The *Guardian*, 1 September 1973.
24. Chiao Kuan-hua at the U.N., 15 November 1971.

**Chapter 14**

1. Jack A. Smith, 'Unite The Many, Defeat The Few', The *Guardian* (A U.S. Communist publication, S.A.C.U., London) p. 89.
2. Stuart Schram, *The Political Thought of Mao Tse Tung* (Pelican, 1969) p. 189.
3. Vladimir Dedijer, *Tito Speaks* (Weidenfeld and Nicolson, 1953) p. 331.
4. Mao, 1 July 1949.
5. Smith, op. cit., p. 89.
6. Fontaine, op. cit., p. 133.
7. John Gittings, *Survey of the Sino–Soviet Dispute* (O.U.P., 1968) p. 62.
8. *People's Daily* editorial of 1971, quoted in Smith, op. cit., p. 22.
9. Gittings, op. cit., p. 62.
10. ibid., p. 73.
11. Mao Tse-tung, *Imperialism and all Reactionaries are Paper Tigers* (F.L.P., Peking, 1958).
12. Edward Crankshaw, *Moscow Versus Peking: The New Cold War* (Penguin, 1963) p. 80.
13. David Floyd, *Mao Versus Khrushchev* (Pall Mall Press, 1964) p. 262.

14. Gittings, op. cit., p. 346.
15. Greene, op. cit., p. 280.
16. A Chinese Government statement in the *Peking Review*, 2 February 1963.
17. ibid., 6 September 1963.
18. *The Times*, 10 May 1974.
19. Theodore C. Sorensen, *Kennedy* (Hodder and Stoughton, 1965) p. 665.
20. The *Observer*, 14 July 1965.
21. *C.C.P. Polemic* (F.L.P., Peking) July 1964.
22. *Pravda*, 10 November 1966.
23. *Peking Review*, 4 February 1966.
24. Gittings, op. cit., p. 20.
25. Sino–Soviet Survey No. 8 (S.A.C.U.) 1969.
26. Gittings, op. cit., p. 160.
27. *Sekai Shuho* (a Tokyo newspaper) 11 August 1965.
28. Sino–Soviet Survey op. cit., p. 71.
29. *Strategic Survey, 1970* (I.I.S.S., 1971) p. 71.
30. *The Military Balance, 1970–1* (I.I.S.S., 1970) p. 101.
31. *Strategic Survey, 1973* (I.I.S.S., 1974) p. 67.
32. *China Reconstructs*, Peking, April 1970.
33. Nixon, Report to Congress 1972, op. cit., p. 51.
34. *The Sunday Times*, 27 January 1974.
35. The *Guardian*, 24 January 1974.
36. ibid., 9 January 1974.
37. *People's Daily*, Peking, 26 October 1973.
38. *Peking Review*, Peking, 4 May 1973.
39 *China Reconstructs*, Peking, January 1974.
40. *Peking Review*, 15 June 1973.

See also:
Harold C. Hinton, *China's Turbulent Quest* (Macmillan, 1970).

## Chapter 15

1. Sir William Hayter, *Russia and the World* (Secker and Warburg, 1970) p. 2.
2. Harry Schwartz, *Eastern Europe in the Soviet Shadow* (Abelard-Schuman, New York, 1973) p. 75.
3. Hayter, op. cit., p. 38.
4. ibid., pp. 38–9.
5. ibid., pp. 40–1.
6. ibid., p. 66.
7. Crozier, op. cit., p. 93.

See also:
Paul Lendvai, *Eagles in Cobwebs: Nationalism and Communism in the Balkans* (Macdonald, 1970).
Kurt Weisskopf, *The Agony of Czechoslovakia '38–'68* (Elek Books, 1968).

## Chapter 16

1. The *Guardian*, 19 January 1970.
2. Prittie, op. cit., p. 247.
3. ibid., pp. 251–2.
4. *Strategic Survey 1971* (I.I.S.S., 1972) p. 18.

5. The *Economist*, 8 September 1973.
6. ibid.

**Chapter 17**

1. Peter Lyons, *Neutralism* (Leicester Univ. Press, 1963) p. 107.
2. Sir William Hayter, *The Kremlin and The Embassy* (Hodder and Stoughton, 1966) p. 146. (Sir William was the British Ambassador in Moscow in 1956.)
3. Fontaine, op. cit., p. 255.
4. D. F. Fleming, *The Cold War and its Origins, 1917–60*, vol. 2 (Doubleday, New York, 1961) p. 889.
5. Fontaine, op. cit., p. 262.
6. *The Economist*, 20 March 1976, p. 54. According to information released by a C.I.A. official at a news briefing on 11 March 1976, Israel had 10–20 nuclear weapons.

See also:
J. D. B. Miller, *The Politics of The Third World* (O.U.P., 1966).
Andrew Boyd. *United Nations, Piety, Myth, and Truth* (Pelican, 1964).
Hugh Thomas, *The Suez Affair* (Pelican, 1970).
Terence Robertson, *Crisis: the Inside Story of the Suez Conspiracy*, 1965.
Walter Laqueur, *The Road to War: the Origins and Aftermath of the Arab–Israeli Conflict, 1967–8* (Pelican, 1969).
John Bulloch, *The Making of a War: the Middle East from 1967–73* (Longman, 1974).

**Chapter 18**

1. *The Times*, 11 October 1974.
2. ibid., 10 May 1974.
3. *The Military Balance 1974–5* (I.I.S.S., 1974) p. 75.
4. *The Times*, 12 January 1974.
5. Nixon, Report to Congress 1973, p. 68.
6. ibid., p. 68.
7. ibid., p. 78.
8. ibid., p. 65.
9. President Ford to U.N.O. General Assembly, 18 September 1974.
10. *The Times*, 25 November 1974.
11. The *Guardian*, 4 December 1974.

**Chapter 19**

1. *The Military Balance 1973–4* (I.I.S.S., 1973) p. 79.
2. The *Observer*, 29 December 1974.
3. The *Guardian*, 17 December 1974.
4. *The Sunday Times*, 24 June 1974.
5. 'Focus on U.S. Foreign Policy', *Horizon Magazine*, 1974. U.S. Embassy Information Service.
6. Nixon, Report to Congress 1973, p. 17.
7. ibid., p. 16.
8. *Peking Review*, 15 June 1973.
9. The *Guardian*, 21 January 1975.

See also:
Alastair Buchan, *The End Of The Postwar Era: a New Balance of World Power*
(Weidenfeld and Nicolson, 1974).

**Chapter 20**

1. *Time*, 14 May 1979.
2. The *Economist*, 8 September 1979.
3. *Time*, 28 April 1980.
4. Oil figures from *Time*, 7 May 1979.
5. *Time*, 29 January 1979.
6. The Military Balance 1979–80, International Institute of Strategic Studies, 1979.
7. Coral Bell, *The Diplomacy of Détente: The Kissinger Era* (Martin Robertson, 1977) p. 76.

See also:
J. M. Collins and A. H. Cordesman, *Imbalance of Power: Shifting U.S.–Soviet Military Strengths* (Macdonald and Janes, 1978).
Sir Terence Garvey, *Bones of Contention: An Enquiry into East–West Relations* (Routledge, 1978).
Sir Peter Hill-Norton, *No Soft Options: The Politico-Military Realities of NATO* (C. Hurst, 1978).
G. Kirk and N. H. Wessell, *The Soviet Threat: Myths and Realities* (New York: Praeger Special Studies, 1979).
*Strategic Survey, 1979* (International Institute of Strategic Studies, 1980).

# INDEX